Soviet Grassroots

Jeffrey W. Hahn

SOVIET GRASSROOTS

Citizen Participation in Local Soviet Government

Princeton University Press
Princeton, New Jersey

Copyright © 1988 by Princeton University Press

Published by Princeton University Press, 41 William Street,
Princeton, New Jersey 08540
In the United Kingdom: Princeton University Press, Guildford, Surrey

All Rights Reserved

Library of Congress Cataloging in Publication Data will be
found on the last printed page of this book

ISBN 0-691-07767-3

This book has been composed in Linotron Palatino

Clothbound editions of Princeton University Press books
are printed on acid-free paper, and binding materials are
chosen for strength and durability. Paperbacks, although satisfactory
for personal collections, are not usually suitable for library rebinding

Printed in the United States of America by Princeton University Press
Princeton, New Jersey

To Maricel and Peter,
for giving the baboon enough
time at the piano.

CONTENTS

List of Tables   ix

Acknowledgments   xi

Introduction   3

1. Studying Soviet Deputies   8
   WHY STUDY LOCAL SOVIET DEPUTIES?   9
   THE SCOPE OF THIS STUDY   15
   METHODS   17

2. The Study of Political Participation in
   Communist Countries   26
   THE DEBATE OVER MASS POLITICAL PARTICIPATION   30
   THE NEED FOR RECONCEPTUALIZATION   38

3. Mass Participation in Local Soviet Government:
   The Background   44
   BEFORE THE REVOLUTION   47
   THE EMERGENCE OF THE SOVIETS, 1905 AND 1917   55
   THE DEVELOPMENT OF THE SOVIETS AFTER THE
   REVOLUTION: THEORY AND PRACTICE   59
   THE DEPUTIES UNDER "DEVELOPED SOCIALISM"   70
   IS THERE A BASIS FOR INCREASED PARTICIPATION?   76

4. How Soviet Local Government is Organized   80
   THE SOVIET POLITICAL HIERARCHY   80
   SOVIET ELECTIONS   92
   THE COMPOSITION OF THE LOCAL SOVIETS   107
   THE INTERNAL ORGANIZATION OF THE SOVIETS   114

5. Deputies and Their Constituents   133
  FORMS OF CONSTITUENT CONTACT   135
  PUBLIC OPINION ABOUT THE DEPUTY'S ACTIVITIES   188
  THE DEPUTY AS OMBUDSMAN   194

6. The Deputy as Council   199
  SESSIONS OF THE LOCAL SOVIETS   199
  THE STANDING COMMITTEES   228
  WHO GOVERNS?   246

7. Is the Deputy an Effective Representative?   261
  POSSIBILITIES   264
  PROBLEMS   269
  THE FUTURE: A SOVIET "CIVIC CULTURE"?   284

  Selected Bibliography   291
  Index   309

LIST OF TABLES

4-1. Number and Size of Local Soviets, 1985   86
4-2. Numbers of Electoral Districts (Deputies),
    RSFSR   99
4-3. Composition of Local Soviets, 1985   110
4-4. Composition of Lenin City Borough Soviet,
    Moscow City Soviet, and Soviets of RSFSR,
    1985   111
4-5. Educational Level of Deputies to Local Soviets
    in Belorussia, 1961 and 1982   113
4-6. Composition of Executive Committees of Local
    Soviets, 1985   116
4-7. Administrative Agencies of Lenin City Borough
    of Moscow and Composition of Directors,
    1982–85 and 1985–87   124
4-8. Budget of the Lenin City Borough of Moscow,
    1985 Budget Plan and 1986 Draft Plan   130
5-1. Voter Mandates and Ratio per Deputy, 1983   137
5-2. Implementation of Voter Mandates, 1980–82
    and 1982–84   148
5-3. Deputy Reports to Constituents, 1983   154
5-4. Deputies Subjected to Recall, Selected Years,
    1970–84   187
5-5. Frequency of Deputy-Constituency Contact in
    Taganrog, RSFSR   194
5-6. Citizen Concerns and Channels of
    Communication, Taganrog, RSFSR   196
6-1. Local Soviet Sessions in 1984   206
6-2. Average Number of Issues per Session, USSR
    and Belorussia, Selected Years   211
6-3. Deputy Participation in Sessions of Local
    Soviets, 1976–84   216

6-4. Use of Right of Inquiry (*Zapros*) in the
     Sverdlovsk, 1983   223
6-5. Use of Right of Inquiry (*Zapros*), 1968–84   224
6-6. Local Soviet Standing Committees, Selected
     Years, 1976–85   231
6-7. Standing Committees, 1985 (by Number of
     Committees)   233
6-8. Participation by Standing Committees in Work
     of Soviet, Selected Years, 1976–84   242

ACKNOWLEDGMENTS

WHILE the ultimate responsibility for any book rests with the author, the book that involves field research and that builds on foundations laid by others incurs great indebtedness.

The institutions that supported my efforts deserve recognition, and it is a pleasure to credit them. The International Research and Exchanges Board (IREX) helped me gather essential data by sending me to Moscow State University's law faculty as a senior exchange scholar for three months in the fall of 1984. A short-term grant from IREX in January 1986 allowed me to return to the Soviet Union to gather important follow-up information in the wake of the February 1985 elections. Two short-term research grants (in June 1984 and 1985) from the Kennan Institute for Advanced Russian Studies in Washington, D.C., provided access to the wealth of Russian-language materials at the Library of Congress as well as to welcome research assistance and vital conversations with colleagues. The National Council for Soviet and East European Studies provided me with what I needed most to complete a draft manuscript—time. A grant from them let me take an unpaid leave of absence from teaching in the fall 1985. Finally, I owe much to the support of Villanova University, especially its academic dean, Father Lawrence Gallen. In addition to a sabbatical, two leaves of absence, and a reduced teaching load, the university provided substantial financial support in the form of a summer research grant, matching funds, and other financial assistance.

Institutional support provides opportunities to pursue research, but the assistance of individuals is essential if the enterprise is to succeed. The list of people who deserve more acknowledgment than I can render by mentioning their names is daunting. At the top of this list is my teacher and dissertation adviser, Profesor Wladyslaw W. Kulski, whose influence was felt throughout the researching and writing of this book and whose standards for the scholarly study of Eastern Europe and the Soviet Union are unexcelled. Western scholars who read all or portions of the manuscript and who took the time to make extensive comments include Archie Brown, Theodore H. Friedgut, Ronald J. Hill, Erik Hoffman, Dan Nelson, Timothy O'Connor, Blair Ruble, and Stephen White. In addition to performing this chore, my friend and colleague at Villanova, Justin J. Green, provided needed criticism and welcome encouragement in equal measure. Jerry Hough rendered valuable advice on research strategy during several lengthy conversations for which he found time in his busy schedule. Holland Hunter, Robert Osborn, Alvin Rubinstein, Maurice Simon, and Mike Urban all became aware of what I hoped to do and helped me accomplish it.

The Soviet scholars who helped me understand how local government worked in their country were without exception courteous, professional, and patient. Some were remarkably candid. While their names and affiliations are listed elsewhere (Chapter 1, note 20) and their contributions are cited often, Professor Georgii Vasil'evich Barabashev, chairman of the Department of State Law and Soviet Construction at Moscow State University, deserves special mention. Without his unstinting efforts on my behalf, this book could not have been written.

I am also grateful to Dan Davidson and his wonderful staff at the Russian Studies Center at Bryn Mawr College, who labored mightily to revitalize my rusty Russian (unless otherwise indicated, all translations of Russian materials are by the author). Carly Rogers, the program officer for the Soviet exchanges at IREX, deserves special thanks, not only for finally getting me over there but also for patiently holding my hand during the anxious waiting period. It is also a pleasure to acknowledge the efforts of Gail

Ullman of Princeton University Press; a steadier guide through the perils of publication would be difficult to find. The work of my graduate assistants in lightening my load also deserves recognition, as does the intellectual stimulation and companionship I received from the students in my courses on the Soviet system over the years. Finally, with the exception of my wife, no one suffered more in the preparation of this manuscript than the one who had to type and retype it but who did so with remarkable goodwill, Anne Bowden.

Soviet Grassroots

APART FROM a professional interest in Soviet politics, the genesis of the present work can be traced to the eight years (1976–84) I spent as an elected official in Radnor, a municipality of nearly 30,000 people in a suburb of Philadelphia, Pennsylvania. The government of this municipality is composed of a board of seven commissioners, elected by district, who serve as a legislative council. Executive responsibilities belong to a professional manager who serves at the pleasure of the board and who supervises the day-to-day operations of the various administrative departments. While generally affluent and disproportionately well educated, the population of this municipality includes segments that are neither. If one wanted to observe firsthand the realities of citizen participation in local government in the United States, it would be difficult to find a better vantage point than that provided by my experience as an elected representative.

I quickly developed a theory to explain what I observed in Radnor regarding local participation. Called the "gored-ox" theory of politics, it holds that most people, most of the time, are uninvolved, ill-informed, and uninterested when it comes to local politics, but if their personal interests are significantly affected, they can quickly become very involved, highly vocal, and if not well informed at least quite opinionated.

This view of political participation in the United States is substantially different from the ideal of the New England town meeting that is perpetuated by high school civics textbooks, but it would not surprise those who study such matters. At least since the early 1960s, when Robert Dahl wrote his classic work *Who Governs? Democracy and Power in an American City*, many political scientists have argued that most people simply do not consider politics an important part of their lives and that when they do get involved it is most often instrumental—that is, to protect their own interests. Indeed, politics can be defined as the process by which governments at various levels resolve the differences between competing interests. In the absence of compelling self-interest, however, citizen participation in political life in the United States is negligible for all but a few "professionals."[1] Empirical research on political participation in the United States conducted by Sidney Verba and Norman Nie reveals that, except for voting, there is no political activity in which more than a third of the American people take part.[2] Dahl points out that for most citizens "politics is a sideshow in the great circus of life."[3]

"Democratic revisionism" is the term that has been applied to this view of citizen involvement in politics,[4] and to a large extent I share this view. The framework for the analysis in this book is behavioral and owes much to David Easton, Gabriel Almond, Karl Deutsch, Robert Dahl, and Harold Lasswell. Politics is the process societies use to decide who gets what. But my experience in local politics suggests that there is another dimension to political participation that is not adequately accounted for by the democratic revisionists. A clear majority of the issues decided by the Radnor board of commissioners are utilitarian and involve the pursuit of private self-interest, but it

[1] Robert A. Dahl, *Who Governs? Democracy and Power in an American City* (New Haven: Yale University Press, 1961). See also Robert A. Dahl, *Modern Political Analysis* (Englewood Cliffs, N.J.: Prentice-Hall, 1963), esp. pp. 59–62.

[2] Sidney Verba and Norman H. Nie, *Participation in America* (New York: Harper and Row, 1972), pp. 30–31.

[3] Dahl, *Who Governs?* p. 306; see also pp. 276–301.

[4] The term "democratic revisionism" is used by Donald W. Keim, "Participation in Contemporary Democratic Theories," in J. Roland Pennock and John W. Chapman (eds.), Nomos 16, *Participation in Politics* (New York: Lieber-Atherton, 1975), pp. 3–7.

soon became clear to me that some citizen participation cannot be accurately described in this way. There were occasionally instances of citizen involvement, often at considerable personal cost in terms of time and energy, in the promotion of what can best be termed the commonweal. Examples would include citizen-initiated efforts to adopt a "home-rule" charter for the municipality, to acquire and preserve open spaces, to construct a new library, and to provide recreational opportunities for those who could not otherwise afford them. Moreover, the Hobbesian view of *homo civicus* offered by the democratic revisionists fails to account for those who hold some position in local government, advisory or elected, who are not "professionals," and who harbor no political ambitions other than public service; at personal cost, these people contribute what they can for the common good. Political participation for the sake of a public benefit rather than a private benefit, and for its intrinsic value rather than as a means to an end, comes closer to the vision of the critics of democratic revisionism, who advocate some form of "participatory democracy," including Peter Bachrach, Jack Walker, Henry Kariel, and Robert Pranger, among others.[5] In short, if it is clear that most citizens behave in the manner that Dahl ascribes to *homo civicus*, it became increasingly apparent to me, as a participant-observer that some do not.

The questions that provide the emotional and intellectual impetus for the present work derive from my sojourn in the "real" political world, which stimulated my curiosity about grassroots political life in the Soviet Union. Specialists, at least, do know that citizens in the Soviet Union elect local representatives, but can these representatives really do anything? The totalitarian model held that there was a good deal of political participation by citizens in the

[5] Keim's chapter (in ibid.) provides an excellent summary of the debate regarding the place of political participation in democratic theory. See ibid., p. 4, on the Hobbesian parallel in Dahl's *homo civicus*, and ibid., pp. 8–24, for a summary of the views of critics of "democratic revisionism."

Soviet Union, but that it was mobilized from above merely for the purpose of propagandizing and socializing citizens and could therefore hardly be considered "genuine." But that model failed to account adequately for the changing realities of Soviet political life after Stalin, and the question of mass political participation was reopened. Quantitatively, at least, participation is impressive, but the key question remains a qualitative one: Is it "meaningful"?[6] This book focuses on that question.

We will be taking a close look at what locally elected representatives, called "deputies," in the Soviet Union actually do. Do constituents come to them with local problems, as my Radnor constituents did? If so, is there much the deputies can do for them? What can citizens do if a representative does not do what they want? What can a deputy do to represent his constituents? What kinds of issues are dealt with at the local level—and what kinds are not? And perhaps most important in trying to establish whether such participation is "genuine," what opportunities exist for citizen-initiated action? Are such opportunities ever used? In short, can we in any way compare the kind of citizen participation in local politics that I observed in eight years as a locally elected official with what takes place at the local level in the Soviet Union?

My preference for the behavioral approach to politics has already been noted. Ideologically, I have a deep and abiding preference for the values embedded in Western traditions of democratic liberalism. Nonetheless, the present work is not polemical. It does not seek to persuade readers that democracy in the Soviet Union does or does not exist. Its goal is to provide an objective picture of what locally elected Soviet representatives do so that debate about the nature of citizen participation in Soviet politics will have a stronger basis in fact. While the point of view

---

[6] The extensive literature regarding political participation in the Soviet Union is reviewed at length in Chapter 2.

taken is often critical, it is not my purpose to show only the shortcomings of the Soviet system.

In pursuit of the goals stated here, the first step will be to show, in Chapter 1, why the subject of political participation in the Soviet Union is of interest and how the author proposes to treat it. Then Chapter 2 gives a thorough review of the often controversial Western scholarship on the subject and offers an analytical perspective that might move the debate forward and that in any case provides a theoretical framework for analyzing activities of locally elected representatives in the Soviet Union. Chapter 3 provides a historical overview of the policies on local government adopted by the Communist Party of the Soviet Union (CPSU) and of major legislation dealing with the soviets. Chapter 4 looks at the structural framework within which the deputies conduct their activities and provides a statistical profile of the soviets and their deputies. Chapters 5 and 6 are the heart of the book and describe, respectively, the ways in which constituents can communicate their goals, problems, and preferences to the deputy and what the deputy can do to respond to their needs. Chapter 6 also focuses on the role of deputies in making decisions and shaping policy. The concluding chapter offers observations on the gap between what seems possible in terms of citizen participation in Soviet local government and what is often practiced, and speculates about what the evolution of the deputy's role may imply for Soviet political culture and indeed for change in Soviet society.

CHAPTER ONE

Studying Soviet Deputies

IN THE SOVIET UNION, citizens are elected to local government to represent the interests of the people who elected them. These individuals are referred to as deputies, and the organs of government in which they serve are called local soviets. Largely neglected during the Stalin years, the activities of the deputies have been the subject of a resurgence of interest since 1956, when Nikita Khrushchev called for revitalization of the soviets as part of the process of de-Stalinization. Over the past thirty years a substantial body of legislation expanding the role of the deputy has been adopted. This legislation was accompanied by assertions that the growing importance of the soviets was stipulated by the theory of "developed socialism," a contribution to the evolution of Marxist-Leninist doctrine emphasized during the tenure of Leonid Brezhnev as General Secretary of the Communist Party of the Soviet Union (CPSU). Thus, the institutional basis for the increased activity of elected deputies received ideological support from the CPSU.

Given these expressions of official support for expansion of the deputies' activities, the primary concern of this book is to understand how the deputy functions in practice. What can deputies actually do, and how do they do it? More specifically, what is the role of the deputy as a representative of constituency interests? What mechanisms do Soviet citizens use to communicate their needs to their elected representatives? How effectively do these mechanisms work? What can deputies do to satisfy the needs and demands of their constituents? Is there any evidence that the role of the deputy has grown over the past years?

WHY STUDY LOCAL SOVIET DEPUTIES?

Answers to the above questions will contribute to our empirical knowledge of political participation in the Soviet Union. The importance of the vigorous debate by Western specialists on this issue (see Chapter 2) should be clear. Quite simply, if it can be shown that Soviet citizens do have legitimate opportunities to participate effectively in political life, and that these opportunities have increased over time, then our conclusions about the nature and evolution of the Soviet system are likely to be different from the conclusions we would make if such opportunities do not exist. In particular, the opportunity to participate is a precondition for the emergence of a "civic culture" in Soviet society; absence of participation would indicate the persistence of a Stalinist political culture with its reliance on coercive means to maintain system stability.[1]

[1] The concept of a "civic culture," while not without detractors, is widely accepted in the professional literature and was first articulated in Gabriel Almond and Sidney Verba, *The Civic Culture* (Princeton: Princeton University Press, 1963), esp. pp. 1–45. Almond and Verba maintain that the perceived ability to participate in political decision-making is the distinguishing characteristic of such a culture. The concept has generated considerable controversy, much of which has been brought together, along with a response, in a collection edited by the original authors, *The Civic Culture Revisited* (Boston: Little, Brown, and Co., 1980). A "civic culture" is only one of several possible types of political culture, a concept that itself has engendered definitional disputation, as discussed by Archie Brown in the concluding chapter of the book he edited, *Political Culture and Communist Studies* (New York: M. E. Sharpe, 1984). The most ambitious attempt to employ the concept of political culture in understanding Soviet politics is found in Stephen White's *Political Culture and Soviet Politics* (New York: St. Martin's Press, 1979). The present work will use the definition offered in Gabriel Almond and Bingham Powell, *Comparative Politics: A Developmental Approach* (Boston: Little, Brown, and Co., 1966): "Political culture is the pattern of individual attitudes and orienta-

The concept of political efficacy provides a link between political participation and system stability. Political scientists use the term "political efficacy" in several ways, but most commonly to describe an attitude of subjective competence found among citizens regarding the actions of their government—a perception that they have the ability to influence governmental decisions that affect their lives. The feeling that one cannot do this is referred to as "political alienation."[2] Because politically efficacious citizens presumably feel a greater sense of personal responsibility for governmental decisions, it is reasonable to expect that they will be more likely to support those decisions voluntarily than individuals who are politically alienated. A feeling of subjective competence in a population should enhance system support and political stability; its opposite, political alienation, would require reliance on coercion to prevent the system from falling apart.

How is political participation related to political efficacy? Does participation lead to feelings of efficacy, or is it that efficacious people are more likely to participate? The relationship between political attitudes and political behavior is a complex theoretical issue, as Archie Brown and others point out.[3] The prevailing view is that the two variables

tions towards politics among the members of a political system" (p. 50). The possibility that a return to the political culture of the Stalinist period could result if efforts to foster political participation in the Soviet Union fail is discussed in Theodore H. Friedgut's groundbreaking work *Political Participation in the USSR* (Princeton: Princeton University Press, 1979), pp. 320–325.

[2] For a recent review of this concept, see Paul Abramson, *Political Attitudes in America* (San Francisco: W. H. Freeman and Co., 1983), chap. 8. See also Ada Finifter, "Dimensions of Political Alienation," *American Political Science Review* 64 (June 1970).

[3] The issues were originally raised by Archie Brown in the introductory chapter of Archie Brown and Jack Gray (eds.), *Political Culture and Political Change in Communist States* (New York: Holmes and Meier, 1977), pp. 12–14. They are elaborated on at much greater length in Brown, *Political Culture and Communist Studies*. In particular, the chapter by Mary McAuley, "Political Culture and Communist Studies: One Step Forward, Two Steps

are interdependently related.[4] Lester Milbrath, summing up the literature, writes, "The safest inference is that political participation and subjective competence are positively related. An increase in the level of one is accompanied by an increase in the level of the other."[5] Political participation may bring about changes in the way people think about politics as much as the reverse.

This hypothesis supports the view that an increase in political participation in the Soviet Union will be accompanied by greater feelings of political efficacy, which in turn will bring about greater support for the system. It is hardly surprising that the study of political participation in the Soviet Union has generated so much controversy and definitional disputation among Western scholars, for evidence that Soviet citizens can effectively participate in decisions that affect their lives would support the view that the stability of the Soviet political system is increasingly based not on coercion but on consensus.

Back," sharply defines the differences of opinion between those she identifies as "subjectivists" and "behavioralists." The chapters by Brown, Jonathan Miller, and Stephen White are, at least in part, rejoinders to McAuley. The approach adopted in the present work is discussed in greater length in the section of the next chapter that deals with reconceptualizing political participation.

[4] See Gabriel Almond, "The Intellectual History of the Civic Culture Concept," in Almond and Verba, *The Civic Culture Revisited*, p. 29; and Almond's review of Stephen White's book on Soviet political culture in *Soviet Studies* 33 (April 1981), pp. 307–309. White also holds this view (*Political Culture and Soviet Politics*, pp. 16–17). Even Brown acknowledges that he is "probably a minority of one" in resisting a broader definition of political culture that would include the behavioral dimension (*Political Culture and Communist Studies*, p. 3). In correspondence with the author, Brown emphasized that excluding behavioral considerations from the *definition* of political culture implies no judgment either way on the issue of the relationship between political culture and political behavior.

[5] Lester Milbrath, *Political Participation*, 2nd ed. (New York: Rand McNally, 1977), p. 59. Brown (*Political Culture and Communist Studies*, pp. 149–155) cites a considerable body of social-psychological literature to support his contention that there is no one-to-one correspondence between participation and subjective competence.

For students of political participation in the Soviet
Union, there are good reasons to take a closer look at the
role of the deputy in local Soviet government. First, there
is the special importance attributed to this position as one
of several institutions in which Soviet citizens may participate. Theodore Friedgut, author of the most thorough examination of Soviet political participation to date, writes,
"Today, the elected deputies of the local soviets have become the most active focus of mass citizen participation in
the USSR."[6] Unlike the practice with other Soviet participatory organizations, each of which claims to represent
one or another specialized constituency, all Soviet citizens
are eligible to vote for the deputies; at least in principle,
the character of the deputies' representative function is
universal. As the elected representatives of all the people,
deputies to the local soviets represent an important point
of connection between the organs of the state and the average citizen. Like the ganglia of the nervous system, the
deputies both receive and transmit the messages that
monitor the well-being of the body politic. Soviet scholars
recognize this too. The leading Soviet textbook on the soviets makes it clear that while the first function of the deputy is to represent the interests of constituents in the government, the deputy is also responsible for representing
the government to the people. Thus, "they [the deputies]
explain and propagandize the policies of the CPSU, and
by personal example sit as a model in the fulfillment of
labor and social duties."[7] The unique position of the soviets as the "political foundation" of the Soviet Union to
which all other state agencies are accountable was further
confirmed by article 2 of the 1977 Constitution.[8]

Second, the sheer number of deputies and amount of

[6] Friedgut, *Political Participation in the USSR*, p. 155.
[7] G. V. Barabashev and K. F. Sheremet, *Sovetskoe stroitel'stvo*, 2nd ed. (Moscow: Iurid. Lit., 1981).
[8] *Kommentarii k zakonu o statuse narodnykh deputatov SSSR* (Moscow: Iurid. Lit., 1983), p. 23.

participation at the local level are reasons to take a close look at the role of deputy. In 1985 there were 52,041 soviets comprising more than 2.3 million deputies.[9] About half the deputies are replaced at each new election, which means that the number of people who have held political office in the Soviet Union exceeds that of any noncommunist political system. Holding office anywhere is itself a participatory act: the deputy is both participant and object of participation. It may be argued that the sheer number of elected officials, in the Soviet case, may dilute their individual weight as effective decision-makers. From another perspective, however, a situation in which one deputy serves fewer constituents could mean that the role of that deputy as a representative of community interests is enhanced.[10] Given the lower constituent-deputy ratio, an emphasis on the constituency-service function of the elected representative may offer a fresh approach to our understanding of political participation in communist countries.

Finally, Soviet leaders themselves have shown increased interest in revitalizing local government generally and activating the role of the deputy in particular. According to the theory of "developed socialism," the concept of the dictatorship of the proletariat has been replaced by a "state of all the people." In this "state of all the people," the functions of the government will be increasingly taken over by mass social organizations, especially the soviets. This ideological imperative has found expression in a number of resolutions increasing the role of the local so-

[9] *Itogi vyborov i sostav deputatov mestnykh Sovetov narodnykh deputatov 1985 godu* (Moscow, Izvestiia, 1985).

[10] During interviews with Soviet specialists and deputies conducted by the author during a three-month visit to Moscow in the fall of 1984, the relatively large number of deputies was frequently defended on pragmatic grounds, as increasing representativeness, and on ideological grounds, because Lenin had referred to the soviets as "schools of self-government."

viets.[11] The deputies' role, in particular, was enhanced by the "Law on the Status of Soviet Deputies" (adopted on September 20, 1972), by the 1977 Constitution, and by subsequent legislation.[12] Consequently, serious interest in the local soviets on the part of scholars in the Soviet Union has grown rapidly over the past two decades. Some of this extensive literature urges reforms that would substantially enhance the deputies' autonomy and jurisdiction.[13] In addition, there is now a monthly journal for deputies called *Sovety narodnykh deputatov* (*SND*; published since 1977).[14] Finally, there are a number of studies of local soviets based on quantitative research, including surveys.[15]

Even though participation in local government is rele-

[11] A concise summary of these developments may be found in Ronald J. Hill, "The Development of Soviet Local Government Since Stalin's Death," in Everett M. Jacobs (ed.), *Soviet Local Politics and Government* (London: George Allen and Unwin, 1983). On the relevance of "developed socialism" to the soviets, see Jeffrey W. Hahn, "Is Developed Socialism a Soviet Version of Convergence?" in Jim Seroka and Maurice Simon (eds.), *Developed Socialism in the Soviet Bloc* (Boulder, Colo.: Westview Press, 1982), p. 28.

[12] *Kommentarii k zakonu o statuse narodnykh deputatov v SSSR; Sbornik normativnykh aktov po sovetskomu gosudarstvennomu pravu* (Moscow: Iurid. Lit., 1984).

[13] Ronald J. Hill, *Soviet Politics, Political Science, and Reform* (New York: M. E. Sharpe, 1980).

[14] This journal was published from 1957 to 1977 as *Sovety deputatov trudiashchiksia* (*SDT*). The title change reflects the 1977 Constitution, which marks the change from the dictatorship of the proletariat to the "state of all the people."

[15] Among the most valuable of these are R. A. Safarov, *Obshchestvennoe mnenie i gosudarstvennoe upravlenie* (Moscow: Iurid. Lit., 1975); A. T. Leizerov, *Demokraticheskie formy deiatel'nosti mestnykh Sovetov* (Minsk: Belorusskii gosudarstvennyi universitet, 1977); B. A. Grushin and L. A. Onikova (eds.), *Massovaia informatsiia v sovetskom promyshlennom gorode: Opyt sotsiologicheskogo issledovaniia* (Moscow: Politkniga, 1980); P. N. Lebedev, *Mestnye Sovety i obshchestvennoe mnenie* (Moscow: Iurid. Lit., 1982); and B. K. Alekseev and M. N. Perfil'ev, *Printsipy i tendentsii razvitiia predstavitel'nogo sostava mestnykh Sovetov (sot siologicheskoe issledovanie)* (Leningrad: Lenizdat, 1976).

vant to the way Soviet citizens view politics in their country, Western scholarly literature has only recently showed much interest in the topic.[16] The next chapter reviews the Western literature on Soviet local government at greater length, but we will note here that there is no work devoted exclusively to describing the role of locally elected Soviet deputies. This book fills that gap.

THE SCOPE OF THIS STUDY

In delineating the scope of the present study, let us begin by clarifying what is not included. Although the growing role of the local soviets in the administration of economic policy is of great interest to Soviet scholars and policy-makers and merits the attention of Western analysts, treatment of that role is not central here.[17] Nor is it the purpose of this book to review exhaustively the activities of the deputy at each level of government, or to com-

[16] The important exceptions to the general lack of research done on Soviet local government in general, and the deputy in particular, are the works by Theodore H. Friedgut, *Political Participation in the USSR*; Everett M. Jacobs, *Soviet Local Politics and Government*; Ronald J. Hill, *Soviet Political Elites: The Case of Tiraspol* (New York: St. Martin's Press, 1977), and much of Hill's *Soviet Politics, Political Science, and Reform*. Portions of all these works contribute much to our understanding of local politics in the Soviet Union, but none deals exclusively with the role of the deputy.

[17] For a good Western commentary on this aspect of soviet activity, see Carol Lewis, "The Economic Functions of the Local Soviets," in Jacobs, *Soviet Local Politics and Government*; and Carol Lewis and Stephen Sternheimer, *Soviet Urban Management* (New York: Praeger, 1979). Recent Soviet literature is voluminous, but among the works worth noting are G. V. Barabashev (ed.), *Rol' mestnykh Sovetov v ekonomicheskom i sotsial'nom razvitii gorodov* (Moscow: Moscow State University, 1983); E. I. Koronevskaia, *Sovety narodnykh deputatov i kompleksnoe razvitie regionov* (Moscow: Sovetskaia Rossiia, 1983); a collection published by the Institute of State and Law of the Academy of Sciences (hereafter IGPAN), *Priniatie reshenii mestnymi organami vlasti i upravleniia* (Moscow: IGPAN, 1983); and S. V. Solov'eva, *Sovety i nauchno-tekhnicheskii progress* (Moscow: Iurid. Lit., 1978).

pare systematically regional or national variations in deputy activities. The work of deputies at different levels and in different regions will be referred to in order to generalize the deputy experience, but the primary focus is deputies in the city (*gorodskoi*) and city borough (*raion v gorode*) soviets. This is partly because of the information available, but also because the *process* of constituency contact, not the degree of its universality, is the focus. Finally, this is a study in Soviet political behavior. A chapter on history and a chapter on institutional setting provide background necessary for understanding the deputies' role, but the main interest of the book is describing empirically what the deputies actually do.

An underlying hypothesis that will be explored derives from studies previously cited that positively correlate effective political participation with citizens' feelings of subjective competence. Specifically, if citizen-deputy contact at the local level is seen as having a reasonable chance of achieving a desired outcome, it may be necessary to reconsider the prevailing view that there is no sense of civic competence in Soviet society. It could be argued that development of a sense of civic competence at the local level does not mean much for the system as a whole, but the local deputy may be the first and most accessible contact the citizen has with the organs of Soviet government. While the substance of the issues involved may be parochial, it is possible that, if such contacts are rewarding, the larger system may come to be regarded in a more favorable light as well.

The experience of being a deputy may in itself change how citizens think about government. Those who participate in government are more likely to know more about the political system, its institutions and personnel, and to have more favorable feelings toward the system than those who do not.[18] If these propositions have any cross-

[18] This is well established in the literature. See Milbrath, *Political Participation*; Sidney Verba, Norman Nie, and Jae-on Kim, *Participation and Po-*

cultural validity, and if the deputy increasingly is able to influence political outcomes on behalf of constituents, then the activities of the deputies could have important implications for development of support for the system in the Soviet Union. Conversely, failure to produce the outcomes sought by constituents could lead to deepened cynicism and to erosion of whatever hopes Soviet citizens may have for the evolution of their system in a more democratic direction.

Methods

The most appropriate means for testing the hypothesis that there is a correlation between political participation and subjective competence would involve the definition of specific variables in such a way that they could be measured quantitatively. Data would then be collected using survey research techniques, and analysis would determine the validity of the original propositions. Unfortunately, the possibilities for conducting systematic social science research in the Soviet context are extremely limited, especially when the variables are attitudinal in nature. While Soviet specialists have conducted some useful survey research, the kind of research on public attitudes about the effectiveness of deputy activities that would enable an objective observer to draw conclusions about variations in levels of subjective competence is simply not available. In view of these limitations, this study is essentially descriptive and will focus almost exclusively on one variable— participation. Any conclusions offered regarding the effect of participation on Soviet political culture must remain more speculative than the standard criteria for behavioral research would require or than the author would wish.

Short of rigorous hypothesis-testing, other empirical research strategies can be employed: field observation, in-

litical Equality (New York: Cambridge University Press, 1978); and, of course, Almond and Verba, *Civic Culture*.

cluding interviews with deputies and specialists; the use of archival materials, such as public records, government documents, and press reports; and analysis of existing statistics.[19] Because the present study is based primarily on these three methods, in combination with an analysis of the published work of Soviet and Western scholars, the data generated by the three methods need further elaboration.

Field Research

The field research that is the basis of much of this study took place during a three-month period in the fall of 1984 while the author was a senior research fellow at Moscow State University. In addition to interviewing Soviet specialists on local government and using Soviet library resources,[20] it was possible to observe the actual workings of local government bodies and to interview about thirty deputies and people who held administrative or executive positions.[21] For example, interviews were held with eight

[19] David Nachmias and Chava Nachmias, *Research Methods in the Social Sciences*, 2nd ed. (New York: St. Martin's Press, 1981), esp. chaps. 7, 10.

[20] Among the Soviet specialists interviewed, some more than once, were: G. V. Barabashev, S. A. Avak'ian, N. Bogdanova, and O. E. Kutafin at Moscow State University; K. F. Sheremet, R. A. Safarov, and N. G. Starovoitov at IGPAN; A. A. Bezuglov and E. I. Kozlova of the All-Union Juridical Correspondence Institute (VIUZI); V. I. Vasil'ev, deputy editor of the journal *Sovety narodnykh deputatov (SND)*; V. A. Perttsik, director of the All-Union Scientific Research Institute on Soviet Legislation (VNIISZ); and Professor V. S. Osnovin of Voronezh University. While these people were all helpful, none is responsible for the points of view expressed in this book or for any errors of fact. The library resources the author used included the Library of the Institute for Scientific Information on the Social Sciences (INION), the Gorky Library at Moscow State University, and the Lenin Library.

[21] The author developed a Russian-language questionnaire measuring approximately forty variables in hopes of systematically interviewing a group of deputies. While a large-scale interview was not possible, the survey was completed by ten deputies of the Lenin district. In addition, interviews of varying degrees of formality were conducted with about twenty other deputies from several districts, some of whom also held executive positions.

deputies, including the chairman of the executive committee in Mitishii, a city on the outskirts of Moscow; with twelve deputies of the Lenin city borough in Moscow; and with two members of the Organizational-Instructional Department of the Moscow regional (*oblast*) soviet. A session of the local soviet of the Lenin city borough, a meeting of its Standing Committee on Socialist Legality and the Preservation of Order, and meetings of deputies with constituents were also observed. Furthermore, the author was able to look at, and in some cases acquire, records of meetings of deputies with constituents during consulting hours (the *priyom*), agendas and minutes of meetings, lists of voter mandates (*nakazy izbiratelei*), collections of complaints (*zhaloby*), and copies of reports by deputies (*otcheti*). In some cases these materials were available not only for the Lenin city borough but also for the city, the region, and other districts.[22]

Because the greatest amount of documentation and personal observation comes from the Lenin city borough, the research data presented here will make frequent use of this district as a case study. The Lenin city borough is one of thirty-two urban districts (*raion v gorode*) that comprise and are subordinate to Moscow's city government. The city of Moscow itself has regional (*oblast*) administrative status within the Russian Soviet Federated Socialist Republic (RSFSR). About 150,000 people live in the borough, which encompasses much of the older part of the city south from Red Square, including Moscow State University on Lenin Hills, and is bordered by the Moscow River. There are 250 electoral districts from which deputies may be elected to the soviet.

It can be said that the borough is atypical because it has a large university population, the Novodevichy Convent,

---

[22] Much of the documentation in this book is not available publicly either in the West or in the Soviet Union. Scholars who want to confirm the existence of any documents cited or to examine them for error of fact or interpretation may request the opportunity to do so from the present author.

and the Kremlin located within it, but otherwise it is not
unlike other urban districts in the composition of its deputies or what they do. As we shall see, the composition
of all soviets is organized to ensure representation of certain demographic and socioeconomic groups in proportion
to national or regional criteria. The organs of the Lenin
city borough soviet include a thirteen-member executive
committee (*ispolkom*), fifteen standing committees, twenty
deputy groups, and about twenty-five administrative agencies, including departments for housing, health, education, public works, and internal affairs, among the largest.
This type of structure is standard for soviets at this level.
While well represented, the university community is a distinct minority among the deputies. There are a number of
factories in the borough and a good deal of retail activity,
so that university representatives can hardly be considered a controlling force in the community's affairs. No one
from the university, for example, sat on the ispolkom during 1982–85. Moreover, the question of whether the activities that take place within the Lenin city borough can take
place elsewhere is answered at least partially by data from
other areas. In any case, the conclusions in this book de-
pend not on how typical the Lenin borough is in terms of
deputy performance but on what the *process* of constituency representation is. If it can be established that effective
constituency representation can take place in one case,
then it is reasonable to assume that it can occur elsewhere
in the Soviet Union.

Archival Research

"Archival" research is used here to refer to other
sources of data that are official or private in character and
that serve to document empirically the phenomenon under investigation.[23] In the case of research on the role of
Soviet deputies, this would include, in addition to materials previously mentioned, all legislative acts pertaining

---

[23] See Nachmias and Nachmias, *Research Methods in the Social Sciences*,
pp. 249–255.

to the activity of the deputy;[24] descriptions in the press of meetings of local soviets or the work of an individual deputy with a constituent; the publication of decisions or resolutions by the Communist Party relevant to the deputy; published letters or reports by firsthand observers about the conduct of a deputy in his or her electoral district or at a meeting; and documents of a semiofficial character, such as handbooks explaining how deputies are to act in different circumstances. Some of these documents are available in the West, but often incompletely, and some are not available in the West at all. A good example of the latter is the *Bulletin of the Executive Committee of the Moscow City Soviet*, a biweekly publication of the resolutions, decisions, and activities of the Executive Committee as they relate to the city and to each of its districts. It is an important source of empirical data on the work of the soviets, but virtually unavailable in the West.

Analysis of Existing Statistical Data

Even though social scientists in the West have been unable to conduct systematic survey research in the Soviet Union, there is a great deal of quantitative data available about almost all aspects of the deputies' activities. There are three major sources of aggregate statistics, each using data collected by the Department on Questions about the Work of the Soviets of the Presidium of the Supreme Soviet of the USSR (the Supreme Soviet of each republic has a similar department). The first is a summary of election statistics, with data about the deputies, and the organs elected by the deputies. It has been published every two years at least since 1961 on the federal and republic levels.[25] The second is a statistical handbook, published an-

---

[24] Virtually all the major federal legislation pertaining to the soviets from 1917 to 1983 has been compiled in a volume published in 1984 by Iuridicheskaia Literatura (Iurid. Lit.) entitled *Sbornik normativnykh aktov po sovetskomu gosudarstvennomu pravu* (hereafter, *Sbornik normativnykh aktov*).

[25] *Itogi vyborov i sostav deputatov mestnykh Sovetov narodnykh deputatov (statisticheskii sbornik).* (Moscow: Izvestiia). Before adoption of the 1977

nually since 1973, that summarizes the activities of the
deputies nationally and by republic.[26] The third source is
the statistical data available in the monthly journal of the
deputies, *Sovety narodnykh deputatov*, especially in the
fourth, fifth, or sixth issue of each year.[27] While the aggregate data published by the Soviet Union are sometimes
tantalizingly incomplete and categories are not always
consistent over time, the figures themselves do appear to
be accurate. Longitudinal analysis of these data will be
used to determine any changes in the composition of the
deputies and in the level of their activity over time.

Besides published aggregate data, some results of survey research, conducted either in the Soviet Union or in
the West from émigré sources, are available. In the Soviet
Union, studies were carried out in Leningrad,[28] Kalinin
Oblast,[29] Taganrog,[30] and Minsk,[31] in the cities of Orel,

Constitution the title was: *Itogi vyborov i sostav deputatov mestnykh Sovetov
deputatov trudiashchikhsia*. Citations in this text will be noted as *Itogi vyborov* unless republic editions are used.

[26] *Nekotorye voprosy organizatsionnoi raboty mestnykh Sovetov narodnykh deputatov* (Moscow: Izvestiia). The title was changed in 1977 from *Nekotorye
voprosy organizatsionnoi raboty mestnykh Sovetov deputatov trudiashchikhsia*.
Citations here will be to *Nekotorye voprosy*.

[27] See footnote 14. Citations in this text will be to *SND* or *SDT*, which-
ever is appropriate, along with the issue number and year of publication.

[28] Alekseev and Perfil'ev, *Printsipy i tendentsii*, a study of 500 deputies
from two urban districts in Leningrad conducted in 1969 and 1971.

[29] Safarov, *Obshchestvennoe mnenie i gosudarstvennoe upravlenie*, a study
of public opinion using a sample of 1,500 people and 1,000 members of
the executive and administrative personnel in Kalinin Oblast, RSFSR,
conducted 1970–1972.

[30] Grushin and Onikova, *Massovaia informatsiia v sovetskom promyshlennom gorode*, a study of mass communication in an industrial city (Taganrog) with data from Moscow and Rostov-on-Don, conducted between
1967 and 1974 using 16,159 questionnaires, 10,762 interviews, the content
analysis of 15,648 texts, personal observations, and aggregate data.

[31] Leizerov, *Demokraticheskie formy deiatel'nosti mestnykh Sovetov*. While
Leizerov's study is not based on survey research, the author does provide a useful quantitative study of deputies' activities in Belorussia. This
is a continuing longitudinal study. More recent data can be found in

Murmansk, Kaluga, and Penza in the RSFSR,[32] in Irkutsk,[33] and in four regions of different republics.[34] There
are, however, limitations on the usefulness of this research
for the present study. First, much of it deals with subject
matter tangential to the topic at hand, exploring deputy
activities or public attitudes toward the soviets only mar-
ginally. Second, in many cases the data were collected in
the late 1960s or early 1970s—before much of the important legislation on the deputies was adopted or, if
adopted, had been very much in use. Finally, Soviet survey data is frequently incomplete, either in the reporting
of results or in describing the methods employed. As a result, it can be difficult to establish reliability.

In the West, survey research has been conducted among
recent émigrés from the Soviet Union.[35] Data from this

A. T. Leizerov, *Konstitutsionnyi printsip glasnosti raboty Sovetov narodnykh deputatov* (Minsk: Belorusskii gosudarstrennyi universitet, 1981), and in
various articles he has written.

[32] Lebedev, *Mestnye Sovety i obshchestvennoe mnenie*. This booklet is
really a review of other works that use survey research to study public
opinion on the local soviets. It is intended to demonstrate the practical
applications of such research. Unfortunately, information about methods
of research, including sample size, are not readily available.

[33] See the discussion of V. A. Perttsik's work in Irkutsk in Hill, *Soviet
Politics, Political Science, and Reform*, pp. 48–55.

[34] *Lichnost' i uvazhenie k zakonu* (Moscow: IGPAN, 1979), a study conducted by IGPAN on the attitudes toward law of people in ten different
occupations in regions in Latvia, Tadzhik SSR, Yaroslav, and Saratov.

[35] There are three major studies of émigré opinion using survey research of which the author is aware. The first is a stratified sample of a
large population of émigrés called the "Soviet Interview Project," which
is being conducted under the direction of Professor James Millar at the
University of Illinois. To date, the data from this study have not been
available for secondary analysis. Second, there is a project entitled "Bureaucratic Encounters in the USSR" administered by Professor Zvi Gitelman at the University of Michigan. Third, Theodore Friedgut has conducted a similar project at the University of Jerusalem. All three efforts
are based on information of the so-called "second wave" of emigrants
from the USSR who left during the past ten years. It is not surprising that
the great majority of the respondents in all three surveys are Jewish.

source have the potential to yield insight into realities of Soviet life that otherwise cannot be studied, but several factors limit their usefulness for this study. First, except for the work of Friedgut,[36] the research design of these studies was very broad, and questions related to deputy activities per se comprise a very small portion of the whole. Second, most of the information collected is simply not yet available for secondary analysis, although publications making use of such data have appeared or are scheduled to appear. Third, the use of émigré data must raise questions of representativeness and bias.[37] Despite the limitations noted here, the survey research conducted by scholars in both the Soviet Union and the United States, when used with appropriate caution, can tell us something about the opinions of both the deputies and the public that would otherwise be lacking. In conclusion, while the empirical evidence available is perhaps inade-

[36] Friedgut's study of 300 former Soviet citizens who emigrated to Israel specifically deals with attitudes toward the deputies as well as toward other local officials. His "The Soviet Citizen's Perception of Local Government," in Jacobs, Soviet Local Politics and Government, contains useful data, some of which complements Soviet source materials in interesting ways. These are examined in the section on public opinion about the deputy in Chapter 5 of the present book.

[37] The respondents in the "Bureaucratic Encounters in the USSR" project (see footnote 35) were disproportionately well educated and at least 77 percent Jewish, although Jews account for less than 2 percent of the Soviet population. A recent article using these data suggests that the assumption of émigré bias can be "exaggerated"; The authors argue that "the ethnic imbalance of the emigration is as much a product of Soviet emigration as it is of special feelings of alienation on the part of those who have left" (Wayne DiFranceisco and Zvi Gitelman, "Soviet Political Culture and Covert Participation in Policy Implementation," American Political Science Review 78 [September 1984], p. 606). While this may be true, it in no way diminishes the unrepresentativeness of the sample, but the authors do not claim that the results can be generalized to the population in the Soviet Union. Conclusions based on such data about the political culture of the Soviet population rest on shaky empirical foundations.

quate for rigorous hypothesis-testing, it does provide a sufficient basis for attempting to answer the research problem stated earlier: To what extent are locally elected representatives in the Soviet Union able to represent the interests of those who elected them?

CHAPTER TWO

The Study of Political Participation
in Communist Countries

FOR THE PAST TWO DECADES, specialists on the Soviet Union have been looking at political participation in communist countries, and not without considerable controversy. Instead of reiterating what has already been written on the subject, it will be useful here to take stock of where the debate stands now and to clarify the concepts employed in the present work.

One of the standard questions used in measuring a sense of civic competence is whether respondents feel there is much they can do if an unjust law were passed by their legislative body. People living in societies with a "civic" or "participatory" political culture are more likely to respond positively than those who do not.[1] When asked to specify what they would actually do if such a law were passed, students in the author's classes over the years responded in a variety of ways. Most frequently mentioned was contacting legislators (individually or through a group) either directly or indirectly through petitions, letters, or the media. Students also said they would get involved in election or campaign activities, including voting or working for a candidate, either in a political party or through a special interest group. Less frequently, reference was made to participating in demonstrations, peaceful or violent, and to using class action suits in the courts.

The most influential effort to provide a conceptual framework for analyzing different forms of political participation and to examine them empirically is the seven-na-

[1] Almond and Verba, *The Civic Culture*, pp. 141–167.

tion comparative study of Austria, India, Japan, the Netherlands, Nigeria, the United States, and Yugoslavia conducted by Sidney Verba, Norman Nie, and Jae-on Kim entitled *Participation and Political Equality: A Seven-Nation Comparison* and published in 1978. The authors adopted the following working definition of political participation: "those legal activities by private citizens that are more or less directly aimed at influencing the selection of governmental personnel and/or the actions they take."[2] Using a factor analysis of different kinds of political activity, the authors generalized four "modes" of conventional participation: voting, campaign activity, communal activity, and particularized contacts.[3]

The four modes of activity used as the conceptual framework of the seven-nation study can be reduced to two: participation in elections, including voting and campaign activity, and what can be called constituent participation, including communal activity and particularized contact. Verba, Nie, and Kim use both "communal activity" and "particularized contact" to describe contact between constituents and the people responsible for making public policy with the object of influencing that policy. Their study explicitly adopted what the authors acknowledged was a "narrower" conception of participation by excluding people who were "professionally involved in politics," including "government officials, party officials, as well as professional lobbyists,"[4] but the present work will expand the definition of constituent participation to include such individuals.

[2] Sidney Verba, Norman Nie, and Jae-On Kim, *Participation and Political Equality: A Seven Nation Comparison* (New York: Cambridge University Press, 1978), p. 46.

[3] Ibid., pp. 51–57. Verba and Nie explicitly exclude from consideration demonstrations, peaceful or violent, and deal with what they call "within the system" participation. Their model has been criticized for this reason. See William Schonfeld, "The Meaning of Democratic Participation," *World Politics* 28 (October 1975): 134–158.

[4] Verba et al., *Participation and Political Equality*, p. 47.

Constituent contact, rather than electoral activity, appears to be the form of participation that interests students of communist political systems most. Elections in communist countries are thought to be largely ceremonial. With the exceptions of Hungary, Poland, and Yugoslavia, only one candidate is nominated for each position, and the nomination process is controlled by only one political party.[5] However, forms of political participation other than elections are widespread, as noted in the case of Yugoslavia by Verba, Nie, and Kim.[6] And given the low rate of participation in local elections in many Western democracies, and the absence of real competition in many electoral districts, there is reason to question the effectiveness

[5] While some prenomination competition may go on in Soviet elections, the lack of choice for the electorate means that this activity is largely ceremonial and therefore less likely to be perceived by Soviet citizens as a way to communicate demands or preferences. See Everett M. Jacobs, "Soviet Local Elections: What They Are and What They Are Not," *Soviet Studies* 22 (July 1970); Friedgut, *Political Participation in the USSR*, pp. 137–146; and Victor Zaslavsky and Robert Brym, "The Structure of Power and the Functions of Soviet Local Elections," in Jacobs, *Soviet Local Politics and Government*. The possibility of competitive elections in the Soviet Union in the future cannot be ruled out. Yugoslavia has had them for some time, and in Hungary in June 1985 a new law requiring at least two candidates for each seat went into effect. See Paul Lewis, "Voter Choice Brings Some Upsets in Hungary," *New York Times*, June 23, 1985, p. 6. The idea of electoral choice has been proposed by a number of Soviet specialists for some years. See Hill, *Soviet Politics, Political Science, and Reform*, pp. 26–30. Professor G. V. Barabashev, in particular, has made specific recommendations that some degree of electoral competition be introduced to allow, say, five candidates to compete for three places. This idea is embedded in a law adopted on February 26, 1987, following M. S. Gorbachev's proposed competitive elections at the January 1987 plenary session of the Central Committee of the CPSU. The law called for the introduction of multiple-candidacy districts on an experimental basis in selected regions of the RSFSR for the June 21, 1987, elections to local soviets. For more on this, see below, chapter 4 and footnotes 31 and 32 of that chapter.

[6] Verba, Nie, and Kim, *Participation and Political Equality*, pp. 53–54, 323–327.

of elections as a mechanism for influencing decisions even in noncommunist systems.[7] Therefore, the focus here will be on constituent participation rather than electoral activity.

Two issues have dominated the Western literature on constituent participation in communist countries: whether politics in these countries is influenced by interest group activity and whether mass political participation is "meaningful." The attempt to use interest group analysis for understanding the Soviet political system has been controversial. A review of these debates can be found elsewhere,[8] but their relevance to the present work deserves at least passing notice. The application of interest

---

[7] Less than one-third of the American electorate report voting regularly in local elections. Sidney Verba and Norman Nie, *Participation in America* (New York: Harper and Row, 1972), chap. 2. If one defines a "competitive election" as an election in which the losing candidate receives more than one-third of the votes, then a large majority of congressional and local elections in the United States are not competitive. When one further notes that voting is often a function of factors other than "rational choice," then electoral participation must be considered a poor mechanism for communicating citizen preferences to decision-makers. At best, it is a blunt instrument that can be used in those relatively rare cases when citizens are sufficiently aroused to change officeholders. See Verba, Nie, and Kim, *Participation and Political Equality*, p. 53. A more recent review of the literature on voting behavior, but one that reaches a generally similar conclusion, is in Ada Finifter (ed.), *Political Science: The State of the Discipline* (Washington, D.C.: American Political Science Association, 1983), chap. 12.

[8] Jeffrey W. Hahn, "Conceptualizing Political Participation in the USSR: Two Decades of Debate," Kennan Institute for Advanced Russian Studies, Occasional Paper no. 190 (1984). Susan Gross Solomon (ed.), *Pluralism in the Soviet Union* (New York: St. Martin's Press, 1983). The storm over "interest group pluralism" appears to have lost some of its fury. In addition to the chapter by Jerry Hough, "Pluralism, Corporatism, and the Soviet Union," in Solomon, *Pluralism in the Soviet Union*, see H. Gordon Skilling, "Interest Groups and Communist Politics Revisited," *World Politics* 36 (October 1983), p. 14; Zvi Gitelman, "Comments," *Studies in Comparative Communism* 12 (Spring 1979), pp. 35–38; and the reviews of Solomon's *Pluralism* by David Powell in *Slavic Review* 44 (Spring 1985), and by T. H. Rigby in *World Politics* 36 (July 1984).

group theory to our understanding of Soviet politics opened up the conceptual possibility that policy-making in the Soviet Union could be influenced by input from below, or at least by those outside the small circle of the party elite normally assumed by the totalitarian model to enjoy an unquestioned monopoly of the decision-making process. What the debates and research over the past two decades on this topic have established is that some sort of constituency participation in the form of interest group activity does take place in the Soviet Union.[9] In affirming the participation of groups in Soviet political life, the groundwork was laid for a reexamination of political participation by individuals.

THE DEBATE OVER MASS POLITICAL PARTICIPATION

Until the mid-1970s, the prevailing view of mass political participation in communist countries was that, with few exceptions, such participation was little more than window dressing used by Soviet leaders to obtain a veneer of legitimacy while enhancing their ability to mobilize citizens and check up on policy implementation. Organizations involving mass activity, such as trade unions, the local soviets, the Komsomol, the People's Control Committees, and the like, served primarily as "transmission belts" used by party leadership to inform, direct, and control the masses.[10]

Not all analyses in this period agreed with the prevailing view. In 1969, James Oliver argued that within limits the avenues open to "citizen demands" had widened and that the local deputy played a significant role in processing these demands.[11] L. G. Churchward suggested that partic-

---

[9] Skilling, "Interest Groups and Communist Politics Revisited," pp. 8, 25.

[10] White, *Political Culture and Soviet Politics*, pp. 16–17.

[11] James Oliver, "Citizen Demands in the Soviet Political System," *American Political Science Review* 63 (June 1969).

ipation had increased in the post-Stalin period and that it varied inversely with the level of government.[12] Henry Morton provided an unusual "inside look" at the workings of an urban district in Moscow based on his attendance at several organizational meetings dealing primarily with housing. His description suggested that an unexpected amount of confrontation took place at these meetings. Other than the present work and that of Friedgut on the Oktyabr' District of Moscow, this appears to be the only firsthand observation of local Soviet government in action by Western observers since World War II.[13] A number of works dealing with the governing of Soviet cities concluded that party-state relations were more complex than previously thought, with the organs of the state playing a significant role in formulation as well as implementation of policy.[14] Despite this, Donald Schulz writes in his critical summary of the literature:

> The functions of participation were thought to be largely limited to the socialization of the populace, the legitimation of the regime and the mobilization of the citizenry in pursuit of goals determined by the elite. Thus participation, it was argued, was neither meaningful nor real, and could be safely ignored by political scientists.[15]

Two articles, one by Jerry Hough in 1976 and one by D. Richard Little in the same year, stimulated new interest in the nature of mass political participation in communist

[12] L. G. Churchward, "Soviet Local Government Today," *Soviet Studies* 17 (April 1966).

[13] Henry W. Morton, "The Leningrad District of Moscow: An Inside Look," *Soviet Studies* 20 (December 1969), p. 206.

[14] William Taubman, *Governing Soviet Cities* (New York: Praeger, 1973), esp. pp. 111–115; B. Michael Frolic, "Decision-Making in Soviet Cities," *American Political Science Review* 66 (March 1972), esp. pp. 50, 51; Philip D. Stewart, *Political Power in the Soviet Union* (New York: Bobbs-Merrill, 1968); and Hill, *Soviet Political Elites*; chap. 6.

[15] Donald Schulz and Jan S. Adams (eds.), *Political Participation in Communist Systems* (Elmsford, N.Y.: Pergamon Press, 1981), p. 2.

countries.[16] Both authors point out that on the basis of numbers alone political participation in the Soviet Union was substantial and had grown steadily in the post-Stalin period, often exceeding in quantitative terms the standard measures of conventional participation used to describe Western democracies, but Hough believes that we do not have enough information to determine whether mass political participation has any effect on decisions. As for the argument that participation in communist countries serves to mobilize and socialize citizens while providing feedback on the effectiveness of local administration, Hough says that this is also true of the West and that we cannot adopt two definitions of participation—one for the Soviet Union and one for the West—if we are to make a true comparison. Neither Hough nor Little denies that differences may exist, but, they argue that we do not have enough empirical evidence to draw the kinds of conclusions that prevail in the literature.[17]

A kind of cottage industry of published work dealing with political participation in communist countries has emerged since these provocative articles were published. Much of the reaction was critical, arguing that crucial distinctions should be made between "genuine" democratic participation and participation that was not "genuine." Donald Barry, in a critique of Hough's views on political participation, cites another Soviet specialist, Walter Connor, to the effect that Soviet citizens lack a participant political culture and that "the only participation worthy of the name that exists among numbers of the general populace is that practiced by the dissidents." Barry then dismisses the participation in public organizations described

[16] Jerry Hough, "Political Participation in the Soviet Union," *Soviet Studies* 28 (January 1976); D. Richard Little, "Mass Political Participation in the US and USSR: A Conceptual Analysis," *Comparative Political Studies* 8 (January 1976).

[17] See also Jerry Hough and Merle Fainsod, *How the Soviet Union Is Governed* (Cambridge: Harvard University Press, 1979), pp. 510–517.

by Hough as "sham participation at best."[18] In a similar vein, T. H. Rigby argues that the essential difference between mass political participation in the West and in the Soviet Union is the opportunity for individuals or groups to organize and express public opposition to Soviet leaders and their policies. He specifically notes the importance of elections in the West as a mechanism for replacing a government when people are dissatisfied with its performance.[19] Indeed, the absence of competitive elections in the Soviet Union is one of the most frequently articulated criticisms uniting those who maintain that political participation in Soviet politics is little more than a charade.[20]

Other scholars argue vigorously on behalf of the utility of studying political participation in communist countries,[21] but there are still relatively few published works on local government in the Soviet Union that are based on empirical field research and deal with political participation as a major theoretical concern. The most extensive

[18] Donald Barry's critique of Hough's views, and Hough's reply, are in *Problems of Communism* 25 (September–October 1976), pp. 93–96.

[19] T. H. Rigby, "Hough on Political Participation in the Soviet Union," *Soviet Studies* 28 (April 1976), p. 260.

[20] Competitive balloting is cited as a major criterion of participation in one of the earliest and most recent articles arguing that "meaningful" participation does not exist in communist countries. See Howard Swearer, "Political Participation: Myths and Realities," *Problems of Communism* 9 (September–October 1960), p. 51; R. V. Burks, "Political Participation Under Socialism," *Studies in Comparative Communism* 15 (Spring–Summer 1982), p. 147. Burks argues that in almost all cases citizen participation in communist countries is "organized from above and involuntary in nature" (p. 142). A recent analysis by a prominent French student of Soviet politics also holds this view. See Helene C. d'Encausse, *Le Pouvoir Confisqué*, published in English translation as *Confiscated Power* (New York: Harper and Row, 1982), esp. chap. 7.

[21] Jan S. Adams, *Citizen Inspectors in the Soviet Union: The People's Control Committee* (New York: Praeger, 1977); Jan F. Triska, "Citizen Participation in Community Decisions in Yugoslavia, Romania, Hungary, and Poland," in Jan Triska and Paul M. Cocks (eds.), *Political Development in Eastern Europe* (New York: Praeger, 1977); and Schulz, *Political Participation in Communist Systems*.

work to date is that of Theodore Friedgut, whose *Political Participation in the USSR* deals primarily with the institutions of local government. Friedgut's work is based on field research carried out while he was an exchange student at Moscow University in the 1969–1970 academic year. He interviewed deputies in the Moscow City Soviet, in the Oktyabr' City Borough Soviet, and, during a week in December 1969, members of the Kutaisi City Soviet in Georgia.[22] In addition, he did extensive interviews with Jewish émigrés to Israel.[23] Friedgut's work is also based on a wide reading of Soviet source materials. After reviewing all the data available to him, Friedgut concludes that efforts to turn the local soviets into a vehicle for citizen participation that would generate popular support for the system have met with, at best, limited success: "The activization of participatory institutions has not eliminated the subject element so prominent in Soviet political culture."[24] Friedgut is "doubtful" about the thesis that successful participation will breed more participation in the Soviet Union, thereby bringing systemic change.[25]

While Friedgut sees relatively little change so far, he differs from those who see the local soviets as institutions that exist solely for the socialization and mobilization of Soviet citizens. Instead, he points out that Soviet citizens can and do "fight city hall" to some extent. "It is a significant development in the Soviet political system that the citizen can and does elicit regime attention for his demands, for the feeling of being able to command attention

[22] Theodore Friedgut, "Community Structure, Political Participation, and Soviet Local Government: The Case of the Kutaisi," in Henry Morton and Rudolf Tokes (eds.), *Soviet Politics and Society in the 1970s* (New York: Free Press, 1974).

[23] Theodore H. Friedgut, "Citizens and Soviets: Can Ivan Ivanovich Fight City Hall?" *Comparative Politics* 10 (July 1978); and T. H. Friedgut, "The Soviet Citizen's Perception of Local Government," in Jacobs, *Soviet Local Politics and Government*.

[24] Friedgut, *Political Participation in the USSR*, p. 302.

[25] Ibid., p. 317.

from the authorities is the precondition of any civic culture."[26] Most recently, he suggests that while a "civic consciousness" is not yet a dominant fact of Soviet political life, "neither is it wholly absent." Further study of the development of a civic consciousness would "enable us to understand more of the dynamics of development of Soviet society, and the prospects for that system's future."[27]

Another study of political participation based on field research in the Soviet Union is the work of Ronald J. Hill, whose *Soviet Political Elites: The Case of Tiraspol* had its origins in his doctoral dissertation, which was based on field research in Tiraspol, the third largest city in Moldavia. Hill conducted some interviews with local officials, but he relied heavily on local newspaper accounts. A second book by Hill, who spent May through July 1975 in Moscow, is *Soviet Politics, Political Science, and Reform*. In this work, he examines the problem of political change in the Soviet Union and provides an excellent review of what professional students of politics in that country are suggesting in the way of governmental reform. In certain respects, Hill's conclusions coincide with Friedgut's. Efforts to revitalize the local soviets and turn them into more-participatory organs have not yet been very successful.[28] Also like Friedgut, however, Hill maintains that local government may become the locus of more significant changes in the future. He suggests that emergence of a participatory political culture would be facilitated by the kind of democratic reforms now being discussed.[29] Finally, Hill too urges further research, especially on the role of the local

[26] Friedgut, "Citizens and Soviets," p. 469.

[27] Friedgut, "The Soviet Citizen's Perception of Local Government," p. 130.

[28] See Hill, *Soviet Political Elites*; p. 186; and Ronald J. Hill, "The Development of Local Soviet Government Since Stalin's Death," in Jacobs, *Soviet Local Politics and Government*, pp. 18, 30, 33.

[29] Hill, *Soviet Politics, Political Science, and Reform*, pp. 175–176.

deputy, which he acknowledges was not a major focus on his original study.[30]

In an article based on field research in Moscow during the 1979–1980 academic year, Michael Urban attempts to separate qualitative aspects of political participation from purely quantitative considerations by looking at the flow of information from administrative organs to the local soviets. He concludes that administrative bodies dominate the elected deputy because they control the flow of information so that the deputy cannot have a participatory role in the "public sphere." As a result, "popular participation in the USSR has little to do with democracy."[31]

The debate over citizen participation in Soviet politics remains unsettled. In an article based on émigré survey data from the project "Bureaucratic Encounters in the Soviet Union," DiFranceisco and Gitelman reject any contention that Soviet citizens can participate meaningfully in the making of public policy. Concentrating on citizen interaction with Soviet administrative organs, the authors conclude that Soviet political culture can best be described as "covert-participant." By this they mean that citizen participation is almost exclusively limited to obtaining outputs from the system by means of personal connections, if the citizen is educated, or bribery, if he is not.[32] Elsewhere, Gitelman terms this covert political behavior a "second

[30] Hill, *Soviet Political Elites*, p. 186.

[31] Michael Urban, "Information and Participation in Soviet Local Government," *Journal of Politics* 44 (February 1982). The distinction between quantitative and qualitative measures of political participation is useful. Mere volume of participation does not make for a "democratic" polity in communist or noncommunist systems. The issue in the present work, however, is not whether the Soviet Union is "democratic" or not, but whether the patterns of participation that do exist are considered useful to the processing of citizen demands, thereby increasing the system's legitimacy in the eyes of those who participate.

[32] DiFranceisco and Gitelman, "Soviet Political Culture and Covert Participation in Policy Implementation," p. 603.

polity" paralleling the "second economy" of the Soviet Union.[33]

The view that citizen contact with local organs of government is largely instrumental and self-interested ("output-oriented") is not new. In their discussion of citizen access to urban administration several years earlier, Carol Lewis and Stephen Sternheimer also come to this conclusion, but they point out that this type of citizen participation in politics is not unique to the Soviet Union.

The composite picture of citizen access to administration that the Soviet data provide suggests that, in many respects, the limits to citizen participation in urban government in the United States and the USSR are remarkably similar. As in the United States and Western Europe, Soviet citizens become involved in the public sector largely out of a concern for their private interests and pursuits. . . . In this respect, the engaged Soviet urban resident differs little, if at all, from his counterpart in other systems.[34]

The renewed interest in Soviet local government, as well as the diversity of views regarding citizen participation, find expression in the volume edited by Everett Jacobs and published in 1983, *Soviet Local Politics and Government*. A number of the articles in this volume offer assessments suggesting that, within limits, the scope of local governmental activity has expanded.[35] In particular, Churchward notes positive changes in the practice of mass participation

[33] Zvi Gitelman, "Working the Soviet System: Citizens and Urban Bureaucracies," in Henry W. Morton and Robert C. Stuart (eds.), *The Contemporary Soviet City* (New York: M. E. Sharpe, 1984), p. 241.

[34] Lewis and Sternheimer, *Soviet Urban Management*, p. 159.

[35] Everett M. Jacobs (ed.), *Soviet Local Politics and Government* (London: Allen and Unwin, 1983). The chapters on legislative developments since Stalin's death by Hill, on political participation by Churchward, on the economic functions of the local soviets by Lewis, and on citizen perception by Friedgut suggest progress, however halting, in enhancing the role of the soviets.

since 1961, including greater professionalism, greater observance of rules, new participatory mechanisms, and increased discussion of public policy.[36] But several of the authors are skeptical about there being any real increase in the role of local government in the making of public policy.[37] These divergent findings offered by the contributors to Jacobs' book, and by those mentioned in the preceding review of the literature, are testimony not only to the vitality of the renewed interest in citizen participation in communist systems but also to the need for further field research.

THE NEED FOR RECONCEPTUALIZATION

Our review of the study of political participation in communist countries suggests two propositions on which most specialists would probably agree. First, some kind of political participation does take place in these countries. Moreover, the literature would seem to support the view expressed earlier that constituent participation, in the form of interest group activity and direct citizen involvement, is likely to be a more fruitful avenue of research than electoral activity. Second, the rush to determine whether such participation is evidence that a democratic polity is emerging in the Soviet Union has far exceeded the field research, which might provide a firmer empirical foundation for accepting or rejecting such a weighty conclusion. In fact, the issue of whether political participation in communist countries is "democratic" or not is, as Skilling observes, something of a red herring, since neither he nor Hough claims that it is. Even if effective popular par-

[36] L. G. Churchward, "Public Participation in the USSR," in *Soviet Local Politics and Government*, pp. 38–45.

[37] The chapters in Jacobs' *Soviet Local Politics and Government* by Bohdan Harasymiw on party control of the soviets, by Morton on housing services, and by Zaslavsky and Brym on elections do not give grounds for optimism.

ticipation can be demonstrated, it would constitute only one of the prerequisites of a democratic polity. In the absence of more field research, however, the rejection of the possibility that the Soviet Union is moving in a more democratic direction simply on the grounds that they are communist and we are not seems to move the discussion from a scholarly arena into an ideological one.[38]

Beyond the points of accord there is wide disagreement. Even if there is participation in Soviet politics, whose purposes does it serve—those of the citizen or those of the regime? How meaningful is it? Can citizens influence policy, or only the distribution of "outputs"? Does comparison with political participation in Western democracies yield more similarities or more differences?

Answers to such questions presuppose a clear definition of political participation that is truly cross-cultural, enabling students of politics to compare communist and noncommunist systems. The call for such a reconceptualization is not new. In 1967, Robert Sharlet noted, "Political scientists have conceptualized political participation primarily on the basis of political behavior in democratic systems" and stated that "a reconceptualization of this key term that takes into consideration Communist data is essential for the systematic study of comparative politics."[39] Donald Schulz discusses Sharlet's efforts to reconceptualize participation.[40] Sharlet uses three defining characteristics of political participation based on Western experience

---

[38] This point has been made by others: Churchward "Public Participation in the USSR," p. 45; David Lane, *State and Politics in the USSR* (New York: New York University Press, 1985), p. 259; and Schulz, *Political Participation in Communist Systems*, p. 7. I am indebted to Friedgut for the reminder that participation is a necessary but not sufficient condition for the emergence of a democratic polity; a free press and autonomous interest aggregation are certainly among the other necessary elements. Signs of progress in these areas are difficult to discern, even at the local level.

[39] Robert Sharlet, "Concept Formation in Political Science and Communist Studies," *Canadian Slavonic Studies* 1 (Winter 1967), pp. 646, 648.

[40] Schulz, *Political Participation in Communist Systems*, pp. 7–19.

(efficacy, voluntarism, and responsiveness) and argues that because none of these is found in communist societies we need a new definition. Schulz argues that all of these characteristics can be found in communist societies, but that what is different is a question of degree and mixture.

The present study of the activities of deputies focuses on whether deputies can effectively represent the interests of those who elect them; that is, is their participation "meaningful"? Therefore we need to define the term "political participation" and the word "effective" (or "meaningful"). In light of the preceding, we shall define political participation as the involvement of citizens in the process by which decisions affecting community life are made and implemented. This represents a modification of the definition used by Verba, Nie, and Kim discussed at the beginning of this chapter. First, my definition does not exclude elected officials as participants. Second, it reduces the emphasis on electoral participation and gives greater weight to nonelectoral forms, or what is termed here "constituent contact." The author believes that this enhances the cross-cultural applicability of the definition with reference not only to communist systems but also to those of the less-industrialized countries of the world as well, where elections are often not a useful indicator of participatory behavior. Finally, this definition weights the output and input aspects of political participation more equally. Constituent contact aimed at influencing decisions relevant to the community's interest, as well as constituent activity aimed at influencing the policy administration within the community, are considered participatory acts of equal weight.

Three criteria are used to determine whether participatory behavior is effective. First, there must be mechanisms by which citizen preferences can be communicated to decision-makers. Second, citizens must make use of these mechanisms. Third, citizens must have a reasonable expectation that such behavior will be rewarded. In addition to these criteria, two other facets of this question merit attention. Not all political participation worthy of the name is initiated from below. For example, referenda on national or local issues that stimulate citizen activity often originate from above. However, for political participation as a whole to be considered "meaningful," the opportunity for citizen initiative must not only be available but also at least occasionally employed. Finally, this book does not exclude participation for the satisfaction of individual self-interest from the class of participatory acts considered "genuine." Verba, Nie, and Kim explicitly include "particularized contact" as one of the four categories they use to describe political participation in Western democracies. And, as noted earlier, Dahl's *homo civicus* rarely participates in politics for any other reason. Adoption of a different standard for the Soviet system would seem hypocritical.

One other theoretical issue requires clarification, or at least a statement explaining the author's approach: the relationship between political attitudes and political practice. As indicated in the introductory chapter, the scope of this book is limited to the analysis of a single variable—the role of deputies in political participation, both as participants themselves and as the objects of constituent contact. However, it was also stated that such a study was justified, at least in part, by what it could suggest about the emergence of a feeling of subjective competence on the part of Soviet citizens, with all that might imply about the foundations of political stability in the Soviet Union.

The pitfalls of such an endeavor are clearly articulated by Archie Brown: you cannot infer political attitudes, value, and beliefs by examining political institutions or practices. He persuasively exemplifies this dilemma by noting that few objective scholars would ascribe a high level of civic competence to East European citizens simply because 99 percent of them vote at each election.[41] Yet, as

[41] Archie Brown, "Introduction" in Brown, *Political Culture and Communist Studies*, p. 4.

Brown also notes, students of political culture in Eastern European communist countries are prone to making such inferences because of the obvious limitations on conducting attitudinal research in these countries. One can observe and analyze their political practices to a considerable extent, but systematic study of their attitudes and orientations toward politics, employing standard methods of the social sciences, remains closed to Western scholars.

Brown's admonition not to infer political attitudes from political behavior, however tempting this may be when studying communist systems, is wholly appropriate. And, as indicated in the methodological section of the previous chapter, any attempts to do so in this work are presented as qualified speculation. However, to deny that there is a connection between how people think about politics and how they behave politically does not make intuitive sense, and Brown does not make such an argument. In the writings of Milbrath and Almond, among others, the relationship between the two variables is held to be more interdependent. In the recent critique of the "subjectivist view of political culture," Mary McAuley writes, "We cannot simply run off attitudes and values from existing political institutions and practices—but neither does that mean we can ignore them entirely. There does seem to be a connection."[42] She approaches the problem by arguing that institutional practices constitute a precondition for the emergence of certain attitudes, values, and beliefs—necessary though not sufficient.[43] She points out, for example, that the positive affective orientation held by the peasants for the Tsar, at least until 1905 (the image of the "Just Tsar"), could hardly have emerged without the institutions of autocracy or of practices that led people to believe that such an attitude was in some way rewarding.

[42] Mary McAuley, "Political Culture: One Step Forward/Two Steps Back," in Brown, *Political Culture and Communist Studies*, p. 19.

[43] Conversely, the present work also assumes that political attitudes, values, and beliefs condition but do not determine political behavior.

   Although McAuley used this approach with reference to the problems inherent in identifying traditional political culture in Russia, its applicability to the present study seems equally compelling. The emergence of feelings of subjective competence on the part of Soviet citizens presupposes the existence of mechanisms for, and the practice of, effective political participation. While demonstration of the existence of such mechanisms would not in itself permit the conclusion that subjective competence is a characteristic of Soviet political culture, the absence of such institutions and practices would clearly preclude such a possibility. More positively, evidence of effective political participation at the local level would indicate that at least one of the preconditions for evolution of a more consensual and even "civic" political culture had been met.

CHAPTER THREE

Mass Participation in
Local Soviet Government:
The Background

THE POLITICAL CULTURE of prerevolutionary Imperial Russia can be summarized by the three principles that comprised the doctrine of "official nationality": autocracy, orthodoxy, and nationality.[1] Of these, autocracy was the keystone. The right to make decisions for all the Russian people was invested in the Tsar, who was accountable to no one. The Orthodox clergy, whose mediation of the official faith stressed ethics and values that were wholly consonant with those of the autocracy, affirmed that the Tsar's absolute authority came from God rather than from the consent of the governed. Nationality (*narodnost'*) emphasized the uniqueness—indeed, the superiority—of slavic culture, and in doing so it distinguished that culture from the culture of the West and mystically reinforced the Tsar's claim that Moscow was the embodiment of a "Third Rome." The Tsar's relationship to his people was patriarchal; like a wise and benevolent father, the Tsar made decisions for his large family and household. Given this perception of politics, notions of popular participation in

[1] See Nicholas Riasanovsky, *A History of Russia*, 4th ed. (New York: Oxford University Press, 1984), p. 324. See also White, *Political Culture and Soviet Politics*, p. 39. In a recent "unorthodox" reinterpretation of Russian political culture, Keenan argues persuasively that "official autocratic ideology" was a "useful myth" employed for external consumption by oligarchs whose real political power was better preserved by concealment (Edward L. Keenan, "Muscovite Political Folkways," *The Russian Review* 45 [April 1986], esp. p. 147).

governance were no less fanciful than the suggestion that
small children be allowed to run the household; the alternative to autocracy was anarchy.

Prevailing Western historiography tends to find more
continuity than change between the political culture and
institutions of autocratic Russia and those of its Soviet suc-
cessor. Especially in its Stalinist variant, the Soviet system
is portrayed as a reincarnation of tsarist Russia with Stalin
as the unlimited autocrat and Marxist ideology as his orthodoxy. There are shades of opinion. One view holds
that in the absence of any democratic experience, Russian
national character became highly authoritarian; political
choices were limited to obedience or violent revolt. Given
their psychological predisposition for a strong leader
whose authority was unlimited, failure to develop institutions of popular participation in government was all but
inevitable.[2] A more optimistic view denies that Russians
are incapable of self-government, or that the transition
from tsarist autocracy to Stalinist dictatorship was inevitable. Without minimizing the importance of Russian political traditions to the evolution of Bolshevism, the emergence of parliamentary forms of government in the late
nineteenth and early twentieth centuries provided a viable
historical alternative, but one that was lost when the Bolsheviks took power.[3] Finally, although many political sci-

[2] Two Russian émigré historians were sources for this view, though it
is held by many others. They are Nicholas Berdaiev, *The Origin of Russian
Communism*, trans. R. M. French (London: Geoffrey Bles, 1937); and
Georgii Fedotov, *Novy grad; sbornik statei* (New York: Chekhov, 1952). In
his *Soviet Man and His World* (New York: Praeger, 1961), Klaus Menhert
succinctly states this view: "Nature and history have combined to im-
plant and develop in the character of the Russians certain traits that have
helped their rulers to establish a dictatorship over them" (pp. 189ff.). For
more recent versions of this theme, see Ronald Hingley, *The Russian Mind*
(New York: Charles Scribner's Sons, 1977), esp. pp. 194–205; and Hedrick
Smith, *The Russians* (New York: Times Books, 1976, 1983) esp. chap. 10,
"Leaders and Led: Nostalgia for a Strong Boss."
[3] Among others, see Neil Weissman, *Reform in Tsarist Russia* (New

entists maintain that Russia under the tsars was an authoritarian system, to be distinguished from the totalitarian character of modern Russia, they too argue the
contemporary relevance of autocratic traditions, adding
only that twentieth-century technology has enhanced the
degree to which Soviet tsars can control their subjects.[4]
Stephen White concludes in his more behaviorally ori-
ented analysis of Soviet and tsarist political systems that

Brunswick, N.J.: Rutgers University Press, 1981); Terence Emmons, "The
Zemstvo in Historical Perspective," in Terence Emmons and Wayne Vucinich (eds.), *The Zemstvo in Russia* (New York: Cambridge University
Press, 1982); and to a lesser extent George Yaney, *The Systematization of
Russian Government* (Urbana: University of Illinois, 1973). Two summaries
of the debates between the optimists and pessimists regarding the evolution of a democratic polity in Russia are Arthur Mendel, "On Interpreting the Fate of Imperial Russia," in Theofanis George Stavrou (ed.), *Russia Under the Last Tsar* (Minneapolis: University of Minnesota Press, 1969);
and Robert McNeal (ed.), *Russia in Transition* (New York: Holt, Rinehart,
and Winston, 1970). In a challenging and unconventional approach to the
question of historical continuity, Keenan concludes that the stability of
Soviet political culture in recent decades rests on the reintegration of
many features of traditional Russian political culture, in which political
authority is highly personalized and informal, in which the good of the
individual is subordinated to that of the group, and in which policy aims
at self-preservation, stability, and risk-avoidance (Keenan "Muscovite
Political Folkways," pp. 167–172). Soviet historiography rejects all parallels between the Soviet and tsarist systems and uniformly dismisses prerevolutionary democratic institutions as part of the temporary bourgeois
phase of history that would inevitably be replaced by socialism.

[4] Merle Fainsod, "Review," in E. J. Simmons (ed.), *Continuity and
Change in Russian and Soviet Thought* (Cambridge: Harvard University
Press, 1955), p. 179; and Merle Fainsod, *How Russia Is Ruled* (Cambridge:
Harvard University Press, 1964), pp. 3–5, 577–581; Carl Friedrich and
Zbigniew Brzezinski, *Totalitarian Dictatorship and Autocracy* (Cambridge:
Harvard University Press, 1956); Zbigniew Brzezinski and Samuel Hun-
tington, *Political Power: USA/USSR* (New York: Viking Press, 1963), pp.
24–29; Adam Ulam, *Russia's Failed Revolutions* (New York: Basic Books,
1981), esp. pp. 412–415; Herbert McCloskey and John Turner, *The Soviet
Dictatorship* (New York: McGraw-Hill, 1960), pp. 21–39. Hannah Arendt,
Origins of Totalitarianism (New York: Harcourt, Brace, 1951).

"an emphasis upon continuity rather than change in Soviet political culture would not appear to be misplaced."[5]

In what follows, the cultural-continuity hypothesis will be reexamined, with particular reference to participation in local government. Are there factors in prerevolutionary Russian political culture that would inhibit the development of participation in local politics in the Soviet Union today? Because it is argued that the presence of such factors has not been convincingly demonstrated, a second issue is whether a sufficient theoretical and legal basis has emerged during the Soviet period to allow for the expansion of political participation in the Soviet Union in the contemporary period.

BEFORE THE REVOLUTION

While there is general agreement among Western scholars that the dominant values of prerevolutionary Russian political culture were antithetical to the development of the institutions and practices of participatory government, most would also agree that elements of participatory government were not wholly absent in Russian history. In identifying these institutions and practices, it is helpful to adopt the image of "two Russias": the "official" Russia of the nobility and the gentry, whose political consciousness was exposed to concerns of national policy, and the "popular" Russia of the peasant, whose political life was limited to the village.[6] Because historical experience appears

---

[5] White, *Political Culture and Soviet Politics*, pp. 167–168.

[6] The concept of "two Russias" used here is an adaptation of the image of a "dual Russia" as described by Robert Tucker, *The Soviet Political Mind* (New York: W. W. Norton, 1971), chap. 6, who uses the terms "official Russia" and "popular Russia" to correspond to the distinction between state and society (p. 122). See also Sidney Harcave, *First Blood: The Russian Revolution of 1905* (New York: Macmillan, 1964), chap. 1, "The Two Russias." The progenitors of this image were the Slavophiles, who iden-

to be relevant to the formation of political attitudes and orientations, any assessment of the problems and possibilities for development of participation in local government in the modern period would be incomplete without reference to the practices that did exist, however attenuated, in the prerevolutionary period. We will look at the experience of local self-government in "official Russia" first, then examine that of the villages.

Local Self-Government in "Official Russia"

The earliest known institution of local self-government in Russian history is the *veche*. As it existed in Kievan Russia of the eleventh and twelfth centuries, the veche was a crude form of direct democracy in which the heads of households gathered as an assembly, usually in the marketplace, to decide issues of war and peace and even conflicts between princes, as well as more local concerns. The veche preceded the establishment of rule by the princes in Kievan Russia, and the latter were obliged to take into account local opinion as expressed in these early town councils. While these institutions were primitive and disappeared in most Russian towns with the Tatar invasions of the thirteenth century, they achieved their most refined expression in the northern Russian city-state of Novgorod and Pskov in the fourteenth and fifteenth centuries. Here the members of the veche invited and dismissed princes, elected executive officials (the *posadnikii* and *tysiatskii*), even bishops, and acted authoritatively on all matters of

tified politics with government and the organs of the state and romanticized that the life of the peasant was free from politics. The definition of "politics" used in the present work is broader, including as political whatever mechanisms were used to arrive at decisions affecting the life of the community as a whole. Keenan ("Muscovite Political Folkways") suggests that three district Russian political cultures developed in the Muscovite period: that of the court, that of the bureaucracy, and that of the village. A summary of these may be found in ibid., pp. 156–157. In Keenan's view, the first two of these—the court and the bureaucracy—do not merge until the Imperial period (p. 159).

importance to the community. Only the expansion of the Muscovite autocracy under Ivan III brought these practices to an end in Novgorod (1479) and Pskov (1511).[7]

Even with the establishment of the Muscovite state, traditions of popular participation in decision-making did not entirely disappear. While in no way restricting the sovereign's ultimate authority, these traditions were manifest in three ways. First, there was the boyar *duma*, a council of the nobility ranging in number from 30 to perhaps 200. While only an advisory body, the duma met frequently and dealt with virtually all matters of state business. Nicholas Riasanovsky suggests that the Muscovite formula to the effect that "the sovereign directed and the boyars assented" resembles the activity of the royal councils of Europe.[8] The institution of the *zemskii sobor* bears an even more intriguing resemblance to Western parliamentary institutions. The *sobori* were assemblies called by the Tsar. In attendance were, perhaps, 200 to 500 representatives of the three estates of Muscovite Russia: the boyars, the gentry servitors, and the clergy. Townspeople and even peasants also took part in the deliberations. The most famous *sobor* resulted in the election of the first Romanov tsar in 1613. Like the boyar duma, the sobory were advisory, and implementation of their decisions depended on the willingness of the Tsar to give them effect. Nonetheless, the issues they dealt with were significant, and their influence cannot be discounted. Finally, local self-government was officially encouraged in this period, in some cases including the elections of local town administrators. Legislation to this effect was adopted by Ivan IV in 1555 in an effort to use popular participation in local affairs as a check on corrupt officials appointed by an ever-growing Moscow bureaucracy.

The Imperial Age of Russia, which began with the acces-

[7] Riasanovsky, *A History of Russia*, pp. 50–52, 81–87.
[8] Ibid., pp. 189ff.

sion of Peter the Great in 1689, witnessed the introduction of precedent-shattering changes in many aspects of Russian life. Ironically, however, for a ruler committed to Westernization, these included a retreat from the tenuous traditions of self-government that had preceded him. The boyar duma and zemskii sobor ceased functioning; efforts to stimulate local participation in government remained stillborn. The objective of the reforms in local government which did take place under Peter I and Catherine II was not the development of popular participation in government, but expansion of the central authority's control over local affairs, especially in the collection of taxes. Whatever "participation" in local government did exist was exclusively the province of the gentry, who accounted for about 1.5 percent of the population. The overwhelming majority of Russians had been serfs for more than one hundred years and would remain so until 1861.

If the emancipation of the serfs was the signal reform of Alexander II's reign, the establishment of the *zemstva* in 1864 followed it in importance. This represented the most ambitious experiment in local self-government in prerevolutionary Russian history. The basic unit of the *zemstvo* was the district (*uezd*) assembly, which met annually. It was comprised of perhaps forty representatives elected for three-year terms from the three classes of the local population: peasants, townspeople, and gentry. Each district assembly in the thirty-four provinces where zemstva were created elected members to a provincial (*guberniia*) assembly, also for three-year terms. At their annual meetings these assemblies elected executive officers who managed the administrative affairs of the zemstvo. These included a variety of basic municipal services, including roads, medicine, education, and famine relief.

It is tempting to see in the zemstva a major step toward the transformation of Russian autocracy into a constitutional democracy. Indeed, those who designed the system clearly did so with reference to the theories of democratic liberalism that prevailed in Europe in the nineteenth century.[9] In reality, the zemstva as institutions of self-government were flawed, perhaps fatally. According to the authors of a recent book on this subject, the notion that the zemstva would promote the kind of social integration upon which a stable democratic polity could be based was a "liberal myth."[10] In the first place, the zemstvo reforms were accepted primarily because of their usefulness to the central authorities; promotion of popular participation in local government was, at best, a secondary purpose.[11]

In addition, the system of proportional representation by which seats in the assemblies were allotted was based on landownership. This ensured control by the gentry, whose decisions naturally reflected their own interests. It is hardly surprising that the peasants, although indirectly enfranchised to elect about one-third of the district representatives, took little interest in zemstvo affairs, correctly perceiving these as organs to preserve a status quo that was unfavorable to them. As William Rosenberg points out, for the peasants "the zemstvo symbolized reaction, not progress."[12] Finally, there was the unequal relationship between the zemstva and the central bureaucracy. The chief administrative officer in the provinces was the governor, who along with heads of other key departments, notably the police, was answerable to the center, not to the zemstvo. Thus, the central bureaucracy could, and did, interfere, at its discretion, in the affairs of the zemstvo. The latter could do little but appeal. Matters worsened with the legislation in 1890 that established a system of land captains (zemskie nachalniki) who had broad

[9] S. Frederick Starr, Decentralization and Self-Government in Russia, 1830–70 (Princeton: Princeton University Press, 1972), chap. 2.

[10] Emmons and Vucinich, The Zemstvo in Russia, p. 434.

[11] Emmons, "The Zemstvo in Historical Perspective," p. 432.

[12] William Rosenberg, "The Zemstvo in 1917 and Its Fate Under the Bolsheviks," in Emmons and Vucinich, The Zemstvo in Russia, p. 402. See also Yaney, The Systematization of Russian Government, pp. 231ff.

authority in the local districts and especially in the peasant *volosts*.

Yet if the zemstvo reforms did not succeed in establishing the principles and practices of local self-government, neither can they be said to have been without any effect at all. They accomplished much in the provision of municipal services and served, perhaps inadvertently, to disseminate liberal and radical ideas, though to what extent is unclear.[13] In trying to draw conclusions about Russian political culture prior to the revolutions of 1905 and 1917, it seems clear that popular participation in state politics—that is, in the politics of "official" Russia—was poorly developed; the political orientations of Russians were predominantly "subject" orientations. They had little, if any, say in the decisions from above that affected their lives. Nevertheless, it is not accurate to conclude that there were no traditions of self-government. Institutions embodying such traditions did exist, and they functioned, however imperfectly, from the veche to the zemstvo.

Politics in the Village

From the beginning there was a second Russian society, separate and parallel yet intimately connected to the first. This was the Russia of the peasant. In trying to comprehend the development of Russian political culture, it is essential to maintain a demographic perspective. Until Stalin's forced industrialization, peasants accounted for at least 85 percent of the population. Equally important for understanding the political consciousness of the peasants is the psychological distance that separated them from the political life of "official" Russia. While certainly aware of the autocracy and hardly untouched by the central bureaucracy that was operated by it, these institutions were of secondary importance in the daily affairs of the village. A

[13] See Emmons, "The Zemstvo in Historical Perspective," esp. pp. 440–441.

peasant proverb neatly captures the greater immediacy of village governance for the peasant: "The whip of the village elder is felt more than the scepter of Tsar."

While the origins of the peasant commune (*mir* or *obshchina*) have been the subject of considerable controversy, contemporary opinion holds that after 1600 an important transition in communal life took place with the development of the repartitional commune system. This development was accompanied by the merging of individual households and small hamlets into larger villages, chiefly for the convenience of the state and the landlord, who found it easier to deal with a village representative than with the peasants' individually.[14] It is not coincidental that these changes occurred at the time of expanding seignorial control over the peasants and were accelerated by the onset of serfdom.

On the eve of the emancipation of the serfs in 1861, the village had become established as the framework for peasant social and political life. Nearly 80 percent of the peasants of central Russia lived in rural villages comprised of six or more households.[15] Decisions affecting the life of the village, and especially those regarding taxes and the periodic redistribution of communal land, were made by the heads of households at a meeting (*skhod*) open to all. Normally the head was male, but women also participated and could vote as proxies. Voting was by a simple majority— or by two-thirds if the issue was of sufficient importance. At the meeting a village elder (*starosta*) would be elected, perhaps with other officers. Several smaller settlements or one larger one would be referred to as a volost, but the volost council was always elected, directly or indirectly, depending on size. This basic organization of political life

[14] Richard Pipes, *Russia Under the Old Regime* (New York: Charles Scribner's Sons, 1974), pp. 17–19; Jerome Blum, *Lord and Peasant in Russia* (Princeton: Princeton University Press, 1961), pp. 504–510.

[15] Blum, *Lord and Peasant in Russia*, p. 505. Most settlements at this time (1859) had between 50 and 300 inhabitants.

in the village seems to have been widespread, despite regional variations.[16]

It is tempting to romanticize the participatory character of village political life. In the first place, given the general absence of literacy and a certain tendency to alcoholic overindulgence, the assemblies must often have been unruly and chaotic affairs. Even where order and sobriety prevailed, the villages exercised their authority only at the sufferance of the landlord and, after emancipation, of the state, with its intrusive bureaucracy and system of land captains. Village decisions found unsuitable by either were overridden, no matter how much they reflected popular sentiment. But this practice seems to have been the exception. As long as taxes were paid and no crimes were committed, both landlord and state apparently preferred to leave local affairs to the peasants themselves.[17] Physical and psychological distance from "official Russia" paradoxically served to nurture institutions and practices of local self-government among the peasants that were almost unknown among the higher classes. While the principle of autocracy dominated the prerevolutionary political culture of "official Russia," the overwhelming majority of Russians engaged in what White refers to as "the rich and democratic community life" of the village.[18]

[16] The organization of government in the 160 to 170 smaller cities and towns of Russia (the posad commune) has much in common with that of the peasant village, at least in the seventeenth and eighteenth centuries. The *posadskii shkod* exercised broad authority over the daily life of townspeople, and did so democratically and with little interference from outside except in matters of taxation. Unlike the villages, they apparently did not escape the expanding influence of the Imperial Tsar and largely ceased functioning after 1800. See J. Michael Hittle, *The Service City: State and Townspeople in Russia, 1600–1800* (Cambridge: Harvard University Press, 1979), esp. pp. 46–57, 129–131.

[17] Ibid., pp. 46–57, 129–131; Blum, *Lord and Peasant in Russia*, pp. 524–525; Geroid T. Robinson, *Rural Russia Under the Old Regime* (London: Macmillan, 1932; Berkeley: University of California Press, 1967), pp. 78–80.

[18] White, *Political Culture and Soviet Politics*, p. 35.

THE EMERGENCE OF THE SOVIETS, 1905 AND 1917

The word "soviet" in Russian means advice, or counsel. Only in the twentieth century has it taken on a second meaning: a council as an institution of government comprised of elected representatives. The absence of such usage before 1905 indicates that these institutions lack roots in the political traditions of either the village or the autocracy but are sui generis in Russian history. In fact, the first use of the word "soviet," in its second meaning of a council, referred not to institutions of government but to committees of factory workers chosen by their peers to negotiate with their employers and with the state during the strikes around the end of the nineteenth century during Russia's period of nascent industrialization. Such committees would arise on an ad hoc basis, often at the request of management, perform their function of communicating worker grievances, and then be disbanded, not infrequently with the dismissal from work of those workers who took part.[19]

The idea of the soviet as a quasi-permanent body with a political character emerged at the time of the Revolution of 1905. The first of bodies is generally considered to have appeared in May 1905 in the textile center of Ivanovo-Voznesensk in Vladimir Province, about 200 miles northeast of Moscow. Particularly bad living and working conditions prevailed in these factories, and on May 12 a strike that quickly spread to include 40,000 workers began. More than one hundred deputies (often called *starosti*, or elders) were elected at individual factories, and on May 15 they constituted the Ivanovo-Voznesensk Authorized Council (*Sovet upolnomochennykh*). They in turn elected a presidium to negotiate not only for improved economic conditions but also for political rights. During the course of the strike,

[19] Oskar Anweiler, *The Soviets: The Russian Workers, Peasants, and Soldiers Councils, 1905–1921*, trans. from the German edition of 1958 (New York: Pantheon Books, 1974), pp. 21–24.

the conduct of local affairs often required the participation, or at least acquiescence of, the soviet. While perhaps one-fourth of the deputies were Social Democrats, the soviet was not affiliated with any one political party.[20] Although the soviet was disbanded on July 18 on its own authority and achieved little in practical results, the former deputies continued to speak for the workers, and the idea of the soviet attracted attention in other parts of the country.

The idea of electing worker representatives was not unknown elsewhere in Russia. The General Strike, which came to a head in St. Petersburg, served as a catalyst for the creation of the Council of Workers' Deputies (*Sovet rabochikh deputatov*), which first met on October 13, 1905. Originally consisting of 30 to 40 deputies elected on a ratio of one deputy per 500 workers, the St. Petersburg soviet grew in a few days to 226 representatives from 96 factories and 5 unions. An executive committee was elected in which the chairman and vice-chairman were Mensheviks and another vice-chairman was a Social Revolutionary.[21] What distinguished the St. Petersburg soviet and made it a model for fifty or so similar organizations that grew up elsewhere in Russia was not only its broad representativeness across different industries but also the revolutionary political intentions of its leadership. As Leon Trotsky wrote in 1922, the St. Petersburg soviet was different "because this purely class-founded, proletarian organization was the organization of the revolution as such. The soviet was the axis of all events, every thread ran towards it, every call to action emanated from it."[22] The St. Petersburg soviet was to become considerably more than just another strike committee. It was a prototype for the Petrograd Soviet of Workers' and Soldiers' Deputies, which was estab-

[20] Harcave, *First Blood*, pp. 152–155.
[21] Ibid., p. 188.
[22] Leon Trotsky, *1905*, trans. Anya Bostock (New York: Random House, 1971), p. 104.

lished on March 12, 1917, and was the basis of Lenin's future government for Communist Russia.

A detailed description of the development of the Petrograd Soviet from its inception to the October Revolution is beyond the scope of the present work and in any case thoroughly covered elsewhere.[23] What is pertinent for this book is the degree to which the deputies to the Petrograd soviet participated in the momentous decisions that led to establishment of political power in their name. Given the uncertainties generated by the overthrow of the Tsar, the first days of the Petrograd soviet were necessarily characterized by a kind of chaotic direct democracy, but one dominated by a small number of socialist intellectuals acting on their perceptions of the workers' interests. The critical decision not to join the Provisional Government, for example, appears to have been made by a self-appointed Executive Government largely on its own authority. The vote was 13 to 8.

The development of the Petrograd soviet as a popular body in whose name a smaller group of leaders made effective decisions facilitated its takeover by the Bolsheviks in September. At first, however, Bolshevik representation was weak. In March 1917 the total number of deputies reached an unwieldy 3,000, of which two-thirds were soldiers. The Bolsheviks accounted for only 40 of these. The 42-member Executive Committee of the Petrograd soviet, which was technically accountable to its working class membership but included only 7 workers, made decisions that were ratified at sessions of the whole. Only two members, Stalin and Kamenev, were Bolsheviks. While Lenin's party fared better in the borough soviets in Petrograd and in the local zemstva, which had been given control of the municipal dumas by the Provisional Government, Men-

[23] The most detailed Western account of the evolution of the soviets between the two revolutions is Anweiler's, *The Soviets*, pp. 97–207. Much of the factual material that follows is based on this source, which makes extensive use of primary source material not readily available elsewhere.

58   Chapter 3

sheviks and Social Revolutionaries clearly dominated the
soviet movement in Russia.[24] Thus, at the First All-Russian
Congress of Soviets, which met on June 16, some 285 out
of 822 voting delegates, were Social Revolutionaries, 248
were Mensheviks, and 105 were Bolsheviks.

Lenin's commitment in the "April Theses" to the soviets
as "the *only possible* form of revolutionary government,"
and his slogan "All power to the soviets," seem paradoxi-
cal in light of Bolshevik weakness in these organs.[25] In
fact, his commitment was ambivalent and pragmatic.
From the outset of the revolution, governing had been the
responsibility of the Provisional Government, but real
power lay with the Petrograd soviet, which controlled the
activities of the workers and soldiers and whose effective
veto over the decisions of the Provisional Government was
established by the famous "Order No. 1." Yet as Lenin
also recognized in his speech to the Bolsheviks on his return to Russia on April 17, the soviets were controlled by
the Mensheviks and the Social Revolutionaries. The strategy Lenin outlined in the "April Theses" was to attack the
leadership of the Petrograd soviet for its support of the
Provisional Government, but Lenin's objective was to gain
Bolshevik control of that body and to use it as an instru-

[24] The infiltration of municipal government by the Bolsheviks to further
their revolutionary aims is described in L. A. Komissarenko, *V borbe
massy: munitsipal'naia deiatel'nost' petrogradskikh bol'shevikov v period podgo-
tovki oktiabriaskoi revoliutsii* (Leningrad: Lenizdat, 1983). The Bolsheviks
were not universally successful in this effort, however. While the Bolsheviks did receive 34 percent of the local vote in Petrograd in August 1917,
they received only 7.5 percent in the provincial cities and 2.2 percent in
the small towns. See Hough and Fainsod, *How the Soviet Union Is Governed*, p. 51. All dates in the text are "new calendar" dates. An excellent
discussion of Bolshevik weakness in rural government, and indeed of the
soviets generally among the peasants, is available in Graeme J. Gill, *Peasants and Government in the Russian Revolution* (London: Macmillan, 1979),
pp. 117–124.
[25] V. I. Lenin, *Collected Works* (Moscow: English trans. by Progress Publishers of the 4th enlarged edition prepared by the Institute of Marxism-
Leninism, 1977), vol. 24, p. 23 (Lenin's emphasis).

ment of revolution. This goal seemed distant when the Petrograd Soviet repudiated Lenin and the Bolsheviks for their participation in the abortive uprising of July 3–5, which was conducted under the slogan "All power to the soviets." Indeed, Lenin abandoned this slogan until September 13, when the Bolsheviks, riding a crest of popularity based on their key role in the defeat of Kornilov, finally gained a majority in the Petrograd soviet. At this time a new Executive Committee comprised of twenty-two Bolsheviks, sixteen Social Revolutionaries, and six Mensheviks was elected. An apostate Trotsky was elected chairman. Now that the *power* of the soviets belonged to the Bolsheviks, the revolution to take over the *government* could proceed.

THE DEVELOPMENT OF THE SOVIETS AFTER THE REVOLUTION: THEORY AND PRACTICE

Lenin's approach to the soviets in 1917 was primarily tactical; they were means to an end rather than the end itself. But when that revolutionary end was secured and the question of how to govern came to the fore, the soviets were projected by Lenin as the incarnations of Marxist democracy.

Lenin drew heavily on Karl Marx's description of the Paris Commune of 1871 in *The Civil War in France*, which was perhaps the clearest expression of Marx's views on governing a communist society, a society in which the state was to become extinct. According to Marx, communal government would consist of elected representatives of the working class, subject to recall. There would be no separation of executive and legislative functions—apparently to ensure that those who passed laws would also be responsible for carrying them out. Public service would be remunerated at "workmen's wages" to avoid the development of a class of professional politicians. All the municipal functions formerly undertaken by the state would now be run by the citizens themselves through their councillors. The Paris Commune was to have been prototypical for all France, with local affairs being decided by local communes while those "few but important functions which would still remain for a central government" would be conducted by instructed delegates sent from district assemblies. The standing army and police were to be abolished; order would be preserved by local militia and the natural comradeship of the working class.[26]

Lenin's efforts to draw parallels between the communes and the soviets are apparent as early as 1908,[27] but the conception of the soviets as organs of state power modeled on the communes was not clearly elucidated until after the Provisional Government was established.[28] The most comprehensive expression of Lenin's views on the state is in *State and Revolution*, where he provides the fullest theoretical definition of the state as the dictatorship of the proletariat. Much of the treatise is an attempt to associate the Paris Commune with this conception, seeing in it "the first attempt by a proletarian revolution to *smash* the bourgeois state machine; it is the political form by which the state machine must be *replaced*."[29] It is significant, however, that we look in vain for references in *State and Revolution* to the soviets as the inheritors of this role. The fact that it was written during his exile, in July–August of 1917, says much about Lenin's disenchantment with the soviets at that time. It was not until after the Bolsheviks gained control of the soviets in September that Lenin resurrected

[26] Karl Marx, *The Civil War in France*, as translated by Progress Publishers in Karl Marx and Friedrich Engels, *On the Paris Commune* (Moscow: Progress Publishers, 1971), pp. 70–72.

[27] V. I. Lenin, "Lessons of the Commune" (March 23, 1908), in *Collected Works*, vol. 13, p. 478 (Lenin's emphasis).

[28] V. I. Lenin, "Letters from Afar" (March 24, 1917), in *Collected Works*, vol. 23, p. 325 (Lenin's emphasis).

[29] V. I. Lenin, "State and Revolution," in *Collected Works*, vol. 25, p. 440.

them from the "purgatory" of Menshevik and Social Revolutionary leadership and again identified them as "the new state apparatus" explicitly modeled on the experience of the Paris Commune.[30]

The evolution of Lenin's thinking on the soviets has significance for understanding the conception of the state in contemporary socialist societies. Neil Harding argues persuasively that two mutually exclusive conceptions of government were contending in Marxist thought on the state: the ideal of the commune, with its emphasis on proletarian self-rule and direct democracy, and the dictatorship of proletariat, with its reliance on coercion to repress class opposition. Harding believes that at least until April 1918 Lenin continued to favor the evolution of the soviets into proletarian instruments of self-government in which locally accountable worker-citizens would run their own affairs—a sort of government by amateurs. But the crises faced by the Bolsheviks during the period of the civil war forced Lenin to rely on the other Marxian theoretical construct of the state as a dictatorship, albeit one acting in the interests of the working class.[31] A contrary view holds that Lenin was never interested in the soviets as instruments of self-government, but always viewed them simply as a means to make revolution and supported them only when they acted according to the directions of the party.[32] The absence of references to the soviets in *State and Revolution*, and the contemptuous repudiation of democratic "forms of government" in *The Proletarian Revolution and the Renegade Kautsky*, written in October 1918, support this.[33]

Any Soviet scholars seeking doctrinal legitimization of

---

[30] V. I. Lenin, "Can the Bolsheviks Retain State Power" (October 14, 1917), in *Collected Works*, vol. 26, pp. 101–104.

[31] Neil Harding, "Socialism, Society, and the Organic Labour State," in Neil Harding (ed.), *The State in Socialist Society* (Albany, N.Y.: State University Press, 1984), pp. 3–30.

[32] See, e.g., Anweiler, *The Soviets*, pp. 161–165.

[33] In Lenin, *Collected Works*, vol. 28, pp. 231–242.

their efforts to resurrect the soviets as institutions for popular participation in government will find ample ammunition in the writings of both Marx and Lenin. The communal model as a political archetype of the kind of
government that would emerge in communist society after
the coercive apparatus of the state was no longer needed
persists in the theoretical formulations articulated by
Lenin *after* the October Revolution. It was even incorporated into the 1919 program of the All-Russian Communist
Party (the Bolsheviks).[34] Emphasis on direct participation
of workers in the running of their own affairs is echoed in
contemporary Soviet writing on the soviets.[35] Much of the
language and spirit of this communal model also found its
way into the legislation on the soviets adopted since
1967.[36] In some of this writing, the dictatorship of the proletariat is presented as a necessary but temporary form of
the state justified by the exigencies of civil war and the
abnormal circumstances of rapid industrialization. In normal times, it is implied, a return to some version of direct
worker participation found in early Bolshevik theory
would become possible.[37]

[34] Ibid., vol. 29, p. 109.

[35] Barabashev and Sheremet, *Sovetskoe stroitel'stvo*, pp. 92–98.

[36] "O statuse narodnykh deputatov v SSSR," September 20, 1972, *Vedomosti Verkhovnogo Soveta SSSR*, 1979, no. 17, item 277. The first ten articles of this law are resonant with the formulations about the activities
of the soviets as "working" bodies found in the section of *State and Revolution* entitled "Abolition of Parliamentarianism."

[37] Soviets often explain any lack of democratic participation in their political system as the result of turbulent events in Soviet history: the civil
war, industrialization, World War II, and reconstruction, and that only
now can the Soviet Union begin to afford popular political participation.
Expressions of this relevant to the development of the soviets can be
found in A. I. Luk'ianov, *Razvitie zakonodatel'stva o sovetskikh predstavitel'nykh organakh vlasti* (Moscow: Iurid. Lit., 1978), pp. 38–42. See also
A. V. Gogolevskii, *Petrogradskii sovet v gody grazhdanskoi voiny* (Leningrad:
Nauka, 1982). On the limiting effects of World War II and the cult of per-
sonality, see A. I. Lepeshkin, *Sovety-vlast' naroda, 1936–1967* (Moscow:
Iriud. Lit., 1967), p. 122.

Whatever visions the Bolsheviks may have entertained about the future evolution of the soviets, practice diverged from theory rather sharply in the period following the October Revolution. Instead of moving toward direct democracy, the state moved quickly in the direction of ever-greater centralization. Any local autonomy that did exist was by default, not design, and even that disappeared with the onset of industrialization. It was one thing to declare at the Second All-Russian Congress of Soviets on October 25, 1917, "All power henceforth belongs to the Soviets," and quite another to erect a government.

The structure of government that emerged initially was minimal and readily adaptable; real power rested with the party from the outset. Nationally, decisions were made by the Council of Peoples' Commissars, chaired by Lenin and nominally responsible to the Congress of Soviets and its Central Committee. Local government was handed over to the Soviets of Workers', Soldiers', Peasants', and Farm Laborers' Deputies by means of a circular from the Commissariat of Internal Affairs issued on January 4, 1918, which simultaneously terminated the authority of the zemstvo organs that preceded them. The commissariat's instructions were less than a page in length: local organs decided local matters, they carried out the decrees and decisions of the central power, and they elected an executive committee from among their members to do this.[38] That was about it.

Not until the Constitution of July 10, 1918, did the principles of government by the soviets receive institutional expression. Here, however, the legal requirements were quite specific. In towns, local soviets of between 50 and

[38] Until the Constitution of July 10, 1918, the local government was defined by two very short documents, "Ob organizatsii mestnogo samoupravleniia" and "O pravokh i obiazannostiakh sovetov," both promulgated by the Commissariat of Internal Affairs on January 4, 1918. These documents can be found in *Sbornik normativnikh aktov* (see above, Chapter 1, footnote 24), pp. 22, 23.

1,000 deputies were elected at a ratio of one per 1,000 inhabitants; village soviets numbered between 3 and 50 deputies, with one deputy for every 100 citizens. The town soviets were to meet once a week, the villages twice. An executive committee (ispolkom) of up to 5 villagers, or 3 to 15 townspeople, would be elected from the membership to conduct current business. Elections to soviets at higher administrative levels (volost, uezd, guberniia, and oblast) were indirect, the deputies being chosen by the executive committee of the subordinate unit. At the summit was the All-Russian Congress of Soviets. While the Constitution specified local control over local questions, central control was ensured both by the Constitution and by the principle of democratic centralism.[39]

Like the theories on which it was based, the Constitution was the expression of an ideal; it described what government should be like, not what it was. In fact, two realities determined the character of the soviets in their formative years: the extension of party control over the organs of government, and the weakness of the soviets outside the major cities. With respect to the first, it should be remembered that in their origins the soviets were independent of any single party control. Their membership was comprised of individuals with varying party affiliations or, frequently, none at all. Following the dismissal of the Constituent Assembly on January 19, 1918, all pretensions that the soviets could act independently of the will of the Bolshevik Party were eliminated. If the party was the "vanguard of the proletariat," then in Lenin's words "the soviets are the Russian form of the dictatorship of the proletariat."[40] Party control over the soviets was ensured not only by the steady abolition of opposition parties but also by the erection in the summer of 1918 of an organiza-

[39] "Osnovnoi zakon RSFSR," July 10, 1918, *Sbornik normativnikh aktov*, pp. 31–43. Articles 53–70 deal with local government.
[40] V. I. Lenin, "The Proletarian Revolution and the Renegade Kautsky," in *Collected Works*, vol. 28, p. 257.

tional structure which paralleled that of the soviets at every level from the center to the periphery. By the 8th Party Congress of March 1919, the highly partisan nature of the relationship between the party and the soviets had been established and codified. According to the resolution "On the Organizational Question" adopted at this congress:

> The Communist Party sets itself the task of winning decisive influence and complete control in all organizations of the working people: in trade unions, cooperatives, rural communes, etc. The party particularly strives to carry out its Programme and establish its complete control in the contemporary state organizations that are the soviets.[41]

The second reality to recognize about the early development of the soviets is that the organization of the political life of the villages, where most Russians lived, bore little resemblance to that prescribed by the Constitution. One district deputy said, "I must note, to my regret, that in some places there are actually no soviets at all; they exist on paper. And even where they do exist, they have no life, there are no meetings; no resolutions or decisions are arrived at." Another stated, "It is fortunate for the village that none of the authorities tries to find out if its orders have been followed. The village becomes completely independent. . . . Hardly anything is known in the countryside of the soviet system, actions, or aims."[42] Nor was the weakness of the soviets confined to the villages. Soviet authors concede that the economic, cultural, and organiza-

[41] The relationship between the party and the soviets was defined in the Resolution of March 22, 1919, "On the Organizational Question" (*KPSS v rezoliutsiiakh* 2 [Moscow, 1970], p. 77). The process by which the party organized its control of the soviets is described in B. M. Morozov et al. (eds.), *Partiia i Sovety* (Moscow: Politizdat, 1982), pp. 21–31.

[42] Quoted in Anweiler, *The Soviets*, pp. 236–237, from *Sovety v epokhu voennogo kommunizma*, vol. 1 (Moscow, 1928), pp. 189, 313.

tional work of the soviets outside the major urban centers was generally of a low level.[43] The weakness of the soviets in these formative years is hardly surprising. Much of the countryside remained hostile to Bolshevik policies, as the efforts at collectivization would soon reveal. Moreover, effective public administration requires administrators who are educated and experienced, qualities that were largely absent even in Soviet cities at this time. The lack of such individuals almost certainly contributed to the vacuum of authority at the local level, a void that could be filled only by the center. This development was not long in coming.

The harnessing of the soviets to the tasks of industrialization and collectivization in the late 1920s and early 1930s did not so much change their character as subordinate them to control from the center. This was the result not only of economic necessity; political reasons also played a role. Whatever vestigial traces of the independent origins of the soviets may have remained, they disappeared by the time the Constitution of 1936 was adopted. Together with the trade unions, the peasants, the scientific community, writers and artists, and ultimately even the party itself, the soviets became fully yoked to the construction of "socialism in one country."[44]

It is tempting to dismiss the 1936 Constitution as one of history's great conceits. In the face of the eradication of perhaps 3 million *kulaks* (private peasant farmers) and at the height of the Great Purges, it was declared that class conflict had been ended in the Soviet Union and that the

[43] Luk'ianov, *Razvitie zakonodatel'stva*, p. 94; also A. I. Luk'ianov, in *Sovety naradnykh deputatov: spravochnik* (Moscow: Politizdat, 1984), pp. 25–26.

[44] Many regulations pertaining to the city and village soviets were passed during transition to the five-year plans and the collectivization of agriculture that began in 1928. Clearly, however, the objective of this legislation was to improve the ability of the local units of government to implement the momentous economic decisions being made in Moscow. These developments, and references to specific legislation, are thoroughly reviewed by Luk'ianov, in *Razvitie zakonodatel'stva*, pp. 97–109.

basis for socialism had been achieved. The transition from the state of the dictatorship of the proletariat to an "all-peoples state" comprised of harmonious classes and nations required a new legal framework. Nevertheless, the document is significant for at least two reasons. First, it symbolized the retreat that had taken place from the more idealistic expectations of early Bolshevism since Stalin's coming to power. It established, for example, a more traditionally parliamentarian system (at least in form) and incorporated certain necessary compromises, such as private plots for the peasants and a degree of official autonomy for the nationalities. Second, it reorganized and consolidated existing institutions and gave them a formal structure that with modifications has remained the basis of the soviet state system to the present.

With respect to the local soviets, the 1936 Constitution contained changes in both nomenclature and structure; it also made explicit the principle of "dual subordination," by which the executive organs of the local soviets were accountable not only to the council that elected them but also to their corresponding administrative departments at higher levels (art. 101). The prerevolutionary terms for the local organs of government (*gubernia*, *uezd*, *volost*, etc.) were replaced. Republics were now subdivided into area (*krai*), region (*oblast*), district (*raion*), city (*gorod*), and village (*selo*) soviets. Equality of suffrage represented a change from earlier days, when the industrial workers were heavily overrepresented. Originally scheduled to meet once or twice weekly, soviet sessions were now to be held four to six times annually, more nearly reflecting local practice.[45]

---

[45] Articles 85 and 86 of "The Basic Law of the USSR," December 5, 1936, *Sbornik normativnikh aktov*, pp. 72ff. See also article 80 of the RSFSR Constitution (trans. Harold Berman and John Quigley, Jr., in *Basic Laws on the Structure of the Soviet States* [Cambridge: Harvard University Press, 1969], esp. pp. 44–49). All three Soviet constitutions are translated with

The activities of the soviets under this constitution and for the rest of the period of Stalin's leadership were not insignificant. Especially during the war years and the period of reconstruction that followed, much of the administration of local affairs was of necessity left to local administrators. Despite the loss during the war of two out of three deputies and over half the ispolkom presidents, the soviets continued to function.[46] Yet the suggestion that "citizen influence on local decisions" may have been a by-product of these circumstances should be carefully qualified.[47] The realities of political life at the local level diverged substantially from what was prescribed by the Constitution. Descriptions provided by the Soviet observers themselves, starting with Khrushchev's inventory of shortcomings to the 20th Party Congress, make it clear that by 1956 the soviets functioned more effectively on paper than in life. More often than not, local decisions appear to have been made by local administrators acting on instructions from above—and then imposed on an indifferent citizenry. It would be difficult to exceed in frankness the description set forth in the resolution adopted by the Communist Party of the Soviet Union (CPSU) on January 22, 1957, "On Improving the Work of the Soviets of Workers' Deputies and Strengthening Their Ties with the Masses." According to this document,

> The most important questions in the practical work of the soviets are rarely brought before sessions for consideration. Many executive committees, heads of administrative departments, and directors of economic organizations are not being held accountable to the soviets, which results in an absence of supervision, and a weak-

extensive commentary in Aryeh Unger, *Constitutional Development in the USSR* (New York: Pica Press, 1981).

[46] Luk'ianov, *Razvitie zakonodatel'stva*, p. 135.

[47] Hough and Fainsod, *How the Soviet Union Is Governed*, p. 190.

ening of the directing role of the soviets as the organ of state power at the local level. In many instances, sessions of the soviets limit themselves to discussions of minor questions, are conducted in a formalistic fashion, at times simply to parade forth approval of the draft decisions prepared by the executive committees. As a result, the sessions are conducted in a passive fashion; shortcomings and mistakes in the work of the soviet organs and of their executives are not criticized; proposals of the deputies often receive no attention, while those decisions which are adopted lack concreteness and are full of generalities.[48]

The resolution cataloged other failings of the system. Sessions were called irregularly; there was a lack of public debate among deputies or of criticism of officials by deputies; both deputies and members of executive committees were reprimanded for a lack of responsiveness to citizen input and for their failure to account for their activities before their constituents. Klement Voroshilov, in his speech to the 20th Congress on the inadequacies of the work of local officials, warned that draft legislation improving recall procedures had been introduced; those not performing their functions properly were put on notice.[49] There was even an acknowledgment in this remarkable document of the party's responsibility for the poor quality of the soviets' work. Communists were ordered to put "an end to needless tutelage over and petty interference in the work of the soviets."

Criticism of the work of the local soviets was long overdue. The resolution of January 22, 1957, is rightly consid-

[48] *KPSS v rezoliutsiiakh*, vol. 7, p. 238. The resolution as a whole is translated in Robert McNeal (ed.), *Resolutions and Decisions of the CPSU*, vol. 4 (Toronto: University of Toronto Press, 1974), pp. 75–81.

[49] Speech by K. Y. Voroshilov to the 20th Congress of the CPSU, February 21, 1956, translated from *Pravda* in Joint Committee on Slavic Studies, *Current Soviet Policies*, vol. 2 (New York: Praeger, 1957), p. 115.

ered a turning point in the revival of interest in promoting citizen participation in local government. But while the deputies were called upon to play a larger role in governmental affairs, the resolution expected them to do it within the existing legislative framework, which, as A. I. Luk'ianov observes, was an insufficient basis for the real expansion of their authority.[50] Adoption of such legislation would fall to Khrushchev's successors.

The Deputies under "Developed Socialism"

The Program of the Communist Party adopted at the 22nd Congress of the CPSU in October 1961 proclaimed the achievement of socialism in the Soviet Union. It further announced that the building of a communist society was under way and, "in the main," would be accomplished by 1980. As to what this meant for the state, Khrushchev's "Report on the Program" informed the congress that "communist construction no longer requires the dictatorship of the proletariat" and that this form had been transformed into a "state of all the people" (*obshchenarodnoe gosudarstvo*). The prospective "withering away" of the state in a fully communist society was reaffirmed, although the "process will be a very long one."[51] Specifically invoking Leninist traditions, Khrushchev publicly committed the party to the transfer of the administration of state affairs to the soviets. He was quite explicit in his promise: "Many of the matters which are today allotted to the competence of the executive bodies of power and government will be handled directly by the soviets and their committees." Khrushchev's speech was nothing less than an official endorsement of future "public self-government" for

[50] Luk'ianov, *Razvitie zakonodatel'stva*, pp. 136, 139, 158–160.

[51] N. S. Khrushchev, "Report on the Program of the Communist Party of the Soviet Union," October 17, 1961 (New York: Crosscurrents Press, 1961), p. 107.

the Soviet system.[52] The CPSU Program itself specified the ways in which the role of the soviets would be expanded.[53]

Ronald Hill points out that Soviet observers, especially P. P. Ukrainets, mark real changes in the development of the soviets only from the Brezhnev period.[54] In a legislative sense, this argument has merit, as we shall see. The structural framework for the expansion of the soviets' role emerged only after Khrushchev was retired in 1964, starting with a Central Committee resolution on the soviets of Poltava Oblast of November 16, 1965.[55] Moreover, many of the efforts in regard to local government were diluted by the economic reorganizations then taking place, later to be abandoned. There was even some discussion of abolishing the rural soviets.[56] However, it would be an oversight to dismiss what was achieved during Khrushchev's tenure. For one thing, the revitalization of the soviets was well under way by 1961. Data published in 1983 by A. S. Pavlov show a significant increase in the activities of the soviets in 1961 when compared with the 1940s. Thus, in 1946 only 25 percent of the soviets held regular sessions; by 1961, it was up to 95 percent. In 1949, only 25.3 percent of the deputies reported to their constituents; by 1961, this had risen to 80.8 percent. The figures for reports by executive committees to the soviets grew from 45 percent in 1948 to 92 percent in 1961. Pavlov also reports an increased use of the voter mandate (*nakaz izbiratelei*), the right of inquiry (*zapros*), and a decline in "formalism."[57] Moreover, a

[52] Ibid., p. 110.

[53] "The Program of the CPSU," October 31, 1961, translated in McNeal, *Resolutions and Decisions*, vol. 4, p. 236; see pp. 234–237 regarding the soviets.

[54] Ronald J. Hill, "The Development of Local Soviet Government Since Stalin's Death," in Jacobs, *Soviet Local Politics and Government*, pp. 22, 24.

[55] Noted in ibid., p. 24; and Luk'ianov, *Razvitie zakonodatel'stva*, p. 309.

[56] Ibid., pp. 154–155. See also Hill's discussion of administrative reorganization, "The Development of Local Government," p. 23.

[57] A. S. Pavlov, *Partiinoe rukovodstvo mestnymi Sovetami v poslevoennye gody* (Moscow: Vysshaia shkola, 1983), pp. 47–65, 76–77.

sharp increase in the number of those participating in local government is evident. Between 1950 and 1957, the number of elected deputies increased by about 60,000 persons to 1,549,777, but from 1957 to 1963 the increase is more than 400,000.[58] While judgment about the quality of such activity can be reserved, the quantitative changes are evidence of renewed official interest during the Khrushchev years.

The second reason 1957, rather than 1965, could have been the pivotal year for the resurgence of interest in the soviets is that insofar as the commitment to their revitalization is concerned, the place of the soviets in the theory of "developed socialism" conforms in most respects to the role outlined for them by the 1961 Program; on the whole, continuity rather than change is characteristic of the policies adopted regarding the soviets after 1964, though in less ebullient language. True, references to the "withering away" of the state do not appear in Brezhnev's formulations about political life under developed socialism, and the arrival of a fully communist society in the Soviet Union is safely put off to an unspecified future date.[59] Nevertheless, in theory the advent of developed socialism is accompanied by a significant expansion of the rights of the soviets and by the more active participation of citizens in the political process. Indeed, the projected transfer of political

---

[58] *Itogi vyborov*, 1982, pp. 226–227.

[59] For a description of the development of the theory of developed socialism, see Alfred B. Evans, Jr., "Developed Socialism in Soviet Ideology," *Soviet Studies* 29 (July 1977), esp. pp. 421–424. See also Jim Seroka and Maurice Simon (eds.), *Developed Socialism in the Soviet Bloc* (Boulder, Colo.: Westview Press, 1982). A Soviet scholar's attempt to deal with these anomalies is E. M. Chekharin's, *Sovetskaia politicheskaia sistema v usloviiakh razvitogo sotsializma* (Moscow: Mysl, 1975), translated under the title *The Soviet Political System Under Developed Socialism* (Moscow: Progress Publishers, 1977), p. 229. On the continuity between Khrushchev and Brezhnev in their treatment of the soviets, see L. G. Churchward, "Public Participation in the USSR," in Jacobs, *Soviet Local Politics and Government*, pp. 36–39.

authority to the people through their elected deputies is intended to be a distinguishing feature of the "state of all the people." This point was emphasized by Brezhnev in his speech to the Central Committee in May 1977, in which he discussed the draft of the constitution:

In general, it can be said that the *main guideline of the new elements contained in the draft is the broadening and deepening of socialist democracy.* Above all, the democratic principles of the formation and activity of the soviets have received further development. Provision has been made for increasing their role in the resolution of the most important questions in the life of society.[60]

The theory of developed socialism received its ultimate legislative expression in the 1977 Constitution. The importance accorded the soviets in the political life of this transitional period between socialism and full communism is visible throughout the document.[61] In constitutional form, at least, the implications of the theory of developed socialism for an increase in citizen participation in local affairs appear substantial.

The establishment of a legal basis for the development of citizen participation in local government had already be-

[60] L. I. Brezhnev, "On the Draft Constitution of the USSR," *Pravda*, June 5, 1977, translated in *Current Digest of the Soviet* 29, no. 23 (1977): 7 (emphasis in the original).

[61] Articles 2, 48, 49, and 58 and chapters 12, 13, 14, and 19 define the role of the soviets and the rights of political participation. The significance of the 1977 Constitution in expanding the role of soviets as instruments of political participation is emphasized by soviet scholars; see esp. K. F. Sheremet, "Konstitutsiia SSSR i razvitie sotsialisticheskoi demokratii," in *Sovetskoe gosudarstvo i pravo* (hereafter *SGiP*) (1982), and *Sovety narodnykh deputatov: Konstitutsionnye osnovy organizatsii i deiatel'nosti* (Moscow: Nauka, 1981), esp. pp. 7–53. However, the two leading Western studies of the 1977 Constitution also acknowledge that the provisions for broader participation represent an important change in emphasis from previous versions. See Robert Sharlet, *The New Soviet Constitution of 1977* (Brunswick, Ohio: King's Court, 1978), pp. 50–55; and Unger, *Constitutional Development in the USSR*, pp. 204–205, 213.

gun prior to the adoption of the 1977 Constitution. After Brezhnev became General Secretary of the party in 1964, a number of important laws were promulgated to define more precisely and to expand what is now referred to as the "competence" (*kompetentsia*) of the soviets and their officials.[62] The first all-union act regarding the activities of the soviets taken since the few general provisions of the 1936 Constitution was the edict (*ukaz*) of April 8, 1968, entitled "On the Basic Rights and Duties of the Village and Settlement Soviets."[63] Another edict, this one defining and expanding the competence of city and district soviets, was passed on March 19, 1971, following a CPSU resolution of March 12, 1971, "On Measures for Further Improving the Work of Raion and City Soviets of Working Peoples' Deputies."[64] Both pieces of legislation substantially expanded the formal authority of the soviets with respect to locally based enterprises, especially those involved in servicing the community.

In order to carry out their expanded functions, the financial resources of both the rural and city soviet executive committees were strengthened by decrees (*postanovleniu*) of the Council of Ministers passed in 1968 and 1971.[65] The most important legislation directly related to the role of the deputy as the representative of citizen interests is the law (*zakon*) adopted on September 20, 1972, "On the Status of the Peoples' Deputy in the USSR."[66]

[62] O. E. Kutafin and K. F. Sheremet, *Kompetentsia mestnykh Sovetov* (Moscow: Iurid. Lit., 1982), p. 36; see also pp. 26–38.

[63] *Vedomosti Verkhovnogo Soveta SSSR*, 1978, no. 49, item 797.

[64] Ibid., item 796.

[65] "On Measures for Strengthening the Material and Financial Basis of the Village and Settlement Soviets," Decree of the USSR Council of Ministers (1968), and "On Measures for Strengthening the Material-Financial Basis of the Executive Committee of the District and City Soviets," Decree of the USSR Council of Ministers (1971), in *Sobranie Postanovlenii SSSR*, 1968, no. 6, item 30; and ibid., 1971, no. 5, item 37.

[66] "O statuse narodnykh deputatov v SSSR," September 20, 1972, as amended on April 19, 1979, *Vedomosti Verkhovnogo Soveta SSSR*, 1979, no. 17, item 277.

This law broadens the rights of the deputies with respect to those who execute their decisions and more clearly defines their obligations to those who elect them. Many key provisions of the 1972 law found their way into the 1977 Constitution and will be discussed in greater detail later. A good deal of legislation regarding the activities of the soviets also appeared after adoption of the Constitution. The competence of the soviets at the regional level was more precisely defined by the law of June 25, 1980, "On the Basic Authority of Area and Regional Soviets and the Soviets of Autonomous Regions and Okrugs," and their rights expanded, especially in the realm of economic development.[67] Economic development was also the primary objective of a joint resolution of the CPSU, the Presidium of the Supreme Soviet, and the Council of Ministers on March 27, 1981, "On Further Increasing the Role of the Soviets in Economic Construction."[68] In this resolution the relations of the soviets with enterprises subordinated to higher ministries are spelled out, and the role of the soviets in complex economic planning for their territories is strengthened. The resolution also grants greater discretion in use of funds for local economic growth. Concerning the function of the deputies as political representatives, a number of measures have been taken, basically clarifying or implementing what appears in more general language in the Constitution. Of particular importance to the present study are the edict of the Presidium of the Supreme Soviet on "The Organization of Work with Voter Mandates" (September 1, 1980) and another edict from the same source, "On the Procedure for Considering Citizens' Proposals, Applications, and Complaints" (as revised on March 4, 1980).[69]

It is worth observing that the legislation discussed here does not include regulations passed by the union-repub-

---

[67] *Vedomosti Verkhovnogo Soveta SSSR*, 1980, no. 27, item 526.

[68] *Izvestiia*, March 28, 1981, p. 1.

[69] Respectively, in *Vedomosti Verkhovnogo Soveta SSSR*, 1980, no. 36, item 736; and amended 1980, ibid., no. 11, item 192.

lics, many of which are also important to the development
of the soviets in the period of "developed socialism." The
Supreme Soviet of the RSFSR, for instance, has passed legislation concerning elections, recall, the formation of deputies groups, and the jurisdiction of standing committees.[70] Such legislative acts, along with laws, edicts, and
regulations developed by other republics, number in the
hundreds and advance the legal basis for citizen participation in local government.

Is There a Basis for Increased Participation?

We have seen that the evolution of the soviets since the
beginning of the twentieth century has resulted in an elaborate theoretical and legislative framework for the expansion of citizen participation in local government in the Soviet Union. The theoretical basis had its origins in the
writings of Marx and Lenin on the nature of the state in a
communist society, but it receives contemporary expression in the 1961 Program of the CPSU and in the theory of
developed socialism. Most of the legal foundations have
appeared only in the past two decades, yet the body of law
is substantial. If implemented, the role of locally elected
officials and citizens generally in the political life of the
country would be greatly enhanced. But it is equally clear
from Russian history, both before and after the 1917 Revolution, that legislative expressions of democratic principles have to a large extent remained the registration of aspirations rather than an accomplishment of fact.

[70] RSFSR legislation on local elections (August 3, 1979) and on recall
(December 12, 1979) can be found in *Sbornik normativnykh aktov*, items 86
and 87. The RSFSR edict on standing committees of March 3, 1983, is in
Vedomosti Verkhovnogo Soveta RSFSR, 1983, no. 10, item 318. The RSFSR
resolution (*polozhenie*) on deputy groups and posts is dated August 2,
1984. Legislation on the standing committees and on the deputy groups
had appeared several years earlier in Kazakhstan and Georgia, respectively, and is only slightly different, reflecting particular national circumstances.

The degree to which current practice regarding the deputies' activities conforms to legal and theoretical expectations is a central concern of the present work. Clearly there is a discrepancy. Even recent Soviet statements indicate there is "a gap" between what the law permits and the party publicly encourages, on the one hand, and what people do, on the other hand. The authority for such a conclusion is no less than the late General Secretary of the CPSU, Konstantin Chernenko, who made these shortcomings the major theme of his remarks to the April 19, 1984, plenum of the Central Committee. Summing up his list of criticisms he concluded, "In general, there exists a definite contradiction, a gap between the rich possibilities of the soviets and how these possibilities are used in fact."[71]

Soviet specialists on local government are also fully aware that the legislative powers granted to the soviets are often underutilized. O. E. Kutafin and K. F. Sheremet refer to this as a problem of raising the effectiveness (*effektivnost'*) of the soviets and offer a number of criteria for doing so.[72] Others argue that effectiveness depends on the more precise legal regulation of soviet activities.[73] In general, Soviet specialists treat the question of the transformation of the soviets into functioning representative organs of state power as an inevitability; the question is only one of improving the mechanisms already in place. Western specialists are far less sanguine and talk in terms of uncertain future potentialities. Nonetheless, specialists on both sides would probably agree with Hill's conclusion: "The prob-

[71] *Materialy plenuma TsK KPSS*, April 10, 1984 (Moscow: Politizdat, 1984), p. 7.
[72] Kutafin and Sheremet, *Kompetentsia mestnykh Sovetov*, pp. 66–86. The criteria include the size of the districts, the number and composition of deputies, the financial basis, the relations between the soviets, and the enterprises under higher jurisdiction and greater democratization.
[73] S. A. Avak'ian, *Pravovoe regulirovanie deiatel'nosti Sovetov* (Moscow: Moscow State Univesity, 1980), pp. 157ff., provides a valuable reference to the considerable specialist literature on this topic.

lem of 'developing' local government seems likely to be severe for the next generation at least; it takes a long time to change a culture."[74]

With respect to the question of political culture, the evidence presented here suggests that the view of Soviet citizens as inherently incapable of political participation because there are no historical predispositions or opportunities to do so is suspect. While it may be true that continuity rather than change characterizes the political thinking of most Russians despite the transition from autocracy to communism, it is not accurate to present the prerevolutionary period as devoid of participatory traditions, especially at the local level.[75] First, most historians have established that the great mass of the populace, the peasants, exercised broad and direct control over their local affairs—the "rich and democratic community life" of the village, as White refers to it. If such was the case, and continuity of political culture rather than change prevailed, why would the sense of civic competence in local matters to which the peasant was accustomed have disappeared? In the early years of Soviet power, Bolshevik control over the villages was highly tentative. Even during collectivization, as long as taxes were paid and there was

[74] See Ronald J. Hill, "Local Government Since Stalin," p. 32; Theodore Friedgut, "The Soviet Citizen's Perception of Local Soviet Government"; and L. G. Churchward, "Public Participation in the USSR," all of which are in Jacobs, *Soviet Local Politics and Government*. Hill does not see any real change as long as the party retains its monopoly of political leadership. Friedgut, and especially Churchward, are more hopeful.

[75] Mary McAuley makes this point strongly in her critique of Stephen White's study of Soviet political culture. If one tries to infer present or future Soviet political thinking from past Russian practices, as she argues White does, there is evidence that is contradictory enough to support conclusions quite the opposite of those drawn by White about the persistence of an authoritarian political culture in the period after the October Revolution. See Mary McAuley, "Political Culture and Communist Politics: One Step Forward, Two Steps Back," in Brown, *Political Culture and Communist Studies*, pp. 16–17; White's response is in the same volume.

no overt political opposition, those peasants who remained in the countryside under the *kolkhoz* system continued to make decisions regarding life in the villages. Even if the peasants during collectivization had no opportunities to take part in local decisions, it is unlikely the perception that they should be able to do so would disappear. It seems equally arguable that, as peasants moved into the cities as a result of industrialization, they may have brought with them the expectation that, regardless of which distant tsar sat in the Kremlin, local matters were something about which they should have a say.

Quite apart from the practices in the village, it is not clear that the development of the highly centralized state system that emerged under Lenin and reached fruition under Stalin was inevitable. However imperfectly they functioned, both the zemstva and the duma represented the institutionalization of liberal democratic ideals that were held by many who sought to transform the autocracy into a constitutional monarchy and that, but for the circumstances, might have been realized. Even the soviets originally expressed the aspirations of the urban proletariat for direct participation in the decisions that affected their lives. In short, it would be a mistake to base any conclusions regarding the possibility of increased citizen participation in local government in the Soviet Union on facile assumptions about the antidemocratic character of prerevolutionary Russian political culture or on the absence of an adequate legislative basis for greater participation in the contemporary period.

CHAPTER FOUR

How Soviet Local Government Is Organized

THE ACTIVITIES of the deputies to the local soviets take place within an elaborate organizational framework. Familiarity with this framework is essential to understanding how the deputies perform their functions in practice. First, we will look at the place of the soviets in the Soviet political system and describe the hierarchy of soviets and the relationships between existing various levels. Second, because it is helpful to know who the deputies are and how they are chosen, we will look at the elections, not only as a set of procedures for selecting those who ostensibly run the government, but also as a mode of political participation. Third, the internal organization of the soviets will be outlined. The present chapter is concerned only with describing how the executive and administrative agencies of local government are organized. The relationship between the deputies and the executive agencies, and the relative contributions of the deputies, the executive committee, and the party to policy-making, are dealt with in Chapter 6. Finally, some attention is paid to how the work of Soviet local government is financed.

THE SOVIET POLITICAL HIERARCHY

As in contemporary Western political theory, the Soviet conception of the political system encompasses nongovernmental institutions, such as political parties and interest groups, as well as the organs of government.[1] What is unique to Soviet-type political systems is the monopoly of legitimacy accorded to one party, the Communist Party. The theoretical justification for this claim rests on an organic view of society in which the interests of one group or person are inextricably bound to the interests of all; one part is not supposed gain at the expense of another. Because there can only be one common interest—the creation of a communist society—there can only be one political party. Article 6 of the Soviet Constitution states clearly that its Communist Party is "the leading and guiding force of Soviet society, the nucleus of the political system and of its state and public organizations." Thus, all other elements of the Soviet political system, governmental and nongovernmental alike, are linked to the policies of the party; the system is built on the interdependence of its parts, not on their independence. In the Soviet political system, the government does what the party deems necessary.

The governmental component of the Soviet political system consists of the soviets and the executive organs formally created by them. Here too an organic view of the relationship between parts prevails. From the national parliament (the Supreme Soviet) to the village council, the soviets are said to constitute a "unitary system of state power."[2] This means that each soviet is considered an integral part of the whole. The resolution of local and particular concerns cannot be viewed separately from how it affects other districts or the larger administrative units of which the soviet is a part. Rather, each local soviet must strive to ensure that what it is doing fits harmoniously

[1] A definition of the "political system of society" is offered in *Kratkii politicheskii slovar'*, 2nd ed. (Moscow: Politizdat, 1980), p. 320.

[2] A concise description of the "unity of the system of soviets" can be found in *Sovety narodnykh deputatov: spravochnik* (Moscow: Politizdat, 1984), pp. 76–79. (A. I. Luk'ianov, S. A. Avak'ian, and P. P. Gureev edited this work.)

with the greater good of Soviet society as a whole. The practice of asserting local or regional interests even though they might be disadvantageous to the larger community— a practice often considered the mark of an effective legislator in American politics—is incompatible with this "unitary system," at least in theory. For this reason, Soviet political theorists vigorously reject the idea of independent local "self-government" (*samoupravlenie*) while at the same time asserting that in strictly local issues the soviets have complete authority.[3]

Ideally, the role of the deputy as representative in this system is to merge dialectically the specific interests of constituents with the general interests of society. According to one textbook description, the deputy represents both simultaneously:

> Each deputy represents the constituents from his or her own electoral district, reports to them and is accountable before them. At the same time, the interests of these constituents are organically connected with the interests of the population living in territory of the soviet as a whole, and in the last analysis, with the interests of all the Soviet people. Therefore, the deputies are also the representatives of all the Soviet people.[4]

The unitary character of the soviets as a system of government is manifest in the universality of the norms and procedures that govern the operations of the soviets. Election procedures, internal organization, and the patterns of

[3] The formulation reaches back to the early years of the revolution, when opposition parties, who often held majority control in local areas, sought to emphasize the autonomous character of local self-rule. Lenin, of course, insisted on the unity of local interests with those of the center. See Luk'ianov, *Razvitie zakonodatel'stva*, pp. 47–51. An important reconsideration of *samoupravlenie* aimed at influencing the 1985 Draft Party Program is offered by G. V. Barabashev, "Glavnoe zveno samoupravlenie," *SND*, no. 1 (1986), pp. 9–17.

[4] Barabashev and Sheremet, *Sovetskoe stroitel'stvo*, p. 67.

interaction between levels of government are essentially the same regardless of location. The Law on the Status of Deputies, for example, applies equally to deputies at every level and in every region.[5] This contrasts sharply with the practice in the United States, where the organization of local government varies widely by region, reflecting diversity of historical experience, differences in political subcultures, and levels of economic development.

Yet, Soviet society is at least as variegated as that of the United States, and probably more so. The needs and resources of a village *aul* in Kirgizia are substantially different from those of a city borough in Moscow; the problems faced by a city on the Black Sea coast can hardly be compared to those of a huge national *okrug* in northern Siberia, even though their population size might be similar. The Soviet response was to create an administrative-territorial hierarchy in which the country as a whole is subdivided and classified according to ethnicity, urbanization, and population size. In principle, each subdivision has its own soviet. In the ensuing discussion of administrative structure, keep in mind that underlying the similarity of organizational principles there are widely varying interpretations of how to implement these principles, depending on the character of the community doing the interpreting. This is especially true given the ethnic diversity of the Soviet Union.

At the top of the hierarchy are the Supreme Soviets of the USSR, the fifteen union-republics, and twenty autonomous republics (sixteen of which are in the RSFSR, two in the Georgian Republic, and one each in Azerbaidzhan and Uzbekistan). Deputies at this level are elected for five years. All soviets below this level are called local soviets and the deputy's term of office is two-and-a-half years.

[5] Some of the aspects of the unified system are noted in I. A. Azovkin and N. G. Starovoitov, "Sovety narodnykh deputatov-politicheskaia osnova SSSR," *SGiP*, no. 11 (1982), pp. 125–127.

The hierarchy of the local soviets is quite complex and confusing, particularly because, as Jacobs points out,[6] the territorial breakdown used by the Soviets does not always accurately reflect the ranking of the soviets based on administrative subordination, especially in the case of cities.

Jacobs' approach will be employed here too. First, the levels of local government used in Soviet statistical reporting will be outlined; this will be followed by a description based on administrative subordination. After the elections of February 24, 1985, there were 52,041 local soviets.[7] Based on the territorial ranking used by the Soviet government, they are broken down as follows. Eight of the fifteen union-republics (the RSFSR, the Ukraine, Belorussia, Kazakhstan, Uzbekistan, Tadzhikistan, Kirgizia, and Turkmenia) are subdivided into 123 regional units (*oblasts*). Equal in administrative ranking to the oblasts, but distinguished by the ethnic composition of their population, are eight autonomous republics (five in the RSFSR), six krai (loosely akin to reservations for Native Americans and all located in the RSFSR), and ten autonomous okrugs (all in the RSFSR). Within the regions and in the remaining union-republics that have no regional subdivisions, are 3,113 district (*raion*) soviets and 2,137 are city soviets. In addition, 152 of the larger Soviet cities (all but 9 with populations greater than 200,000) are subdivided into 645 city boroughs (*raion v gorode*). At the base of the pyramid are 3,823 settlement soviets (*poselkovye*) and 42,176 village soviets (*sel'skie*). Settlement soviets represent a single population point, while village soviets are comprised of clusters

---

[6] Everett M. Jacobs, "The Organizational Framework of Soviet Local Government," in Jacobs, *Soviet Local Politics and Government*, pp. 4–5.

[7] These and the following figures come from *Itogi vyborov i sostav deputatov mestnykh Sovetov narodnykh deputatov 1985 goda (statisticheskii sbornik)* (Moscow: Isvestiia, 1985), pp. 10–13. Hereafter, this annual publication will be cited as *Itogi vyborov*, with the year to which the data apply.

of several small rural communities. Table 4-1 gives the number and size of the local soviets.

An examination of the Soviet political hierarchy from the perspective of administrative subordination reveals a different picture of the relative importance of the various levels in the hierarchy, a difference that accentuates the importance of Soviet cities as the nerve centers of the Soviet state system. Although more than 81 percent of the local soviets are found in rural areas, more than 65 percent of the Soviet population live in the cities and are subject to city government. In terms of subordination, cities fall into one of three categories, depending on their importance or their size. In the first category, which includes the capitals of all the union-republics, are the cities that are directly subordinated to the union-republic or autonomous republic in which they are located. In 1983, there were eighty-seven of the former and eighty-five of the latter. Administrative subordination for this group of cities does not appear to be based on size, however, because forty-three of the eighty-seven cities subordinated to union-republics had populations of less than 50,000.[8] The second group includes cities that are subordinated to the regional, krai, or okrug subdivisions. Because inclusion in the regional and krai category is determined by the governments of republics having such subdivisions, the minimal population size varies.[9]

[8] These figures were calculated using SSSR. Administrativno-territorial'noe delenie soyuznykh respublik (Moscow: Izvestiia, 1983), pp. 642–652, and the list of cities with populations over 50,000 in Narodnoe khoziaistvo SSSR v 1983 god (statisticheskii ezhegodnik) (Moscow: Tsentral'noe statisticheskoe upravlenie 1984), pp. 18–23. Minimal population standards for cities of republican subordination vary. In the RSFSR there is no fixed number; in the Ukraine, the standard is at least one million, "as a rule." See "Polozhenie o poriadke resheniia voprosov administrativno-territorial'nogo ustroistva RSFSR," Vedomosti Verkhovnogo Soveta RSFSR, 1982, no. 34, item 1271, art. 7; and "Polozhenie o poriadke resheniia voprosov administrativno-territorial'nogo ustroistva Ukrainskoi SSR," Vedomosti Verkhovnogo Soveta USSR, 1981, no. 12, item 179, art. 6.

[9] Union-republic-level legislation defining the categories of administra-

TABLE 4-1. Number and Size of Local Soviets, 1985

Level of soviet	Total no. of soviets	Percent of all soviets	Total no. of deputies	Percent of all deputies per soviet	Average no. of deputies per soviet	Aggregate no. of registered voters at each level	Average constituency size
Krai, oblast	129	0.25	31,745	1.40	246	136,952,903	4,417
Autonomous oblast	8	0.01	1,360	0.06	170	1,390,657	1,023
Autonomous okrug	10	0.02	1,120	0.05	112	1,290,498	1,152
Raion	3,113	6.00	256,009	11.10	82	81,124,097	317
City	2,137	4.10	291,042	12.60	136	114,664,283	394
City borough	645	1.20	139,574	6.10	216	62,094,489	445
Settlement	3,823	7.40	216,301	9.40	57	16,876,714	78
Village	42,176	81.00	1,367,679	59.30	32	61,173,845	45
For all levels:	52,041	99.98[a]	2,304,830	100.01[a]	44	185,321,639[b]	—

SOURCES: *Itogi vyborov*, 1985, and *Nekotorye voprosy organizatsionnoi raboty*, 1984.

NOTE: Figures as of elections of February 24, 1985. Interested readers may obtain a longitudinal perspective by comparing this table with a similar one for 1980 in Jacobs, *Soviet Local Politics and Government*, p. 9. A comparison of the figures shows their stability over time.

[a] Percents do not add up to 100 because of rounding.
[b] The sum of this column and the total are different because Soviet electors vote in a varying number of districts, depending on their location.

In general, the minimum size for cities subordinated to regions or to krai is 50,000 (30,000 in some republics); in cities of okrug subordination it is 15,000. There are 782 cities of the first type and 14 of the second. Finally, there are 1,156 smaller cities subordinated to the district (*raion*) subdivisions; normally their population size would be between 10,000 and 30,000. Towns with a population of 2,000 to 10,000, a majority of whom (65 percent to 85 percent) work in nonagricultural production, are classified as "urban settlements" (*poselkov gorodskogo tipa*).[10] There were 3,936 of these in 1983, and they are administratively subordinate to districts or to cities of regional subordination.

In principle, each administrative-territorial subdivision has its own soviet. Changes in these subdivisions as a result of economic development, population dynamics, or the increased authority of local government should be reflected in changes in the number of soviets at each level. But this has apparently not happened to the extent that it should, in part because there is no uniform, optimal system for creating administrative subdivisions. As one Soviet observer critically observes, "It is not the system of soviets that is adjusted to administrative-territorial subdivisions, but more often, on the contrary, administrative-territorial subdivisions are bound by the already established number of local soviets."[11] The result is that more and more soviets are no longer classified correctly; rapidly

---

tive subdivision and establishing the procedures by which such subdivisions are made and changed appeared in all the republics between 1982 and 1983. As noted in the preceding footnote, there are variations. A list of *Vedomosti* references by republic, as well as the statute (*polozhenie*) for the Ukraine, can be found in the *Sbornik normativnykh aktov*, pp. 302–307.

[10] The use of the "settlement" designation varies. In Uzbekistan they are called city settlements (*gorodskoi poselok*), while in the RSFSR they are broken down as workers settlements (*rabochik*), health resort settlements (*kurortnyk*), and vacation settlements (*dachnykh*). See *Sovety narodnykh deputatov: spravochnik*, p. 79.

[11] A. V. Moskalev, "Sistema mestnykh Sovetov i ee sovevershenstvovanie," *Pravovedenie*, 1982, no. 6, p. 16.

developing areas that should be governed by a higher-level soviet are still with a lower organ, and vice versa. The same observer concludes that while reform has been slow in coming, at best, when it does come it will be incremental.[12]

Like the party, the system of soviets is linked together by the principles of "democratic centralism" and "dual subordination." The principle of democratic centralism, now incorporated as article 3 of the Soviet Constitution, is usually broken down into its component parts. The democratic element refers to the electability of all the representative organs of state power from bottom to top; to the requirement that members of these organs regularly report to and be accountable (through periodic reports and recall) to those who elected them; and to the rights of the lower units to discuss and make proposals regarding the legislation of superior organs that affects them. In theory, local governments independently resolve all issues "of local significance" within the limits of their competence, determine how they will spend the funds available to them, and have the exclusive right to appoint and remove their members. According to the centralist element, however, it is the obligation of all lower organs to carry out the decisions of superior authorities, including the policies of the CPSU as embodied in legislation enacted by the national organs of power. Any decision made by a lower soviet that its superior soviet considers illegal will be overturned. In addition, the bulk of the revenue available to local units comes from above and must be spent within the parameters established by the annual economic plan.

The second principle, that of dual subordination, ensures that the interests of the center are communicated to the local authorities. Heads of executive departments at the local level are responsible not only to the local soviet that appointed them (horizontal subordination), but also

[12] Ibid., p. 18.

to the administrative official in charge of their branch of the economy at the next highest level (vertical subordination). Thus, for example, the chief administrator of internal affairs (police and fire) of one of the thirty-one city boroughs in Moscow reports not only to his council but also to the head of the corresponding Moscow city department, who in turn is responsible to the RSFSR minister of internal affairs. The latter must oversee the implementation of policies designed and administered by the USSR Ministry of Internal Affairs. Most Western observers see the principle of dual subordination primarily as a guarantee of control by the center,[13] but Soviet specialists reject this view. For example, Barabashev and Sheremet state: "It is necessary to emphasize that the leadership of the apparatus of the local soviets 'horizontally,' that is, from the side of the corresponding soviet, as a rule, is the prevailing line of leadership in comparison with leadership 'vertically,' that is, from the side of the superior soviets."[14] Practice probably lies between these views, with influence of the local soviets being stronger in less important or primarily local issues, and with central authority taking precedence in issues of national or regional importance.

This question of the division of labor between central and local authority is also determined legally. Questions of jurisdiction or "competence" are defined for each level of the soviets by national- and republican-level legislation.[15] The Constitution (in articles 145–148) establishes the general framework of local government jurisdiction and

[13] See, e.g., Jacobs, "The Organizational Framework of Soviet Local Government," p. 7.

[14] Barabashev and Sheremet, *Sovetskoe stroitel'stvo*, p. 91.

[15] This legislation is noted along with the *Vedomosti* citations in the previous chapter. The texts themselves are in *Sbornik normativnykh aktov*, items 125, 127, 129, 131. It is important to add that national legislation with respect to other aspects of social and economic development is controlling for the local soviets. The national law on education, for example, creates certain rights and obligations for local government regarding education.

indicates the areas of activity for which each jurisdiction is responsible. The list is far more extensive than the powers accorded local government by articles 97 and 98 of the 1936 Constitution. In particular, the local soviets' control over enterprises, institutions, and organizations of higher subordination on their territory has been strengthened: the execution of the soviets' decisions by these bodies is "mandatory" (art. 148). Areas specified in which local soviets "coordinate and control" the activities of the entities include land use, conservation, construction, labor resources, production of consumer goods, and provision of everyday consumer services. In short, by law their authority is supposed to be greatest in areas where the needs of the community are most direct.

A detailed description of changes in administrative and legislative jurisdiction for each level of the soviets is beyond the scope of the present work,[16] but it can be said here that the rule-making authority of the local soviets in 1986 is greater than it was even twenty years earlier, not only in the number of areas in which their competence has grown but also in their ability to make decisions (*reshenia*) that contain normative prescriptions. It would be incorrect

[16] A number of "commentaries" published in recent years by Soviet specialists on the laws of local government provide lengthy analyses of each article of laws on local government. They constitute a semiofficial interpretation of these laws. Students seeking details on the rights and obligations for each level of the soviets should consult these commentaries. They are: *Kommentarii k zakonodatel'stvu o poselkovykh i sel'skikh Sovetakh*, 2nd ed. (Moscow: Izvestiia, 1982); *Kommentarii k zakonodatel'stvu o gorodskikh, raionnykh v gorode Sovetakh narodnykh deputatov* (Moscow: Izvestiia, 1983); and *Kommentarii k zakonodetel'stvu o raionnykh Sovetakh narodnykh deputatov* (Moscow: Izvestiia, 1985). A similar volume on the regional and area soviets is under way. While the legislative powers of the local governments relative to the center have increased steadily over the past twenty years, practice has been slow in following. A useful summary of the continued sources of imbalance, as well as a description of an experiment to overcome them in the city of Poti in Georgia, is in Darrell Slider, "More Power to the Soviets? Reform and Local Government in the Soviet Union," *British Journal of Political Science* 16 (October, 1986).

today to conclude, as Max Mote did in 1963, that the deputy to the local soviet "has no power in the Western sense of the word," that "Soviet statutes do not originate with the soviet, as ordinances do with an American city council."[17] In fact, while many local decisions are specific for certain classes of the population and therefore "nonnormative," the local soviets are empowered to adopt public regulations that establish general rules of conduct for the local community, from procedures for collecting garbage to the manner in which retail sales can be conducted.[18]

One intriguing ambiguity in Soviet legislation regarding the jurisdiction of local government is whether local authorities are free to make rules in areas not expressly addressed by superior legislation. In the American system, for example, the principle of "residual powers" applies to states and to municipalities opting for "home rule." Local governments can legislate in areas not reserved to or covered by superior legislation. Soviet specialists appear to differ on this question. One specialist on administrative theory, P. N. Lebedev, writes that "existing legislation does not exhaustively define the spheres of activity of the city and city borough soviets" and that the local soviet can "by its own discretion define the circle of questions related to its jurisdiction."[19] An apparently contradictory view is expressed by S. A. Avak'ian:

It is impossible to agree that local governments might have the right to publish normative acts when a particular issue is not forbidden by the center or if in general it is not found reflected in an act of the central organ. . . . Therefore, no general principle is seen whereby the

[17] Max Mote, *Soviet Local and Republic Elections* (Stanford, Calif.: Hoover Institution, 1965), p. 119.

[18] W. E. Butler, *Soviet Law* (London: Butterworths, 1983), pp. 39, 42, 45–46.

[19] P. N. Lebedev (ed.), *Sistema organov gorodskogo upravleniia* (Leningrad: Leningrad University Press, 1980), p. 21.

local soviet is given the scope to regulate when the center is "silent."[20]

In a recent theoretical discussion, Barabashev and Sheremet argue that two principles are simultaneously operative: "By one principle, the soviet can do only that which it is permitted or instructed to do. By the other principle, the soviet may do that which is not forbidden to it."[21] When asked in separate interviews to explain the differences in these positions, Barabashev and Sheremet gave essentially the same answer: in some areas, like finance, the more restrictive interpretation prevails, but in others— for example, the regulation of the activities of local social clubs or organizations—the principle of residual authority seems to apply. In general, the trend appears to be in favor of a broader interpretation of what the local soviets may do.

Soviet Elections

Soviet specialists on government insist that elections in the Soviet system are the most democratic in the world. To back up this contention, they refer to the Soviet Constitution (articles 95–102), and to the electoral laws of the thirty-five union and autonomous republics, which specify the principles and procedures governing Soviet elections.[22] According to this legislation, elections of deputies

[20] Avak'ian, *Pravovoe regulirovanie deiatel'nosti Sovetov*, pp. 109–110.

[21] G. V. Barabashev and K. F. Sheremet, "Protsess priniatiia reshenii mestnymi Sovetami (teoreticheskie voprosy)," in *Priniatie reshenii*, p. 13.

[22] Other than the articles in the 1977 Constitution, there is no single national electoral law. In 1979, however, electoral laws were adopted in all the fifteen union-republics and the twenty autonomous republics. With only the most minor variations, they conform to the law used in the RSFSR. This law, along with extensive commentary prepared by the Department on Issues in the Work of the Soviets of the Presidium of the Supreme Soviet has been published as *Kommentarii k nekotorym stat'iam zakona o vyborakh v mestnye Sovety narodnykh deputatov RSFSR* (Moscow:

to all soviets are conducted on the basis of universal, equal, and direct suffrage and by secret ballot. Anyone age eighteen or older can be elected to any soviet except the national Supreme Soviet, for which the age requirement is twenty-one. All elections are paid for by the state. To bolster their argument, Soviet observers point to the enormous numbers of people who take part in the organization of the elections, to the campaign itself, and to the all but universal participation by those eligible in the actual vote. They also emphasize that the results are more quantitatively representative of the population as a whole. All these qualities contrast favorably with elections in bourgeois democracies, which Soviet critics contend are highly unrepresentative, characterized by relatively low turnout—indicating the indifference of the masses—and controlled by monopoly capitalists who are the only people able to afford the enormously high costs of running a campaign.

Most Western specialists on the Soviet political system portray Soviet elections as little more than a ritual used by the party to maintain the fiction of democratic legitimacy while propagandizing and mobilizing the population on behalf of their goals. As expressions of the people's will, they are seen as essentially meaningless.[23] The reality, as

Iurid. Lit., 1979). The most comprehensive Soviet discussion of this legislation as it pertains to the local soviets is V. K. Grigor'ev and V. P. Zhdanov, *Vybory v mestnye Sovety narodnykh deputatov i poriadok ikh provedeniia* (Moscow: Iurid. Lit., 1982).

[23] Given the general lack of importance that most Western observers ascribe to Soviet elections, the volume of specialist literature on the topic is remarkable. See George B. Carson, *Electoral Practices in the USSR* (New York: Praeger, 1955); Mote, *Soviet Local and Republic Elections*; Jerome Gillison, "Soviet Elections as a Measure of Dissent: The Missing One Per Cent," *American Political Science Review* 62 (September 1968); Jacobs, "Soviet Elections: What They Are and What They Are Not"; Everett Jacobs, "The Composition of Local Soviets, 1959–1969," *Government and Opposition* 7 (Autumn 1972); Ronald J. Hill, "Patterns of Deputy Selection to Local Soviets," *Soviet Studies* 25 (October 1973); Ronald J. Hill, "The CPSU

Western specialists see it, is that the process of nominating candidates is controlled by the Communist Party, whose monopoly of power and claim to be the sole legitimate representative of the public interest preclude any real competition. The result is that only one candidate is nominated for each position. Soviet voters are harassed into going to the polls by the army of agitators whose function it is to organize elections. All but a courageous few obediently place their ballot with the name of the nominee in the ballot box and leave. For the Western critic, the fact that 99.98 percent of the electorate participates in this exercise, and that all but an insignificant handful of nominees are elected with by a 99.8 percent majority, is not a demonstration of popular support but instead further evidence that in the face of such predetermined results nobody takes elections seriously. One recent Western textbook on the Soviet political system referred to Soviet elections as "the ultimate mark of hypocrisy and sham in Soviet government operations,"[24] while the author of another standard work concluded, "Applying the term election to this procedure does semantic violence to the word as defined in the Western democratic lexicon."[25]

On balance, it is difficult to accept the Soviet contention. How can citizens meaningfully participate in the selection of those who run the government when the nomination of candidates is largely predetermined and no alternatives are offered? In the absence of competition, it is hardly sur-

---

in a Soviet Election Campaign," *Soviet Studies* 28 (October 1976); Ronald J. Hill, "Soviet Literature on Electoral Reform," *Government and Opposition* 11 (Autumn 1976); Victor Zaslavsky and Robert Brym, "The Functions of Elections in the USSR," *Soviet Studies* 30 (July 1978). In addition, Friedgut devotes nearly one-quarter of his book *Political Participation in the USSR* to elections. There are two chapters in Jacobs, *Soviet Local Politics and Government*, chaps. 4 and 5.

[24] Donald Barry and Carol Barner-Barry, *Contemporary Soviet Politics*, 2nd ed. (Englewood Cliffs, N.J.: Prentice-Hall, 1982), p. 91.

[25] Frederick Barghoorn, *Politics in the USSR*, 2nd ed. (Boston: Little, Brown, and Co., 1972), p. 246.

prising that many Soviet citizens exhibit a lack of interest in the outcomes of elections or, worse, develop an active cynicism that is the antithesis of the legitimacy that is ostensibly the object of this exercise.[26] This lack of interest has also been noted by Soviet observers. Roy Medvedev, a socialist-oriented Soviet dissident, wrote in his book *On Socialist Democracy* that phony balloting was widespread, and he urged multiple candidacies and greater participation in the nomination process as the only antidote for public disinterest.[27]

Multiple candidacies are not prohibited by Soviet law, and as Hill points out, the possibility of contested elections has been the subject of a lively debate among Soviet specialists for some time.[28] For example, Barabashev believes that constituency interest would be stimulated if, for example, five candidates ran for three seats.[29] Competitive elections are not unknown in other socialist countries, including Poland, Yugoslavia, and most recently Hungary.[30] Recent events indicate that Soviet leaders may be prepared to overcome the inertia of past experience and introduce changes along these lines. Mikhail Gorbachev, in his speech to the 27th Congress of the CPSU on February 25, 1986, averred, "The time is apparently ripe for making necessary corrections to our electoral practice as well."

[26] Zaslavsky and Brym ("The Functions of Elections in the USSR") argue that it is precisely this cynicism that the leadership seek to foster. In their view, the regime's stability is enhanced by cynicism: citizens who accept the gap between the public commitment to democratic procedures and the reality of Soviet practices with respect to elections will accept it in other areas as well. Zaslavsky, who served for eighteen years on an electoral commission before emigrating, rejects the idea that Soviet elections provide "legitimacy."

[27] Roy Medvedev, *On Socialist Democracy* (1972), trans. Ellen de Kadt (New York: Random House, 1975), p. 143.

[28] Hill, "Soviet Literature on Electoral Reform." See also Hill, *Soviet Politics, Political Science, and Political Reform*, pp. 24–30.

[29] Personal interview, 1984.

[30] *New York Times*, June 23, 1985, p. 6.

What Gorbachev had in mind was spelled out in greater detail in his speech to the January 27–28, 1987, plenum of the CPSU Central Committee, when he described "democratization" as a key element of his policy for "reconstruction" (*perestroika*) of Soviet society and proposed changes in the way members of the local soviets were to be elected.[31] On February 26, 1987, the Presidium of the RSFSR Supreme Soviet adopted legislation that required the formation of multimember districts (*mnogomandatnye izbiratel'nye okrugi*) for the election of deputies to district (*raion*), city, settlement, and village soviets in the elections scheduled for June 21, 1981.[32] The legislation stipulates that in certain regions of the USSR selected single-member districts will be combined into new, larger districts electing the same number of deputies as before, but that the number of candidates will exceed the number to be elected. The actual numbers will vary from one multimember district to another, but roughly seven or eight candidates will run for five seats. Names will appear on the ballots in alphabetical order, with voters crossing off the names of those they do not want to vote for. An absolute majority (50 percent) is required for election, and if the number of those elected exceeds the number of places available, those receiving the fewest votes (but more than 50 percent) will become "reserve deputies" who will fill any vacancies that might occur during the term of office of those who were elected.

It should be emphasized that the multimember district elections are being held as an experiment in selected areas

[31] Speech of M. S. Gorbachev to the January 27–28 plenum of the CPSU Central Committee, in *Materialy plenuma TsK KPSS, 27–28 Ianvaria 1987* (Moscow: Politizdat, 1987), pp. 15, 30.

[32] *Vedomosti Verkhovnogo Soveta RSFSR*, 1987, no. 10, item 310, "Postanovlenie Presidiuma Verkhovnogo Soveta RSFSR o provedenii v poriadke eksperimenta vyborov v mestnye Sovety narodnykh deputatov RSFSR po mnogomandatnym izbiratel'nym okrugam." Similar legislation has been adopted in the other republics.

of the Soviet Union. My conversations with Soviet specialists in May 1987 indicated that about 5 percent of the total number of deputies would be affected. In fact, according to *Pravda* (June 27, 1987) 94,184 deputies were elected from among 120,449 candidates in the June 21, 1987, local elections. That would represent about 4.4 percent of all the deputies elected at the district, city, settlement, and village level. The results of this experiment are to be analyzed and generalized prior to the elections of January 1990. Depending on the outcome of this assessment, a new election law requiring competitive elections for all local soviets, and possibly the Supreme Soviets as well, will be adopted.

The results of Soviet elections to date, however, can hardly be considered an expression of the people's preference about who will govern. Nevertheless, the electoral process itself does have some opportunities for citizens to present their views. In order to understand how citizens participate in local Soviet government, it is necessary to look at these participatory elements.[33] For our purposes, the electoral process will be divided into four sequential stages: the organization of the elections, the nomination process, the campaign, and the voting. A description of each stage will give special attention to occasions when voters can to some extent express themselves.

Organization of Elections

The organization of elections gets under way following an edict from the republican-level Supreme Soviets establishing the dates of the election. This must occur no less than two months before the terms of office end—every two-and-a-half years at the local level. Within five days of the edict, the executive committee (*ispolkom*) of each soviet at each level of the hierarchy publishes a list of electoral districts (*izbiratel'nyi okrug*) of roughly the same size for its

[33] See footnotes 22 and 23 for references to more detailed descriptions of election procedures.

territory, based on the number of voters. Legislation adopted in each republic in 1979 established minimum and maximum numbers of districts for each type of soviet; the figures for the RSFSR are presented in Table 4-2. In addition, the executive committee establishes the number of polling places (*izbiratel'nyi uchastok*), which now may number no fewer than one for every 100 voters and no more than one for every 3,000, with exceptions for sparsely settled areas.[34] Because of the large number of districts, it is normal for constituents from several different districts to vote in a single polling place.[35] The executive committees are also responsible for preparing a voter list based on records kept by their Housing Committees. Except for the insane, anyone who is eighteen years old by the day of the election is included. The list must be published twenty days before the election to give voters the opportunity to verify that they are properly registered.

From the point of view of political participation, the most important aspect of the organizational stage of elections is the formation of the election commissions. There are three types of these: one for the territorial soviet as a whole called the "election commission" (*izbiratel'naia kommissiia*), one for each electoral district in the soviet (*okruzhnaia izbiratel'naia kommissiia*), and one for the precinct or polling place (*uchastkaia izbiratel'naia kommissiia*). In rural and settlement soviets, precinct commissions report directly to the territorial election commission. The function of all the commissions is to ensure that the proper election procedures are followed. They register the candidates for office, organize the balloting, conduct the vote count, examine complaints of impropriety, and certify the results.

---

[34] The information in these sections comes from Grigor'ev and Zhdanov, *Vybory v mestnye Sovety*, pp. 22–35; and *Kommentarii k nekotorym stat'iam zakona o vyborakh*, pp. 17–23. The norms for polling places (art. 17) are discussed on p. 20 of the latter.

[35] Mote states, e.g., that in Leningrad in 1963 there were 5,746 districts but only 1,637 polling places(*Soviet Local and Republic Elections*, p. 20).

TABLE 4-2. Numbers of Electoral Districts (Deputies)
RSFSR (as of 1987)

Level of soviet	Minimum	Maximum
Krai, oblast	1500	500
Autonomous oblast	100	250
Autonomous okrug	75	200
Raion	75	150
Cities subordinate to the RSFSR[a]		
Moscow	1,000	1,000
Leningrad	600	600
Cities subordinate to krai, oblast, autonomous okrug	75	500
Cities subordinate to raion	50	150
City borough	75	350
Settlement	25	75
Village	25	75

SOURCES: *Kommentarii k nekotorym stat'iam zakona o vyborakh v mestnye sovety RSFSR* (Moscow: Iurid. Lit., 1979), pp. 17–18; V. K. Grigorev and V. P. Zhdanov, *Vybory v mestnye Sovety narodnykh deputatov i poriadok ikh provedeniia* (Moscow: Iurid. Lit., 1982), p. 25.

NOTE: There is some variation by republic, though it is not very great. The norms of the RSFSR are the same for the Ukraine, Belorussia, Uzbekistan and Kazakhstan, the four other largest republics. In Kirgizia, Tadzhikistan, and Turkmenia, the other three republics with regional subdivisions, the maximum number of oblast electoral districts is 300, instead of 500. The remaining seven republics are not subdivided into areas, or oblasts.

[a] These two cities are the only cities subordinate to the RSFSR, and their size is exceptional; in the other cities subordinated to the republics the range is 50–500.

Commission members are nominated by social organizations (CPSU, Komsomol, trade unions) or at general meetings held at the workplace and chosen at a public meeting. There is some effort to be quantitatively representative; women, for example, accounted for 51 percent of the commission members in 1985. Like the deputies themselves, members are generally respected in the workplace and apparently look on their appointments as a relatively easy form of public service.[36]

The participatory element is largely quantitative: an enormous number of people are engaged in this form of civic duty. The smallest commission (at the village level) consists of three officers and one to five additional members; the largest (e.g., Moscow or Leningrad) will include fourteen members and three officers. In the February 24, 1985, elections, a total of 8,683,421 people participated on 948,862 commissions.[37] The election commission, like the rest of the electoral process, is dominated by the CPSU (the percentage who are party members has grown steadily from 27 percent in 1961 to 41 percent in 1985), but a large number of individuals actively perform the role of "good citizens," ensuring the integrity of the process. That the activity itself is ritualistic does not necessarily diminish the symbolic satisfaction that comes from performing it.

The Nomination Process

The second stage in Soviet elections centers around the nomination of candidates. Although Soviet deputies represent territorial election districts, they are nominated at their place of work, a procedure that in a different system might raise questions of potential conflict of interest. Since the adoption of the 1977 Constitution, the right to nominate is limited to the CPSU, trade unions, the Komsomol, and cooperatives. This precludes dissident groups from at-

---

[36] See Friedgut's description in *Political Participation in the USSR*, p. 79.
[37] *Itogi vyborov*, 1985, p. 237.

tempting to nominate candidates, which happened in the early 1970s. In villages and army units, nominations can take place at a general meeting of the whole community. The decision to nominate is made formally at a general meeting of the work collective, following discussion of the candidates' qualifications, by a majority of votes of those present or by a majority "of the general composition of the appropriate body of the social organization." The candidate is then informed of the nomination, the electorate is informed who the candidate will be, and the candidate is registered with the election commission in the district in which he or she will stand for election. Nominations must be completed at least twenty-five days before election day, and registration no more than five days after nomination. Unless the nominee's name is withdrawn, it will appear, along with the identity of the nominating body, on a white, blue, red, green, or rose-colored ballot, depending on the level of the soviet to which the candidate will almost certainly be elected.

In reality, the question of who will be nominated has been prepared in advance. First, a certain number of places are already set aside *ex officio*. At the highest level these go to major party figures who are often nominated honorifically from several districts and then chosen by one. Leonid Brezhnev, for example, was a representative to the Supreme Soviet from the Bauman district in Moscow but was nominated by thirty districts in 1975. At the local level, key figures in the local party organization will hold seats along with officers of the executive committee and the heads of administrative departments.

National data about the composition of the local deputies elected in 1985 indicate that 7 percent of the deputies are workers in the soviet organs, while 2.7 percent work in the party full-time, for a combined average of almost 10 percent. At the oblast level the total figure reaches 25.3 percent, in the cities about 10 percent, and in the rural soviets 6 to 8 percent of those elected are workers in party or state organs. In the Lenin city borough of Moscow from 1982 to 1985, for example, 27 of the 250 available seats were held by those employed full-time by the party or the soviet. Among the 27, some 15 were heads of administrative departments.[38] According to one deputy who was interviewed, the executive committee requests renomination of such individuals from the body originally nominating them, in effect overlapping the *nomenklatura* system with that of the election process. This effect has also been noted by Victor Zaslavsky and Robert Brym, who see it as major impediment to competitive elections because some seats must in effect be reserved for such people.[39]

Two other factors figure into the preselection of candidates. One is the quota system, by which the party ensures the quantitative representation of certain population segments in the composition of the soviets' membership. Every local party must see to it that the right mix is achieved (see discussion and Table 4-3, below).[40] With *nomenklatura* and compositional considerations in hand, a meeting before the general nomination meeting is held. In that meeting the leaders of the designated social organizations—usually less than ten individuals for a given collective—will determine the places to be filled. Then, on the basis of the work records available to them and preliminary discussions to determine candidate suitability and availability, they decide who will be presented for what is usually a unanimous vote by the public meeting of the col-

[38] The national figures are from ibid., pp. 24–25. The figures for the Lenin district are for 1985 and were made available to the author during a research visit to Moscow in January 1986.

[39] Victor Zaslavsky and Robert Brym, "The Structure of Power and the Functions of Local Soviet Elections," in Jacobs, *Soviet Local Politics and Government*, pp. 74–75. See also Friedgut, *Political Participation in the USSR*, p. 83. The *nomenklatura* system refers to a list of positions for which party approval is required. For more on this system, see Chapter 6, below.

[40] The party's role in the nomination process is examined by Hill, "The CPSU in a Soviet Election Campaign," pp. 592–596.

lective. To the extent that citizen input is taken into account in the nomination process, it occurs during these informal consultations with others in the workplace or in those relatively rare instances at the public nomination meeting when those attending take advantage of their legal right to participate and to criticize the proposed nominees. The chances of rejection appear to be less than one in 1,000.[41]

The Campaign

From the point of view of direct citizen participation, the most interesting phase of the election process is the campaign itself, for it is during this phase that constituents have the greatest opportunity to communicate their problems, proposals, and preferences to those who make decisions. There are basically two ways in which this can be done: through the network of agitators and at the meetings with the candidates prior to the election.

To some extent, the agitator functions as a Soviet equivalent of the committeeman in American politics. His job is to inform the voter about the time and place of the upcoming election, to disseminate information on the party's platform, and to get out the vote. Such activity begins almost as soon as elections are announced and is separate from working for a particular candidate; the agitator is really campaigning for the system, not for the deputies, per se. Agitators are drawn almost exclusively from members of the party and the Komsomol, and they carry out their activities from hundreds of brightly decorated *agit-punkti* and voter clubs located at factories, educational institutions, apartment buildings, and the like. While exact figures are not available, it appears that between two-thirds and three-fourths of the total party membership

[41] V. K. Grigor'ev, *Vybory v mestnye Sovety deputatov trudiashchikhsia* (Moscow: Izvestiia, 1969), p. 37.

perform this function.[42] Estimates vary, but each agitator is responsible for personally contacting between ten and thirty voters in their homes.[43] It is during these visits that voters have the opportunity to make demands ranging from apartment repairs to improved public service or, according to one former agitator, even express dissent about the regime. While citizens may take advantage of this opportunity relatively rarely, there is some evidence that this function has grown in recent years.[44]

The other opportunity for citizen participation in the campaign comes during the preelection meetings with candidates. Such meetings take place in the district or the workplace following the registration of the nominee, that is, twenty to twenty-five days before the vote. Voters can voice their concerns at these meetings in two ways. Following brief nomination and acceptance speeches, the floor is opened to questions, which can and reportedly does on occasion prompt a lively exchange of opinions on matters of community interest. The lower the level of the soviet, the more likely this is to occur. Minutes are kept of these exchanges. Proposals, problems, and complaints considered reasonable can expect to receive further attention. In addition to informal discussion, there is a more

[42] Friedgut estimates that in 1975 5 percent of the electorate were involved in the elections, or more than 8 million people (*Political Participation in the USSR*, p. 99). Zaslavsky puts the figure at 6 to 8 percent, which in 1985 would mean between 11.1 million and 14.8 million individuals, roughly 95 percent of whom are party or Komsomol members (Zaslavsky and Brym, "The Functions of Elections in the USSR," p. 365).

[43] Zaslavsky's figure is fifteen to twenty electors per agitator (Zaslavsky and Brym, "The Functions of Elections in the USSR," p. 365); Mote puts the figure between ten and thirty (*Soviet Local and Republic Elections*, p. 66).

[44] See Zaslavsky and Brym, "The Functions of Elections in the USSR," p. 367; and Friedgut, *Political Participation in the USSR*, p. 101. The present author's personal experience as a committeeman in the American system is that perhaps one voter in fifty wanted to discuss any issues, preferring to receive the minimum of information offered on the elections, the candidates, or their positions.

institutionalized mechanism for communicating the community's wishes, called the voter mandates (*nakaz izbiratelei*). These mandates are requests for specific community
projects; they are formally proposed, discussed, voted on,
and, if approved, become the personal responsibility of
the deputy to whom they are addressed. The importance
of the mandates as a means of constituent contact, and the
complex procedures surrounding their adoption and implementation, will receive detailed treatment in Chapter 5.
Here we note that roughly two-thirds of the mandates accepted are eventually carried out and that their proposal
by the voters constitutes an apparently spontaneous and
genuinely participatory element of the Soviet election
process.[45]

The Voting

Given the emphasis in the earlier phases of the Soviet
electoral process on developing a consensus in favor of
one candidate representing one point of view, the vote itself seems anticlimactic, if not ceremonial. The polls are
open from 6 a.m. to 10 p.m., though there is an effort to
get 100 percent of those registered out early so the poll
workers and others involved can join in the holiday. The
effort required to vote is minimal. Voters have their names
checked off the voter list, receive one to four ballots depending on where they live, vote for or against the candidate, using a cabin for a secret vote if they wish, and de-
posit the ballot in the ballot box. The ballots are tabulated
at the polling place by the election commission, which also
determines their validity. The district election commission
certifies the results, and the territorial (soviet) election
commission registers the winners or declares invalid elections, all according to procedures spelled out in great de-

[45] An excellent firsthand account of a local preelection candidates'
meeting can be found in Mote, *Soviet Local and Republic Elections*, pp. 59–
64.

tail. Both the turnout and support for the candidate exceed 99 percent in all but a handful of cases.

Despite the ritualistic quality surrounding the actual balloting, there are two participatory aspects worthy of note. First, a certain number of voters use the ballots to write comments—favorable as well as unfavorable—about the candidates or about the activities of the governing soviet. According to one Soviet source who was involved in counting the ballots, these comments are taken seriously and systematically scrutinized by appropriate local officials. In this way, the ballots themselves become one more way decision-makers can gather information about the views of those they govern.[46]

The other participatory aspect relative to the actual vote has to do with citizens who vote negatively, citizens who refuse to vote, or citizens who avoid voting by using absentee ballots. Whether the extent of such behavior can be considered a "measure of dissent" is open to question, but the fact that it occurs is not.[47] In the 1985 elections, 356,855 votes against the nominated candidates were cast. Because election to office requires at least 50 percent of the ballots cast, nominees who fail to receive a majority are defeated. In about half the 127 districts in which no candidate was elected in 1985 the result was due to negative votes, and almost all of these were rural districts, where the average number of voters per district is 45.[48] Avoidance of voting by registering to cast an absentee ballot and then not doing so is difficult to measure because the procedure is

[46] Verification of this practice in a published Soviet source can be found in Yu. Shabanov, *Partiinoe rukovodstvo sovetami deputatov trudiashchikhsia* (Minsk: Belorusskii gosudarstvennyi universitet, 1969), pp. 52–53.

[47] One of the earliest efforts to treat this behavior seriously is Gillison, "Soviet Elections as a Measure of Dissent." The most comprehensive treatment of these phenomena is in Friedgut, *Political Participation in the USSR*, pp. 116–130. As Friedgut points out (p. 123), such behavior may be as indicative of subject competence as dissent.

[48] *Itogi vyborov*, 1985, pp. 3, 10, 17.

not subject to verification. Any citizen can request a "certificate of the right to vote" (*udostovereniia na pravo golosovaniia*) which will allow them to vote in a district other than the one in which they reside. If they receive a certificate, they are listed as having voted on the voter list in their home precinct. If they present the certificate and vote at another polling place, they are enrolled on a supplementary list of voters for that precinct; if they do not, no one will notice. Friedgut estimates that about 2.5 percent of the electorate engages in this practice, with the figure reaching 10 percent in Moscow and Leningrad. Zaslavsky and Brym put the figure closer to 25 percent.[49] Finally, there are those who appear on voter lists but out of apathy or active dissent do not vote, despite the massive effort and pressure to get all voters to the polls. Although the number choosing not to vote in 1985 was small—32,175, or less than 0.2 percent of those eligible—their behavior is a noteworthy form of participation because by refusing to vote they risk drawing considerable unfavorable attention to themselves.[50]

THE COMPOSITION OF THE LOCAL SOVIETS

Soviet spokesmen insist that their elections are more democratic than those in the West because the resulting composition of elected deputies is more nearly representative of the population at large. Segments of society whose interests are allegedly ignored by bourgeois governments are thereby brought systematically into public life in the Soviet Union. The party apparently takes considerable pains during the nominating phase to ensure that certain

[49] For a discussion of these differences in figures, see Zaslavsky and Brym, "The Structure of Power and the Functions of Local Soviet Elections," pp. 70–71.

[50] For a detailed discussion of this issue, see Rasma Karklins, "Soviet Elections Revisited: Voter Abstention in Non-competitive Balloting," *American Political Science Review* 80 (June 1986).

quantitative norms are met with respect to gender, party membership, education, age, social structure, occupation, and nationality, among other criteria. The similarity of the data for these criteria from one republic to another, as well as the incremental nature of the changes from one election to the next, are clearly not accidental. How these norms are determined, for what purpose, and how much local deviance is tolerated are questions that have attracted the attention of Western specialists.

In an article published in 1983, Everett Jacobs, building on the work of Ronald Hill and Soviet research by B. K. Alekseev and M. N. Perfilev, attempted to answer these questions by developing a "hierarchy of variables" based on the application of a modified chi-square test to measure whether the differences between data across republics were statistically significant.[51] Jacobs found that the differences were "so small that we can assume that norms are in operation for all traits," but that the variance for political-demographic characteristics (gender, CPSU and Komsomol membership, age, and medal-holding) was less than for social-occupational characteristics (education, occupation, social group). His conclusion regarding nationality composition of the soviets was that representation varied considerably with whether the ethnic group lived in its own territory; when this was the case, the group was overrepresented. The picture that emerges from the work of Jacobs and others is one in which the CPSU at the top decides what the composition of the soviets will be according to its own political or ideological preferences and then applies these norms in a "relatively strict" manner in all the republics. The result is that "the composition of the local soviets is chosen to reflect, at least roughly, the social strata of Soviet society."[52]

[51] Everett M. Jacobs, "Norms of Representation and the Composition of Local Soviets," in Jacobs, *Soviet Local Politics and Government*. See also Alekseev and Perfil'ev, *Printsipy i tendentsii*.

[52] Jacobs, "Norms of Representation," p. 79.

The emphasis in the Jacobs study is on comparing norms between republics, but a somewhat different view emerges when the composition of the local soviets is analyzed not by geographical area but by the level of the soviet.[53] Table 4-3 contains data for such an analysis that suggests two conclusions. First, if the difference between the highest and lowest percentages (see "Range difference" in the table) is used as a rough measure of relative uniformity, and if a difference of less than 10 percent is used as an operational definition of relative uniformity, then only for gender, age, and Komsomol membership do we find a relatively high degree of uniformity between levels of government. For all other norms there is considerable variation, with deputies at the regional level more likely to have higher education, to be party members, and to work in non-manual jobs than those at the village and settlement level; they are also slightly more likely to be male.

The second conclusion these data suggest is that the composition of the soviets mirrors the characteristics of the population at large only for gender. With respect to the other traits considered here, the degree of representativeness is very rough indeed, with party members, those with higher education, the young, employees, and kolkhozniks overrepresented, the latter because the overwhelming majority (81 percent) of the soviets are located in the villages.

Considerably more variation in composition may be tolerated *within* republics. On the basis of data from Tiraspol, a city in Moldavia, Hill concluded: "The example of Tiraspol tends to suggest that, while it seems certain that some kind of norm can be identified for some variables, it may be applied in a flexible way, within republics, perhaps to take account of local conditions."[54] Table 4-4 contains data from the Lenin city borough in Moscow that can

[53] The point was made by Hill, "Patterns of Deputy Selection," p. 197.
[54] Ibid., p. 207.

TABLE 4-3. Composition of Local Soviets, 1985 (In Percent)

Level of soviet	Women	CPSU members or candidates	Komsomol member	With higher education	With secondary education	Age 18–30 years	Workers	Kolkhozniks	Employees	Industrial worker	Agricultural worker	Holding office for first time
Krai, oblast, okrug	47.7	54.6	26.5	44.9	55.1	35.7	43.7	13.3	43.0	33.8	26.9	55.9
Raion	49.3	49.0	24.6	39.7	60.1	35.7	39.2	24.6	36.2	17.1	49.8	51.3
City	50.1	46.3	25.1	32.6	67.3	37.2	63.0	0.9	36.1	61.3	3.9	52.8
City borough	50.1	46.8	25.0	35.8	64.2	36.6	62.4	0.04	37.6	64.3	0.7	54.3
Settlement	50.7	41.1	22.1	24.3	75.4	34.7	61.7	5.0	33.3	52.1	14.5	48.7
Village	50.6	40.5	21.0	22.0	76.3	32.9	36.9	35.8	27.3	8.0	66.1	44.4
Percent range difference	2.9	14.1	5.5	22.9	21.2	4.3	26.1	35.8	15.7	56.3	65.4	11.5
Percent of all deputies	50.3	42.8	22.3	26.7	72.2	34.2	44.4	24.8	30.8	23.7	47.0	47.4
Percent of general population[a]	53.1	6.5	15.4	8.2[b]	60.4[b]	20.7[c]	61.5	12.5	26.0	—	—	—

SOURCES: *Narodnoe khoziastvo SSSR v 1983; Itogi vyborov*, 1985, pp. 16–27.
NOTE: The total number of deputies elected in 1985 was 2,304,830. For a longitudinal perspective, compare these figures with those of 1977 provided in Jacobs, *Soviet Local Politics and Government*, p. 83.
  [a] These figures are as of 1983 or 1984.   [b] For population over ten years old.   [c] Estimate.

TABLE 4-4. Composition of Lenin City Borough Soviet, Moscow City Soviet, and Soviets of RSFSR, 1985 (In Percents)

	No. of soviets	No. of deputies	Percent women	Percent CPSU	Percent Komsomol	Percent under 30	Percent first time	Percent workers	Percent kolkhoznik	Percent employee	Percent with secondary education
Lenin city borough of Moscow	1	250	47.6	50.4	21.6	33.3	48.8	47.6	0	52.4	99.0
Moscow City	1	1,000	45.6	50.7	22.9	30.0	50.4	47.2	0	52.8	97.3
RSFSR city borough	383	85,634	50.4	47.3	24.9	36.0	55.7	60.9	0	39.1	96.7
Total for RSFSR	28,278	1,148,051	50.9	42.5	22.3	34.2	48.8	48.8	19.0	32.2	83.8

SOURCE: *Itogi zyborov, RSFSR*, 1985, pp. 13, 24–31. The data on the Lenin City Borough and Moscow City Soviet were obtained by the author during a research visit to Moscow in 1986.

be used to test this hypothesis further. The figures indicate that the composition of the Lenin district soviet and that of the city in which it is located are nearly identical, but comparison with the republic as a whole shows somewhat greater variation in all categories, but more so in education and employment than in the political and demographic characteristics. In this sense, the data tend to support the conclusion of Jacobs noted earlier, while confirming Hill's argument that for some variables local diversity is tolerated, reflecting different local conditions.

Because the compositional norms for the election of deputies are clearly determined in accordance with political and ideological criteria deemed appropriate by the CPSU, comparison of these norms over time can provide insight into what qualities the party thinks are important in its governmental personnel. Jacobs' analysis of the trends in the composition of the soviets nationwide between 1959 and 1980 shows a steady increase in the percentage of female deputies, in the level of education of deputies, and in the proportion of deputies classified as "workers." Party membership norms stabilized after 1971 at about 44 percent, while Komsomol representation continued to grow.[55]

Of these changes, probably the most significant is the rising level of education among deputies, an increase which exceeds that found in the population as a whole and which appears to reflect a concern with the quality of the deputies at a time when their responsibilities were being greatly expanded. The biggest increases in educational level coincided with adoption of the new legislation on the soviets in 1967–72, when the percentage of those with higher and secondary education rose from 44.1 percent to 64.3 percent and those with only an elementary education dropped from 23.5 percent to 7.7 percent.[56] A longitudinal analysis of compositional data for deputies in

[55] Jacobs, "Norms of Representation," pp. 81–83.

[56] *Itogi vyborov*, 1985, pp. 248–249. The years of comparison are 1965 and 1973.

Belorussia published in 1984 by A. T. Leizerov shows that the most dramatic changes occur in levels of education at the lowest levels of the soviets, as one might expect (see Table 4-5). It should be noted, however, that while the dynamics of compositional change may reflect party policy in some areas, at a microlevel of analysis changes in personnel may actually run counter to policies pursued by the party in other areas. Leizerov, for example, points to the decline of medical personnel in the soviets of Belorussia at all levels between 1961 and 1982 and then comments, "This is a negative tendency. It is well known how much significance the Party and State attach to the problem of improving medical services in which a central role has been assigned to the soviets.[57]

TABLE 4-5. The Educational Level of Deputies to Local Soviets in Belorussia, 1961 & 1982 (In Percent)

Level of soviet	Higher 1961	1982	Secondary 1961	1982	Incomplete secondary 1961	1982	Elementary 1961	1982
ALL LOCAL SOVIETS	13.9	29.6	28.4	59.5	25.8	10.3	31.9	0.6
Oblast	49.2	49.0	21.7	50.5	16.9	0.5	12.2	—
Raion	27.2	43.6	30.4	51.0	20.8	5.4	21.6	—
City	26.1	31.5	35.7	66.5	24.8	2.0	13.4	—
City borough	30.8	33.2	34.4	66.6	27.9	12.0	5.9	0.2
Settlement	14.5	24.7	36.4	67.2	24.8	7.8	24.3	0.3
Village	9.3	25.9	26.4	58.4	26.8	14.7	37.5	1.0

SOURCE: Leizerov, "Issledovanie dinamiki sostava deputatov mestnykh Sovetov," SGiP, no. 12 (1984), p. 16.

[57] A. T. Leizerov, "Issledovanie dinamiki sostava deputatov mestnykh Sovetov," SGiP, no. 12 (1984), p. 14.

Our analysis of the composition of the local soviets provides a quantitative basis to support Soviet arguments that their electoral system is more representative. In theory, and to some extent in practice, it creates the potential for a greater diversity of voices to be heard. At the same time, it is clear that the norms used do not necessarily reflect the composition of the population as a whole, and indeed that the higher the level of the soviet, the less proportionate representation becomes. Moreover, as we shall see, among executive personnel all pretense at representativeness disappears. Actual participation in the sessions of the soviet also appears to be skewed in favor of older males with higher education and white-collar occupations. Despite these caveats, there does seem to have been a genuine effort in recent years to encourage broader participation by all members of the soviet, an objective that is undoubtedly enhanced by the higher levels of education of those recruited to hold office.

The Internal Organization of the Soviets

With the exception of the Supreme Soviet of the USSR, which meets twice a year, and the settlement and village soviets in the RSFSR, Kazakhstan, Azerbaidzhan, and Moldavia, which meet six times a year, the remaining soviets are convened four times annually, usually for one day or a part of it. Because it would be impossible for a large number of deputies meeting for a short time only a few times a year to run the daily affairs of government, an executive committee (*ispolnitel'nyi komitet*, or *ispolkom*) is elected from among the deputies at the first session following each new election. The ispolkom is empowered to make legally binding decisions and functions as the executive and administrative organ of government between sessions of the soviet. The role of the deputies at the subsequent sessions is largely to confirm the decisions made by this body, although in recent years the potential for more active participation has grown (see Chapter 5). The size of the executive committee is also determined at the first session after elections and varies with the level of government. In addition to the officers—a president, vice-president(s), and secretary—membership in the executive committee of village and settlement soviets is from two to seven people; at the raion level four to nine people; for city and city borough soviets, five to fifteen people; and for oblast soviets, seven to twenty-one people. The Moscow city executive committee has twenty-five members, including a president, nine vice-presidents, and a secretary.[58] Executive committees of soviets governing more than 1.5 million inhabitants may, with the approval of the republican government, designate officers as a presidium with all the authority of the committee as a whole.[59]

Unlike the composition of the soviets, membership in the executive committees appears to be determined less by a desire to ensure representation of certain social or economic categories than by a need to include people with managerial skills. The typical member of the executive committee is far more likely to be male, a party member, older, and better educated than the deputies who elected him. (Table 4-6 provides data on the composition of executive committees; Table 4-4 does this for the deputies as a whole.) The differences are even more accentuated for presidents at higher levels of the soviets (see Table 4-6). Soviet specialists argue that disproportionate representation is totally justified because the executive committee must have knowledgeable and experienced personnel to deal with the increasingly complicated tasks facing municipal government. The concern for professional competence is also reflected in the fact that all presidents and

[58] Soviet sources differ on the range of membership. These figures are from *Iuridicheskii spravochnik deputata mestnogo Soveta narodnykh deputatov* (Moscow: Moscow State University, 1981), p. 80.

[59] A. A. Bezuglov (ed.), *Sovetskoe stroitel'stvo* (Moscow: Iurid. Lit., 1985), pp. 409–410.

TABLE 4-6. Composition of Executive Committees of Local Soviets, 1985

Level of soviet	Total no. of members	Average size of committee	Percent Women			Percent CPSU	Percent YCL[a]	Percent With Higher Education			Percent under age 40	Percent age 40–49	Percent serving for first time
			All	Presidents	Secretaries			All	Presidents	Secretaries			
Krai	114	19.0	15.8	0	16.7	90.4	3.5	89.5	100.0	100.0	10.5	38.6	28.1
Oblast	1,982	16.1	18.3	0.8	18.7	90.4	5.7	87.7	100.0	98.4	13.2	36.0	29.0
Autonomous oblast	108	13.5	20.4	12.5	25.0	90.7	5.6	88.9	100.0	100.0	13.9	41.7	16.7
Autonomous okrug	122	12.2	17.2	30.0	10.0	89.3	5.7	83.6	100.0	100.0	27.9	45.1	32.8
Raion	34,580	11.1	25.9	5.0	53.3	88.1	6.8	81.1	99.8	95.6	38.7	40.8	30.2
City	23,030	10.8	29.2	11.6	79.4	85.7	6.3	72.9	89.8	75.8	39.4	38.8	34.8
City borough	7,837	12.2	30.8	13.4	80.3	88.2	6.2	81.8	99.5	98.9	36.0	44.7	35.2
Settlement	31,674	8.3	36.2	25.0	92.8	73.0	7.4	50.8	67.3	38.9	47.4	31.8	40.7
Village	294,517	7.0	38.8	31.2	85.9	67.2	8.7	44.0	55.3	23.4	52.1	29.9	37.8
For all levels:	393,964	7.6	36.6	28.0	84.0	71.1	8.2	50.5	60.9	32.2	49.2	31.9	37.1

SOURCE: *Itogi vyborov*, 1985, pp. 210–223.
[a] YCL = Young Communist League.

secretaries, and occasionally vice-presidents, work full-time as administrators, an apparent repudiation of Lenin's warnings against creating a "professional class" of politicians. Although all officers formally resign their posts at the end of the term, the great majority are reelected at the next session for the sake of "continuity." This was true for 82 percent of the presidents and 84.2 percent of the secretaries in 1985.[60] Another indicator that specialist competence is the key criteria for selection to a seat on the executive committee is that administrative department heads are often chosen as members of the ispolkom, an arrangement that could lead to a conflict of interest and is generally forbidden in American municipalities.[61]

The activities of executive committees fall into one of two general categories: administrative or organizational. In the first, the executive committee has the authority to decide all matters that fall within the jurisdiction of the soviet from which they are elected, with the exception of items that can be resolved exclusively at sessions of the soviet as a whole.[62] Administrative activity includes implementing the economic plan, overseeing the work of enterprises within the soviet's jurisdiction as well as those subordinated to higher ministries, supervising the activities of subordinate soviets, and making personnel changes. Any personnel decisions affecting department heads and nongovernmental employees must be ratified by the deputies at their next meeting, although the executive committee controls its own nomenklatura for those working in the executive branch. Organizational matters that are handled

[60] *Itogi vyborov*, 1985, pp. 219, 223. The full employment of officers is discussed in Bezuglov, *Sovetskoe stroitel'stvo*, p. 405.

[61] Barabashev and Sheremet, *Sovetskoe stroitel'stvo* (see footnote 4), p. 327.

[62] The items are specified in the laws on soviets and deal mostly with the formation of the soviet and its organs, as well as the confirmation of plans, budgets, and personnel changes. See, e.g., article 45 of the Edict on the Rights and Duties of City and City Borough Soviets.

by the executive committee include convening sessions of the soviet, coordinating the work of the standing commissions, helping the deputies in their dealings with constituents, implementing voter mandates, and preparing elections.

In carrying out these functions, the executive committee makes decisions (*resheniia*) and issues orders (*rasporiazheniia*) that are obligatory for those affected by them.[63] Such actions are taken at meetings (*zasedaniia*) held at least once a month and require the presence of one-half to two-thirds of the members for a quorum. Items for the agenda can be proposed by any of the organs of government, by deputies through their standing committees, or by social organizations (including the party, of course). While a substantial portion of the agenda is taken up with matters specified in a general plan drawn up at the beginning of the term, as much as 50 percent of the time is devoted to matters of an "individual character," that is, constituency problems or matters of interest purely to the district.[64] While only executive committee members vote, the code (*reglamenty*) of city borough executive committees in Moscow gives an advisory voice to the heads of standing committees, deputies of superior soviets, chairs of deputy groups, and administrative department heads. The district procurator and a juridical consultant are expected to be present, as well as specially invited guests who have an interest in or expertise about the matters being discussed.[65]

Assisting the executive committee in its work, but separate from the administrative departments overseeing the economy (discussed below), are two other bodies: the "ap-

[63] P. T. Vasilenkov, *Sovety narodnykh deputatov: organizatsiia i deiatel'nost'* (Moscow: Iurid. Lit., 1983), p. 75.

[64] Lebedev, *Sistema organov gorodskogo upravleniia*, pp. 60–62.

[65] The detailed procedures for holding these meetings are outlined in *Reglament Ispolkoma Leninskogo Raionnogo Soveta*, November 19, 1980, pp. 7–13, which is typical of Moscow city boroughs. See also Barabashev and Sheremet, *Sovetskoe stroitel'stvo*, pp. 331–337.

parat," comprised of full-time professionals (staff), and the executive commissions, made up largely of volunteers. The apparat serves the executive committee and is not responsible "vertically" to superior ministries. Apparatchiks also have no normative powers, as do departmental heads. While the number and types of units into which the apparat is divided varies with the level of government, most local soviets include the following.[66]

1. *The Organizational-Instructional Department.* This department is generally responsible for organizing all the work of the executive committee in the district, for example, contact with constituents, assistance in the preparation of deputies' reports, oversight of lower soviets, collection of statistical information, conduct of elections, interaction with public organizations.

2. *The General Department.* Here is where all the clerical work is done. The apparatchik in the general department keeps records, updates codes, prepares and distributes materials and minutes, makes recommendations regarding personnel qualifications, and so on.

3. *The Reception Department (priyomny otdel).* Staff in this section are responsible for organizing and preparing the meetings (*priyom*) between members of the executive committee and the inhabitants of the district (see also Chapter 4).

4. *The Juridical Bureau.* Apparatchiks working in the juridical bureau advise the executive committee on legal questions and help them prepare draft legislation.

5. *Others.* In addition to the above, there are a variety

---

[66] *Ispolnitel'nyi komitet mestnogo Soveta narodnykh deputatov* (Moscow: Iurid. Lit., 1983), pp. 103–120. See also *Iuridicheskii spravochnik deputata mestnogo Soveta*, pp. 83–89. A useful and detailed description of these departments, especially the important "Org-Instruct" department, can be found in Michael E. Urban, "Roles, Responsibilities, and Incentives in a Soviet Department: Whom Do the Helpers Help?" (Paper presented at the Annual Meeting of the Midwest Political Science Association, Chicago, April 20–23, 1983).

of staff positions—permanent or ad hoc—depending on the level of the soviet or the particular needs of the community it serves. In the Lenin city borough, for example, the regulations specify an assistant to the president, a cadres sector, a senior engineer, an engineer, an inspector, and a corresponding secretary for the Commission on Juvenile Affairs, in addition to the other departments and bureaus.

Executive committees are assisted in their work by special executive commissions similar to advisory councils established by local governments in the United States. These commissions are comprised of citizens with a particular interest or expertise on a functional area who make recommendations in these areas to the legislative or executive authority. While some of these commissions are purely advisory, others have legal authority in individual cases.[67] Again, there is considerable variation in the Soviet case by level of government and region. City and city borough soviets, for example, are assisted in their work at least by the following commissions: the Commission on Juvenile Affairs, the Commission to Assist the Preservation of Monuments of History and Culture, the Commission to Fight Drunkenness, the Administrative Committee, and the Mandate Commission.[68] Other executive committee commissions may be formed on a permanent or ad hoc basis. For every city or city borough soviet there are perhaps five to ten such commissions at the oblast level, and there can be thirty or more. Members are appointed by the executive committees and include staff workers and deputies as well as individuals outside government. The Commission on

[67] Bezuglov, *Sovetskoe stroitel'stvo*, pp. 481ff. For a detailed treatment, see P. F. Chalyi, *Pravovoe polozhenie komissii pri ispolkomakh mestnykh Sovetov narodnykh deputatov* (Kiev: Naukova dumka, 1979).

[68] Article 70 of the RSFSR law adopted on August 3, 1979, "O gorodskom, raionnom v gorode Sovete narodnykh deputatov RSFSR," lists these commissions (see *Vedomosti Verkhovnogo Soveta RSFSR*, 1979, no. 32, item 786). Others are discussed in Barabashev and Sheremet, *Sovetskoe stroitel'stvo*, pp. 366–369.

Juvenile Affairs in the Lenin city borough in Moscow, for example, had seventeen members, which included five deputies and two staff members; the rest were doctors, teachers, legal specialists, and the head of the district Komsomol's Department on Sports and Civil Defense.[69] While there are no statistics available on how many individuals participate in the work of these commissions, a figure of 750,000 or more does not seem unreasonable.[70] If so, the executive committee commissions appear to be an important mechanism for bringing a large number of citizens into administrative activity. They may also function as a means of focusing any interest group activity that may exist within the community.

While the ispolkom exercises general executive and administrative authority between the sessions of the soviets, the daily administration of local government in specific areas is the responsibility of the heads of departments (otdely) and administrations (upravleniia), who are appointed by the executive committee subject to confirmation by the soviets in session. The distinction between "administrations" and "departments" is not established by law, but in practice the former is used for administrative agencies in charge of a larger number of economic organizations, while the latter have few or no directly subordinated enterprises, although they do oversee economic activity; the agencies administering social and cultural activities are usually called departments. This distinction, however, is not strictly followed.[71]

Some Soviet specialists divide administrative agencies

[69] Lists of members of this executive committee commission and two others from the Lenin city borough were made available to the author.

[70] The higher the level of the soviet, the more executive committee commissions one finds, ranging from perhaps 2–3 at the lowest levels, to 30 or more at the oblast level. Taking as a basis for estimation an average of 25 commissions with 15 members each at the oblast level, 5 commissions with 8 members per executive committee at the city and district level, and 2 commissions with 5 members each at the level of the settlements and village, there would be a total of nearly 740,000 members.

[71] Ispolnitel'nyi komitet mestnogo Soveta, p. 142.

into those with branch (*otraslevyi*) and functional (*funktsional'nyi*) responsibilities.[72] The former have specific institutions or activities that they oversee (industry, education, health, trade, police, etc.) and that are usually linked by the principle of dual subordination to superior ministries in charge of their branch of the economy. Organs with functional responsibilities deal with the district as a whole (the Planning Commission, the Financial Department, etc.), and while they may affect the activities of organizations not under their subordination, they are primarily responsible to their own executive committees and through them to executive committees at higher levels. There are no administrative staffs at the settlement and village level; administrative functions for those areas are the responsibility of the rural district (*raion*) executive committees.

Regardless of their formal designation, these administrative agencies are distinguished from other organs serving the executive committee (see the discussion of apparat above) by having the status of juridical persons and by being able to issue legally binding injunctions (*prikazy*) and instructions (*instruktsiia*) within their areas of competence.[73] Areas of competence are defined not only by the rights and obligations of the level of soviet they serve, but also by the regulations of the ministries to which they are subordinated as well as by the legislative acts of higher soviets. All these factors create a degree of independence for the administrative agencies relative to their own executive committees and for the heads of these agencies as well. Examples of this independent authority can be found in health regulations, architectural standards, and the police department, to name a few.[74] Prevailing Soviet scholarship, however, insists that generally the rights of the local

[72] Bezuglov, *Sovetskoe stroitel'stvo*, p. 465.

[73] Ibid., pp. 470–472.

[74] *Ispolnitel'nyi komitet mestnogo Soveta*, pp. 148–150.

soviet take precedence over higher authorities. On paper, this may be so.[75]

The number and size of the administrative agencies is fixed by each soviet at its first session according to what the executive committee recommends. Since 1982, however, a minimal list of such agencies has been established by republican edict for each level of government.[76] Table 4-7 offers a microcosmic view of the organization of administration at the local level using data from the Lenin city borough in Moscow.[77] It also offers a comparison of staff composition over two terms of office. The data are noteworthy in several respects. First, this soviet created slightly more than double the numbers of agencies required by the RSFSR edict of 1982 (those marked by an asterisk in Table 4-7), although not all of them are staffed. Second, in terms of composition, party membership seems to be almost an informal prerequisite for appointment—all but two are party members—and to a lesser degree so does higher education. The breakdowns by age, gender, and years of service are not remarkable, except perhaps for the number of women (about 50 percent) who head administrative agencies.

The most interesting observation from this data is the degree of continuity from one election to the next for the large majority of these administrators; in the agencies required by law, only in the General Department was there a change. Given this apparent emphasis on continuity of experience (the average length of service increased from

[75] Ibid., pp. 145, 150. See also Slider, "More Power to the Soviets?" which documents the continued dominance of the superior ministries.

[76] RSFSR edict of July 1, 1982, "Ob otdelakh i upravleniiakh ispolnitel'-nykh komiteta," *Vedomosti Verkhovnogo Soveta RSFSR*, 1982, no. 27, item 941.

[77] For comparison with a soviet having the administrative status of an oblast, the administrative organization of the Moscow city soviet is described in detail in E. S. Savas and J. A. Kaiser, *Moscow's City Government* (New York: Praeger, 1985), pp. 30–35, 49–51.

TABLE 4-7. Administrative Agencies of Lenin City Borough of Moscow and Composition of Directors, 1982–85 and 1985–87

Title of administrative agency & size	Chief administrator's gender & deputy status	Age (1982)	Year admitted to CPSU	Level of education	Position (1982)
Organizational Instructional Dept.[a] (4)	Female deputy	33	1979	Higher	3
General Dept.[a] (5)	Male (male)	59 (58)	1944 (1956)	Higher (higher)	1 (1)
Dept. of Public Reception[b]	Vacant				
Engineers (3)	Vacant				
Planning Commissioner[a] (4)	Female deputy	38	1973	Higher	0
Dept. of the Architect (2)	Male deputy (male deputy)	30 (34)	1978 (1977)	Higher (higher)	3 (3)
Financial Dept.[a] (2)	Female deputy	53	1949	Higher	20
Lenin Central Bank Savings[b]	Vacant				
Administrative Inspection (5)	Male	58	1945	Higher	6
Dept. for the Calculation & Distribution of Living Space[a] (10)	Male	57	1951	Higher	1
Dept. of Fruits & Vegetables[b]	Male (male)	42 (39)	1962 (1981)	Higher (higher)	1 (2)
Dept. of Trade (3)	Female deputy	47	1964	Higher	13
Labor Dept.[a] (2)	Male	42	1963	Higher	3
Health Dept.[a] (6)	Female deputy	48	1971	Higher	5
Sanitary Station[b]	Vacant				
Dept. of Education[a] (10)	Female deputy	57	1962	Higher	15
Dept. of Culture[a] (2)	Female	36	1976	Higher	1
Physical Education & Sports Dept.[a] (1)	Male	32	1975	Higher	4
Repair & Construction Trust[a] (2)	Male deputy (male)	49 (43)	1961 (1977)	Higher (secondary)	9 (2)

TABLE 4-7 (*cont.*)

Title of administrative agency & size	Chief administrator's gender & deputy status	Age (1982)	Year admitted to CPSU	Level of education	Position (1982)
Material & Technical Supplies (2)	Female	49	Non-CP	Secondary (secondary)	5
Dept. of Roads & Public Works (3)	Male	33	1978	Technical	1
District Food Trade (4)	Female deputy (vacancy)	46	1965	Higher	3
Cafeteria Trust (3)	Female deputy (female)	44 (49)	1965 (1972)	Higher (higher)	5 (2)
Dept. of Public Service (1)	Female deputy	45	1977	Higher	7
Administration of Internal Affairs (Police)[a] (10)	Male deputy	55	1957	Higher	9
Dept. of Social Security[a] (2)	Male deputy	57	1948	Higher	14
Dept. for Registering Acts of Civil Status (ZAGS): births, marriage, deaths, etc.[a] (2)	Female	60	Non-CP	Secondary	31

SUMMARY FIGURES

Years appointed	Women	Deputies	Average age	CPSU membership	Higher education	Average years of service
1982	12/23	13/23	47	21/23	19/23	7
1985	11/22	10/22	49	21/23	18/23	9

SOURCE: List of department and administrative leaders, District Executive Committee (Raiispolkon), Lenin City Borough, Moscow, 1982, 1985.

NOTE: In all but six cases, the personnel appointed at the beginning of the eighteenth term (1982–85) were reappointed at the beginning of the nineteenth (1985–87). Where there was a change, information about the new chief administrator is indicated in parentheses and is data as of 1985. The size of the departments refers to paid personnel as of 1982.

[a] Required by RFSR Edict of 1982 (see footnote 74).

[b] No figure on size available.

seven years to nine years in this period), and given that these bureaucrats are party members of long standing (the average is eighteen years; five of them became members in Stalin's time), it is likely that resistance in the middle and lower levels of the bureaucracy to any "radical reforms" will be substantial unless the next Gorbachev leadership introduces some fairly dramatic personnel changes. Apparently the case of the Lenin city borough is not unusual in this regard, and precisely these kinds of changes are being contemplated. In his speech to the 27th Congress on February 25, 1986, Gorbachev bluntly confronted this issue.

> One cannot ignore the fact that apparatus workers who have been in position for a long time often lose a taste for what is new, shut themselves off from people by means of instructions compiled by them, and sometimes even slow down the work of elective bodies.
>
> It is evidently time we worked out a system that would enable local soviets and all public bodies to assess senior officials working in their apparatus and make the necessary cadre changes in it after every set of elections.[78]

From the perspective of citizen participation in local politics, it is important to note that there are several ways citizens can become involved in the work of administration on a voluntary basis.[79] The first of these is through the nonstaff (*vneshtatnyi*) departments. Originally created in the early 1960s to provide administrative personnel where no departments existed, many were changed over into permanent positions only to be abolished in the latter part of the decade in response to criticism that they were unnecessary or were preempting the functions of the depu-

[78] M. S. Gorbachev, "Report to the CPSU Central Committee" (February 25, 1986), Foreign Broadcast Information Service (FBIS), *Daily Report*, February 26, 1986, p. O-26.

[79] A detailed treatment is not offered here because much is covered by Friedgut, *Political Participation in the USSR*, pp. 215–220.

ties acting through their standing committees.[80] Today they are found in rural areas where there is no permanent staff or as adjuncts to administrative staff when specialist expertise is needed in particular branches of the economy. Activities include helping draft legislation, carrying out studies, and making recommendations. There appears to be a reverse of the decline in nonstaff departments reported by Friedgut. There were 10,994 nonstaff departments in 1982 with 91,798 citizens working in them, an increase of more than 40 percent of the 7,684 such departments existing in 1975.[81]

A second way citizens can participate in administration is through public councils (obshchestvennie sovety) and the commissions comprised of administrators, deputies, and members of the community nominated by one of the social organizations. Examples would include a library council or a commission on the preservation of monuments attached to a Department of Culture. Primarily advisory, such bodies may also conduct on-site meetings to examine firsthand whatever situations have been brought to their attention. Finally, there are public inspectors and instructors who may be attached as individuals to one or another administrative agency and whose function is to observe and report on any problems in the district pertaining to the work of their agency—for example, whether stores are open when they are supposed to be, whether pensions are delivered on time, whether streets are in need of repair. In 1982 there were more than 410,000 of these individuals. Potential abuse of these voluntary activities exists. One author reports instances of citizens "volunteering" to work in the Housing Administration in order to improve their position in the list waiting for new housing.[82]

[80] See the discussion in Ispolnitel'nyi komitet mestnogo Soveta, pp. 168–172.

[81] Friedgut, Political Participation in the USSR, p. 217. The 1982 figures are from Sovety narodnykh deputatov: spravochnik, p. 197.

[82] Bezuglov, Sovetskoe stroitel'stvo, p. 478. The work of public inspectors

No discussion of the organizational structure of the local soviets would be complete without at least a brief discussion of how their activities are financed. Given the broader range of activities administered by the state in a command economy, the preparation and execution of a soviet's budget is even more time-consuming than for noncommunist municipalities of comparable size. A centrally planned economy also means that local budgets must reflect spending priorities determined at the top. Because most of the money needed to run local government comes from the center, discretionary authority over how the money will be spent is limited, although it has grown considerably in recent years and may become even broader if Gorbachev moves to decentralize administrative decision-making, a direction he forcefully endorsed at the 27th Congress of the CPSU.[83] Given these constraints, it is hardly surprising that the budget process in Soviet local government is dominated by the executive committee and especially by its Finance Department. The role of the deputies is largely limited to voting at the last session of the year their unanimous approval for a draft budget that the professional administrators worked out for the next year.[84]

---

is described in detail in Jan S. Adams, *Citizen Inspectors in the Soviet Union: The People's Control Committee* (New York: Praeger, 1977).

[83] In his speech to the Central Committee of February 25, 1986, Gorbachev stated; "Excessive centralization exists in tackling issues that are far from always clearly visible from the center and can be handled much better on the spot. That is why we are resolutely directing one course toward enhancing the independence and the level of activity of local organs of power" (FBIS translation), *Daily Report*, February 26, 1986, p. O-25. On the issue of discretionary authority, even in the United States the portion of the budget open to change by legislators is really a small percentage of the total. This is as true at the federal level as it was in my experience at the municipal one.

[84] This was also Friedgut's conclusion based on his firsthand observation of the session at which deputies adopted the 1970 budget in the Oktyabr' City Borough soviet. On the basis of my attendance at a similar session, the process has changed little. Changes are apparent in the structure of the budget, however, as well as in how the funds may be

Where does the money come from, and where does it go? Table 4-8 provides data that answer these questions for the Lenin city borough of Moscow in 1985–86. While these figures are probably typical for this level of soviet, the proportions of budgetary allocations differ considerably from one level of government to the next.[85] The table presents *planned* budgets; actual income and expenditures may be as much as 300,000 to 400,000 rubles higher, because while the planned income-expenditure balance is exactly equal, the soviet may in fact receive more income in the course of the year and make adjustments to spend it. The reverse is also true. While a deficit budget is not unheard of at this level, it is rare; generally, a very small positive balance is shown. Although actual figures may differ from those shown in these planned budgets, the proportions of budgetary allocations change hardly at all.

On the income side, the proportions of revenue obtained from different sources show considerable variation from one year to the next. Nonetheless, it is clear that most comes from the center: approximately three-fifths to two-thirds is derived from the district's share of the taxes it collects for the central authorities, particularly the turnover (or value-added) tax and the personal income tax (together accounting for 57 to 61 percent of the total revenues). The remaining source of income comes from the planned profits of enterprises and other economic organizations under the soviet's jurisdiction (36 percent to 41

---

spent. For comparison, see Friedgut, "A Local Soviet at Work: The 1970 Budget of the Oktyabr' Borough Soviet in Moscow," in Jacobs, *Soviet Local Politics and Government*, chap. 9. Another detailed study of the budgetary process in the local soviets is found in Frolic, "Decision-Making in Soviet Cities," esp. pp. 39–42, and by the same author, "Municipal Administrations, Departments, Commissions, and Organizations," *Soviet Studies* 22 (January, 1971), pp. 376–393.

[85] A detailed examination of the Moscow city budget for 1975 can be found in Savas and Kaiser, *Moscow's City Government*, pp. 60–79. The authors compare the different proportions of revenue and expenditures between the city and its districts (p. 69).

TABLE 4-8. Budget of Lenin City Borough of Moscow, 1985 Budget Plan and 1986 Draft Plan (in Thousands of Rubles)

	Approved 1985 plan	Percent of total	Draft 1986 plan	Percent of total	Percent Change (plus or minus)
I. INCOME					
Total	19,476	100.0	19,981	100	− 2.9
A. *From enterprise profits:*	4,092	21.0	3,625	18.1	
1. Construction	140	0.7	88	0.4	− 0.3
2. Trade	2,185	11.2	1,812	9.1	− 2.1
3. Housing	1,371	7.0	1,298	6.5	− 0.5
4. Communal	164	0.8	186	0.9	+ 0.1
5. State housing insurance	230	1.2	239	1.2	0
6. Health organs	2	0.0	2	0.0	0
B. *Taxes on property* (e.g., movie theaters, hotels)	3,923	20.1	3,467	17.4	− 2.7
Subtotal from profits & property taxes	8,015	41.1	7,092	35.5	− 5.7

C. *From government income & taxes:*	11,461	58.8	12,889	64.5	
1. Turnover tax	4,069	20.8	7,482	37.5	+16.7
2. Income tax	6,971	35.8	4,844	24.2	−11.6
3. Tax on social organizations	169	0.8	320	1.6	+0.8
4. Lottery	252	1.3	243	1.2	−0.1
II. EXPENSES Total	19,476		19,981		
A. Borough economy	5,401	27.7	5,891	29.5	+1.8
B. Education	5,310	27.2	5,979	29.9	+2.7
C. Health	7,501	38.5	6,859	34.3	−4.2
D. Recreation	4	0.0	3	0	0
E. Social insurance	798	4.0	808	4.0	+0.1
F. Administration	291	1.4	305	1.5	+0.1
G. Other	171	0.8	136	0.6	−0.2

SOURCE: "Spravka o proekte biudzheta Leninskogo raiona na 1986 godu," December 1985, pp. 4, 8.

percent of the total). While not as important a source of revenue as the share received from the central government, even the 36 percent expected by the Lenin city borough in 1985 represents a threefold increase over the 12 percent reported from this source by Friedgut in his study of the Oktyabr city borough of Moscow in 1970.[86]

Turning to expenditures, two changes over the past thirty years are apparent for local government in general. First, the local governments have much more money to spend and much more flexibility in how they spend it. The Lenin city borough spends perhaps four times as much as it did in 1955 and within centrally established categories may spend it as it deems necessary. The chief exception is in the area of personnel; wages in each category are fixed by the Moscow city executive committee and cannot be increased without their approval.[87] Most of these categories are self-explanatory, with the exception of "borough economy" (*raionnoe khoziaistvo*). The major outlay here is for the repair of housing, which accounts for nearly 70 percent of this category; the remaining 30 percent go to public works, street-cleaning, park maintenance, pothole repair, and garbage collection. The "other" category is unusual: 136,000 rubles were set aside in 1986 to compensate those getting married for the first time for increases in the cost of gold wedding bands![88]

[86] Friedgut, "A Local Soviet at Work," p. 163.

[87] This appears to be the case throughout Moscow. See Savas and Kaiser, *Moscow's City Government*, pp. 63–64. I am indebted to Professor Friedgut for noting that the 1.4 percent spent on administration represents a significant increase from the 1 percent norm used in the 1970s.

[88] "Spravka o proekte biudzheta Leninskogo raiona na 1986 godu," p. 11.

CHAPTER FIVE

Deputies and
Their Constituents

HAVING DESCRIBED the theoretical and institutional frameworks within which the activity of local soviet deputies takes place, we now turn to the question of how effectively the deputies perform in practice.

According to Marxist-Leninist theory, the role of the elected representative is to represent constituency interests according to the "instructed delegate" model. V. F. Kotok, in particular, refers to this model by its French form, the *mandat imperatif*, and claims that it is the key characteristic distinguishing the genuinely democratic nature of representation in socialist societies, although he acknowledges that the roots of this conception lie in the traditions of the Estates General in sixteenth-century France.[1] Other Soviet specialists have been quick to caution that the imperative character of the deputy's mandate does not mean that deputies should persist in representing their constituents' views if they become convinced that the general welfare is best served by voting contrary to their expressed wishes.[2] Nevertheless, there is a strong element of direct democracy in Soviet thinking about the role of the deputy as a representative; Barabashev and Sheremet invoke Lenin to underscore their contention that the soviets

[1] V. F. Kotok, *Nakazy izbiratelei v sotsialisticheskom gosudarstve* (Moscow: Nauka, 1967), pp. 5–7, 14. In the Soviet view, the concept of the representative who acts as a "trustee" on behalf of what he or she believes in good conscience to be the best interests of constituents regardless of their will is a practice to be found only in bourgeois parliamentary systems.
[2] A. A. Bezuglov, *Sovetskii deputat* (Moscow: Iurid. Lit., 1971), pp. 15–16.

represent a synthesis of representative government and direct democracy, and they devote a major section of their textbook on the soviets to the forms of direct democracy found in Soviet law.[3]

The 1972 Law on the Status of Deputies deals separately with the deputy's activities as a legislator in council and as a representative in his or her electoral district. This approach is adopted here as well. The present chapter describes the mechanisms available to citizens in the district for communicating individual and community needs. The next chapter will discuss what deputies do in council to translate their constituents' interests into action. In defining the obligations of the deputies in their relations with the electorate in their district, the 1972 law enjoins the deputy to establish close contacts with those who elected them. In particular, the deputy is required by article 18

> to inform his constituents about the work of soviets in accomplishing their tasks, to study public opinion, to communicate the needs and demands of the people he represents to the organs of the soviet and to adopt measures to satisfy them, and to introduce for consideration by the appropriate state organs and officials any proposals on issues that pertain to his activity as a deputy.[4]

Several formal mechanisms make it possible for the deputy to ascertain the "needs and demands" of constituents and so perform his or her assigned task. Most if not all of these mechanisms have existed since early in the Soviet period and received frequent attention in the literature. In

[3] Barabashev and Sheremet, *Sovetskoe stroitel'stvo*, pp. 484–485. See also Kotok, *Nakazy izbiratelei*, p. 7. A more extended discussion for a broader audience is G. V. Barabashev and K. F. Sheremet, *Neposredstvennaia demokratiia v SSSR* (Moscow: Znanie, 1984).

[4] From article 18 of "O Statuse narodnykh deputatov v SSSR," September 20, 1972, as amended on April 19, 1979, *Vedomosti Verkhovnogo Soveta SSSR*, 1979, no. 17, item 277.

reality, their use was erratic at best, especially under Stalin, and more often than not it was largely confined to going through the motions. The reactivation of these institutions in the contemporary period is the focus of the present work. The following will be examined in turn: voter mandates, reports to constituents, procedures for submitting proposals and complaints, and use of the right of recall. In addition to these formal means for communicating citizens' preferences, other forms of contact between deputies and constituents will be considered.[5] Finally, there will be an assessment of what citizens think of the deputies' activities.

Forms of Constituent Contact

The Voter Mandate

In an interview, a deputy with twenty years of experience in the Novosibirsk regional soviet described his work with the voter mandates:

Implementation of the voter mandates occupied a special place in my activity as a deputy. Their realization required the expenditure of a good deal of time and effort. The constituents at the time they nominated me as a candidate, and during my reports to them, continually

---

[5] One other mechanism by which the public can express its opinion on matters of concern is the referendum. A proposal that "the most important draft laws should be put to a nationwide referendum" was included in the 1961 Party Program and elicited scholarly interest. See Hill, *Soviet Politics, Political Science, and Reform*, pp. 100–103; and V. F. Kotok, *Referendum v sisteme sotsialisticheskoi demokratii* (Moscow: Nauka, 1964). As a result of these discussions, the 1977 Constitution included article 5, which in entirety states: "The most important matters of state life shall be submitted for nationwide discussion and also to a nationwide vote (referendum)." While nationwide discussion has been used and does open up real possibilities for the expression of public opinion on major political issues, the referendum has never been used. See Friedgut, *Political Participation in the USSR*, pp. 147–152.

asked about the progress of construction on Factory Road, where a trolleybus line was to be laid. Who did one have to see in order to bring attention to the resolution of these matters? . . . A meeting took place with the president of the executive committee present. The question was then discussed at a conference of the executive committee of the soviet. As a result of measures taken, the street was repaired and the trolleybus line was laid.[6]

Voter mandates consist of proposals made by the voters to the candidates who will represent their district at each level of government. At meetings held prior to each election, any constituent or group of constituents is free to propose whatever projects they wish. If they are serious proposals, aimed at improving the communities' well-being, and are approved by a simple majority of those present, implementation becomes an obligation the deputy is expected to fulfill. As one would expect, the content of the voter mandates varies considerably, depending on the level of government in which the deputy serves. At lower levels, the mandates deal with such matters as the paving of roads and the repair of buildings and landscaping; at the higher levels, examples might include bridges over major rivers, hospitals, irrigation projects, or increases in specific areas of economic production. Quantitatively, each soviet received an average of fifteen mandates in the course of the 1982 elections, one mandate for every third deputy. However, within these averages there is considerable variation, with deputies at higher levels receiving proportionately more mandates than their counterparts at lower levels. Thus, at the regional level there is an average of at least one mandate per deputy, while in the villages every third deputy is responsible for a mandate,

[6] I heard numerous similar examples during my interviews with deputies, but this interview is reported in N. E. Sukhanov, *Izbiratelei dali nakaz* (Moscow: Iurid. Lit., 1981), p. 41.

and in the cities one out of every four or less (see Table
5-1).[7] This may reflect the greater amount of resources
available to higher levels of government.

At all levels, the adoption of a mandate is taken seriously by the deputies to whom they are addressed. The
mandates are considered to have an "imperative" character: deputies must try to do what their constituents have
demanded, or if there are good reasons why they cannot,
they must explain these publicly. This partly helps account
for the high rate of fulfillment: more than 90 percent of
those accepted at the beginning of the term were reported
to be fulfilled (see Table 5-2, below). The imperative char-

TABLE 5-1. Vote Mandates and Ratio per Deputy, 1983

Level of soviet	No. of soviets	No. of deputies	No. of mandates accepted	Average per soviet	Mandates per deputy
Regional	129	31,501	33,853	262	1.07
Autonomous region	8	1,360	1,103	138	0.81
Okrug	10	1,090	699	70	0.64
Raion	3,114	254,193	158,252	51	0.62
City	2,123	287,401	74,995	35	0.26
City borough	644	136,961	20,719	32	0.15
Settlement	3,792	213,663	54,734	14	0.25
Village	41,963	1,362,854	417,625	10	0.31
For all levels:	51,482	2,289,859	761,980	15	0.33

SOURCE: *Nekotorye voprosy (satisticheskii sbornik)*, 1983, pp. 8, 9, 34.

[7] While there is regional variation, the general pattern shown in the
national statistics seems to hold elsewhere. Sukhanov, e.g., reports a
similar pattern for the Chitinskii region in Siberia. See ibid., p. 6.

acter of the voter mandates derives from the "instructed delegate" model of representation noted above. Soviet scholars trace this model to Marx's description of the Paris Commune, where it was agreed that "delegates should be strictly bound by the *mandat imperatif* [precise instructions] of their constituents and can be recalled at any time."[8] According to N. G. Starovoitov, the first use of voter mandates in Russia occurred in 1905, when striking workers at the Ivanovo-Voznesensk textile factory formed the first soviet and gave a list of twenty-six demands to the delegates whom they had elected to represent them.[9] More important in establishing the practice of taking mandates was the specific use of this term by Lenin to justify adoption of the Decree on Land at the Second All-Russian Congress of the Soviets, which met on November 7, 1917. According to Lenin, this decree was "a fulfillment of 242 mandates" he had received from peasant deputies by the First Congress of Soviets, held in June 1917.[10]

Despite their impeccable ideological credentials, the mandates were apparently used only sporadically in the period following the Revolution of 1917, and they received scant attention in the legislation on the soviets. The 1936 Constitution formalized the centralization of the state that had taken place under Stalin, and the use of the mandates declined even further. Only after Stalin's death was the practice of the voter mandates revived. Their use was encouraged in the January 22, 1957, resolution of the Party Control Committee, "On Improving the Work of the Soviet Deputies," and received legislative expression in union-republic statutes on local government, notably in Belorussia and Estonia. However, not until the edict of 1968 on the rural soviets and the edict of 1971 on the city and district soviets did the institution of the voter man-

[8] Kotok, *Nakazy izbiratelei*, p. 22.
[9] N. G. Starovoitov, *Izbiratelei dali nakaz* (Moscow: Znanie, 1984), pp. 8–9.
[10] Ibid., p. 10; Kotok, *Nakazy izbiratelei*, p. 28.

dates receive any attention in federal laws. Through the lobbying efforts of Soviet legal scholars led by Kotok,[11] article 7 of the Law on the Status of Deputies (1972) was devoted to the voter mandate and for the first time gave legal definition to its use. It was also incorporated into the 1977 Constitution as article 102, the only wholly new article to be inserted in the Constitution following nationwide public discussion. Only on September 1, 1980, was a federal edict finally adopted that defined in detail what the mandates were and the procedures by which they were to be accepted and carried out.[12]

As specified by the edict and described in the specialist literature, the process by which the voter mandates are given effect consists of several stages: introduction of the mandate at the preelection meeting, preliminary review by executive committees, adoption of the mandate by the soviet, and implementation of the mandate.[13] These will be examined in turn. First, as indicated earlier, the law guarantees the right of any elector to introduce and discuss a mandate at meetings of the candidates with the voters before the election. Normally the mandate will be introduced at a designated point in the meeting, at which time individuals will be invited to present their proposals. In practice, this speaker often represents a larger group in the community who will have prepared the mandate beforehand. However, interviews with specialists suggest that spontaneous proposals may occur more often in the villages, where procedure is less rigidly adhered to. In either case, those present are free to offer amendments and dis-

[11] Kotok, *Nakazy izbiratelei*, p. 132. Writing in 1967, Kotok called for strengthening the mandate by including it in the Constitution and by developing a special law for its use. While both eventually came to pass, Kotok himself did not live to see it.

[12] "Ob organizatsii raboty s nakazami izbiratelei," September 1, 1980, *Vedomosti Verkhovnogo Soveta SSSR*, 1980, no. 36, item 736.

[13] These stages are adapted from *Sovety narodnykh deputatov: spravochnyk*, pp. 128–130.

cuss the proposal, which can turn into a lively debate, especially when opinion on a particular project is divided.[14]

There are no legal requirements regarding the number of people who must be present before a mandate is voted on, so it is questionable whether a mandate introduced at a poorly attended meeting really represents the will of the community. However, poor attendance seems to be the exception rather than the rule, with turnouts of fifty to one hundred people apparently not unusual.[15] Part of this is undoubtedly the result of the efforts of the agitators, whose responsibility it is to get the electorate active.[16] It is also likely that issues of particular interest to the community, especially if at all controversial, will generate attendance quite independently of the agitators.

One problem frequently encountered by deputies before the edict of 1980 was that proposals were often frivolous, intended for personal benefit, or unrealizable. N. E. Sukhanov reports that one constituent berated his deputy at a preelection meeting for failing to obtain a motorcycle he had requested, arguing that it was a mandate.[17] Noting that this problem was particularly acute before the adoption of the Law on the Status of Deputies in 1972, A. A. Bezuglov proposes a return to an older practice when a platform of proposals would be prepared by the party before the preelection meetings and then presented to the

[14] The only Western eyewitness account of which the author is aware was Max Mote's account of preelection meetings in Leningrad in 1963. Although this predates the substantial legislative attention given the procedures for taking mandates since then, it does capture the element of spontaneity present at such meetings. See Mote, *Soviet Local and Republic Elections*, pp. 56–63.

[15] E.g., Sukhanov reports, (*Izbiratelei dali nakaz*, p. 6) that in the Kemerovskii region in 1977 more than one million people attended some 10,000 preelection meetings at all levels, at which 750,000 mandates were introduced. Average attendance would thus be 100, with mandates being taken at three meetings out of four.

[16] Friedgut, *Political Participation in the USSR*, pp. 95–102.

[17] Sukhanov, *Izbiratelei dali nakaz*, p. 10.

voters for discussion and debate. This, he argues, would ensure that the proposals and discussions would be conducted on a more informed and realistic basis. Indeed, an experiment was carried out along the lines of Bezuglov's suggestion in the city of Konakovo in the Kalinin Oblast.[18] Other scholars argue that this practice would reduce popular initiative and vitiate the significance of the mandate as an instrument of direct democracy.

The issue seems to have been resolved by the edict of 1980 and by the republic-level legislation that ensued. Article 2 of the edict states that discussion of all proposals must proceed from their "social importance, rationality, and feasibility." In addition, in each republic the regulations stipulate that members of the executive committee, as well as members of other social organizations (e.g., the Communist Party), are to participate in preelection meetings to explain the procedure for adopting mandates and apparently which kinds of mandates are "realistic."[19] While such measures will help ensure that only serious proposals are considered, they also reduce the openness with which they are put forth.

The next stage of work with the mandates involves a preliminary review by the executive committee. At each preelection meeting, minutes (*protokol*) are kept in which basic information is recorded: the district in which the meeting was held, the date, the number attending, which candidates were present, and the mandates approved—including the name of the deputy to whom a mandate was addressed, its general content, any debate, and the final vote. The minutes are given over to the executive commit-

---

[18] A. A. Bezuglov, *Deputat v Sovete i izbiratel'nom okruge* (Moscow: Iurid. Lit., 1978), pp. 50–52.

[19] Article 4 of "Polozhenie ob organizatsii raboty s nakazami izbiratelei v RSFSR," May 6, 1982, *Vedomosti Verkhovnogo Soveta RSFSR*, 1982, no. 19, item 587. Starovoitov indicates (*Izbiratelei dali nakaz*, p. 18) that the experience of the 1982 elections showed "unrealistic or inadvisable" mandates had generally been avoided.

tee of the district, city, or village soviet of the territory in which the meeting was held, ideally the next day. Within a fixed period (ten days in the RSFSR) mandates that the executive committee determines fall within the jurisdiction of higher authorities are sent to the executive committees of those soviets. The remainder are sent on to the appropriate administrative department; they are also sent to those economic enterprises located on the territory in the soviets' jurisdiction. Within an established period, these bodies must render reasonable (*motirovannyi*) advice about how to achieve the mandates—specifically about the scope of the project, financial resources, and time needed for completion. The executive committee or, in larger soviets, a special commission established by it, meets with department heads, members of standing committees, planning and finance committees, and anyone else it chooses to invite, to work out a draft plan to submit to the soviet.[20] The plan specifies who is responsible for carrying out the mandate and when. They must also indicate which mandates they do not recommend for adoption and why.

The third stage is the actual adoption of the plan for fulfilling the mandates. This is done by the deputies at the first or second meeting of the soviet during its term of office; the lower the level, the earlier the meeting. The scholarly literature puts a good deal of emphasis on the exclusive right of the deputies to take action regarding the mandates. This right derives, it is argued, from the fact that the deputies receive their mandates directly from their constituents and are the people ultimately held responsible for fulfillment of the mandates. This emphasis is understandable, because it was common practice in the Stalin period (and after it) for such decisions to be made by executive committees who apparently did not consider it

[20] In 1982, e.g., the Moscow regional soviet formed a special commission for studying voter mandates; it consisted of seventeen people, including the executive committee secretary, leading members of the financial and planning commissions, and officers of standing committees.

necessary to consult with the deputies to whom the mandates were given. Since 1980 this practice is clearly illegal.[21] It is true that, by the time the draft plan is presented to the soviet, unanimous approval is generally the rule. While this opens up the possibility that the executive committee will control the decision about which voter mandates are to be given effect, it is also true that a very large portion of the mandates originally approved by the voters are ultimately adopted by the soviet. Moreover, deputies can exercise some oversight over the preliminary review process through their standing committees (see Chapter 6).

The actual plan adopted by the soviet specifies several categories of mandates depending on how they are to be achieved. The experience of the Lenin district in Moscow in dealing with the mandates received before the election of June 20, 1982, illustrates how the plan works out in practice.[22] Forty-five mandates were received by deputies to the Lenin soviet, approximately one for every four or five deputies. These were divided into five categories. The first included thirteen mandates to be accommodated in the economic plan for 1982 already adopted in the previous year. Of the thirteen, eight pertained to asphalt construction needed for courtyards, doorways, and entrances at specific addresses. Roof repair, lighting, repair service

[21] Article 3 of the 1980 USSR edict on the voter mandates, and articles 12–15 of the RSFSR regulations, make the responsibilities of the deputies and executive committee clear. References to the need for clarifying the legislation on this point can be found in A. A. Bezuglov, *Soviet Deputy* (Moscow: Progress Publishers, 1973), p. 88; Starovoitov, *Izbiratelei dali nakaz*, p. 21; and Bezuglov, *Deputat v Sovete i izbiratel'nom okrug* (Moscow: Iurid. Lit., 1978), pp. 53–54.

[22] The voter mandates were adopted at the second session of the Lenin district soviet and are found in "Plan meropriiatii po vypolneniiu nakazov izbiratelei," made available to the author. Similar decisions adopted by the soviet of the Moscow region and the Moscow and Mitishii city soviets, in 1984, 1983, and 1982 respectively, differ only in scale, but not in character or format, from the decision of the Lenin district.

improvement, and the apportionment of space in a local drugstore for the taking of prescriptions accounted for the rest. The second category of mandates (twenty-one in all) were those to be included in the plans for 1983–84 and following years: seven dealt with the construction of new housing, some specifying special areas for children, libraries, or clubs; nine had to do with various public works projects, such as water runoff, landscaping, and the paving of streets and courtyards; four items to be included in next five-year plan called for capital repairs of housing. Finally, one item, which must have been desperately sought, was the removal of a warehouse for the storage of fish from the vicinity of an apartment on Usachev Street.

The remainder of the mandates for the Lenin district in the plan adopted in 1982 fell into the following categories: those accomplished even before the election (four), those rejected by the soviet (three), and those sent on to the Moscow city soviet to which the Lenin district is subordinate (four). Included in the first category were a decision to seek construction of an underground garage, a revision of the regulations involving housing funds, and the development of a plan to deal with litter. Items deemed inadvisable by the deputies included closing a liquor store and replacing it with a store selling dairy products, establishment of a new newsstand in a particular neighborhood (there were two already), and finding room for a children's club (this request duplicated an earlier mandate that was late in being filled). The category of items sent on up to the Moscow city soviet included a new public toilet, relocation of a trolleybus line, and assignment of part of a Moscow University campus for development into new buildings.

It is one thing to decide to undertake the tasks proposed by constituents and another to carry them out. There are two major problems when it comes to implementation: finding the resources and making sure they are properly used. With respect to resources, as the Lenin district case indicates, a sort of triage is performed at the time the decision is made. Some mandates require no funds or can be taken care of in the current plan of the year in which they are adopted; some are set aside for future plans; a few are rejected outright; others are sent to higher administrative levels. In cases where financial resources are required to realize the mandates, the sources of funds are basically two: the soviet's own resources as found in the economic plans and budgets it approves, and the resources of the economic organizations and enterprises located in the territory over which the soviet exercises jurisdiction. Legislation adopted since 1979 has significantly broadened the rights of the soviets in their dealings with the enterprises. The edicts of 1980–82 on the mandates, and the decree of March 19, 1981, "On Raising the Role of the Soviets in Economic Construction," give the soviets the right to coordinate and control the activity of all economic organizations on their territory.[23] Any use by an enterprise of resources affecting the welfare of the population, including road and housing construction, the provision of education, health, and cultural services, and the production of food or goods, requires the agreement of the local soviet. In addition, enterprises subordinated to higher ministries must now submit to the corresponding local soviet its plans for fulfilling the local mandates. Finally, a portion of any above planned profits received by an enterprise is also to be earmarked for this purpose.

Evidence regarding the actual practice of funding the mandates is mixed, and regional variation is great. To some extent the local soviets are apparently successful in using their new authority. Thus, for example, in 1982 the Moscow regional soviet fulfilled more than one-quarter of

[23] Articles 8–10 of the 1980 edict on the mandates specify the financial means on which the soviets may draw to accomplish the mandates. The decree of March 19, 1981, is found in *Sobranie Postanovlenii SSSR*, 1981, no. 13, item 78. A good discussion of financial practices can be found in Starovoitov, *Izbiratelei dali nakaz*, pp. 31–35.

its 2,172 mandates (costing 43 million rubles) using means
made available by enterprises in its territory.²⁴ In Stavro-
pol the regional soviet received about 100 million of the
221 million rubles it spent on mandates in 1980–82 from
this source.²⁵ However, practice does not always live up to
legal expectations. The most persistent problem is that enterprise managers are responsible not only, or even primarily, to the local soviets, but also to higher ministries in
charge of their branch of the economy. For managers
whose principal concern is to fulfill their economic obligations, the mandates most often represent an unsought expenditure of time and money, to be avoided if possible.
Given this outlook, and the inertia of past experience in
the face of newly adopted legislation, both managers and
the bureaucrats to whom they are responsible may not always take the mandates seriously.²⁶ Nevertheless, local soviets now have greater leverage, and they can use their
control over planning and land use in particular as a lever
to obtain from recalcitrant managers the money needed to
complete their constituents' projects.²⁷

If finding resources to implement the mandates is primarily the job of the executive committee, supervision of

²⁴ *Leninskoe znamia*, August 24, 1982.

²⁵ *Kommunist*, September 25, 1982.

²⁶ A classic example of this problem can be found in an article entitled
"Istoriia odnogo nakaza" in *Izvestia*, November 15, 1984, p. 2. The object
of the unfulfilled mandate was a dining room at a sugar factory in a rural
district. Despite the best efforts of local officials, neither the enterprise or
the ministry showed much awareness of their responsibility or any desire
to find the funds. The indifference of managers to the mandates is also
cited as a major shortcoming by the chairman of Belorussia Supreme Soviet Presidium (I. E. Poliakov, "Nakazy izbiratelei-iarkoe proiavlenie sotsialisticheskoi demokratii," *SGiP*, no. 9 [1980], p. 11). The problem continues to plague the soviets despite legislative changes. See V. I. Vasil'ev,
Gorodskii Sovet: zakon i praktika (Moscow: Iurid. Lit., 1984); and Slider,
"More Power to the Soviets?"

²⁷ Starovoitov, *Izbiratelei dali nakaz* (1984), p. 49. Sukhanov (*Izbiratelei
dali nakaz* [1981], p. 36), also discusses this problem and proposes that
ministries be made directly responsible for achieving certain mandates.

the project, or what the soviets refer to as *kontrol*, requires the active participation of the deputy. Deputies are expected to check up on the performance of the administrators or managers responsible for the job, to keep their constituents informed about the progress being made, and whenever feasible to mobilize those who made the proposal in the first place to participate in its realization.[28] In recent years, deputies have acquired a number of rights in this regard. Executive committees and economic enterprises involved in the implementation of mandates must now report regularly to the deputies. If the deputy is dissatisfied with the progress being made, he or she can demand an explanation from those responsible and take part in the resolution of the issue either individually, or through the appropriate standing committee. The agencies responsible are obligated to respond to such requests, especially if they are the subject of a formal inquiry (*zapros*). In practice, the effectiveness of these measures varies with the zeal and ability of the individual deputy. Some deputies simply take their work with the mandates less seriously than others.[29] However, even a dedicated deputy, one informed and experienced in the use of these procedures, is almost totally dependent on bureaucratic goodwill for fulfilling a mandate.

On the whole, however, there is data to suggest that more often than not the voter mandates are an effective way for constituents to communicate their demands for community action. As indicated earlier, the reported rate of fulfillment for the Soviet Union as whole is more than

[28] A good example of community mobilization is cited in Friedgut, *Political Participation in the USSR*, p. 105.

[29] There is evidence of deputy indifference in the popular press as well as in the specialized literature. A recent example can be found in the journal *SND*, no. 7 (July 1985), p. 87, in which a worker at a furniture store in the city of Shar'ia complains he sees his deputy only at the pre-election meeting and that nothing has been done to fulfill two relatively minor mandates that had been adopted at that time.

90 percent (see Table 5-2). But the data also show that the number of mandates approved for implementation has been declining. Some 770,085 had been approved in 1975.[30] Soviet scholars explain this decline by saying that mandates are more difficult to implement today because they are more demanding. In an interview with the author, Starovoitov made the case that the easier mandates have already been fulfilled and that, besides, people's

TABLE 5-2. Implementation of Voter Mandates, 1980–82 and 1982–84

Level of government	No. of mandates accepted for implementation, 1980–82	Percent implemented	No. of mandates accepted for implementation, 1982–84	Percent implemented
Regional	34,020	83	31,674	83
Autonomous region	1,103	87	1,075	89
Okrug	700	82	654	83
Raion	158,425	90	154,134	91
City	74,482	90	73,022	91
City borough	20,424	91	20,069	93
Settlement	55,074	92	54,055	93
Village	416,991	93	413,713	94
For all levels:	761,219	91.5	748,396	92.6

SOURCE: *Nekotorye voprosy (statisticheskii sbornik)*, 1982 (v. 1984), p. 34.

[30] *Nekotorye voprosy organizatsionnoi raboty mestnykh Sovetov deputatov trudiashchiksia v 1976 godu* (Moscow: Izvestiia, 1977).

needs have changed.[31] That seems plausible. People will require fewer preschools as population growth declines, but more tailors and cafés as the standard of living rises, and for the same reasons, less housing, but better quality. Whether other factors are at work is difficult to say. The presence of higher officials at preelection meetings, stipulated in the 1980 edict, has had the effect of reducing frivolous requests or inhibiting spontaneous participation. Nevertheless, as a mechanism that citizens can use to send a message to decision-makers about their needs, the system of the voter mandates retains considerable viability.

Reports to Constituents

Preelection meetings are not the only place constituents can confront their elected representatives with community concerns. Since the 1972 Law on the Status of Deputies, representatives have been required to meet periodically with the voters after elections as well. At these meetings, deputies are to give formal reports on the work of the soviet and on their activities on behalf of their districts. In addition, they are to listen to the problems, proposals, and questions of the people attending. These meetings, like the preelection meetings, are intended as an institutional expression of the theory of direct democracy discussed at the beginning of this chapter.[32]

In his analysis of postelection meetings, which is based on Soviet specialist literature published before 1977, Hill reports a number of legislative deficiencies and unanswered questions related to this form of deputy-constituent contact.[33] Some of these have been resolved by the

[31] Starovoitov also makes this argument in *Izbiratelei dali nakaz*, pp. 17–18.

[32] Barabashev and Sheremet, *Sovetskoe stroitel'stvo*, p. 505.

[33] Hill, *Soviet Politics, Political Science, and Reform*, pp. 59–60. Article 107 of the 1977 Constitution, and articles 20 and 21 of the Law on the Status of Deputies, as amended on April 19, 1979, constitute the governing legislation for the reports.

1977 Constitution and by conforming amendments introduced into the Law on the Status of Deputies in 1979. In
particular, it is specified that reports must be made both to
constituents in the district and to the workers' collective
that nominated the deputy, no less than twice a year in
each case (art. 20). Deputies must also inform their soviet
about what went on in the meeting and any proposals put
forward by constituents. In practice, this is done through
the records kept by the ispolkom. Also new is right of
either the constituents or the collective to demand a report
by the deputy at any time, although this rarely occurs.[34]
While deputies apparently determine when the meetings
are to be held, according to article 21 of the Law on the
Status of Deputies the meeting itself is arranged by the executive committee, which is responsible for finding a location, informing constituents about time and place, and
providing deputies with the information they need to
make their reports. On the whole, these revisions appear
to have strengthened the legislative basis for this form of
popular accountability.

While there is no federal or republic legislation governing the actual conduct of postelection meetings, procedures are described in the specialist literature and are
based on general practice or guidelines approved by the
soviet itself. What follows is a description of how these
meetings are conducted in Moscow, with some references
to experience elsewhere in the Soviet Union.[35]

[34] Based on interviews with thirty-seven village soviet presidents and
an analysis of minutes from meetings held in the Sverdlovsk region in
1980 and 1981, V. A. Kriazhkov reported ("Otchet deputata," *Pravovedenie,* no. 3 [1983], p. 33) that 92 percent of the respondents knew of no
cases of this right being used. Nor did the minutes establish its usage.

[35] The following description is based on a list of recommendations prepared for deputies of the Moscow city soviet and of the district soviets of
that city. It was made available to the author by one of the deputies of
the Lenin district in Moscow, who used it as the basis of meetings he
conducted, one of which the author observed. The document is entitled
"Rekomendatsii po podgotovke i provedeniu otchetov deputatov mest

Meetings are held by deputies in the spring and fall, usually after sessions of the soviet, at a time and place designed to encourage maximum attendance. "In accordance with the wishes of the deputy," the Organizational-Instructional Department of the executive committee prepares a schedule of reports listing the time and place of the meetings, the deputy's full name, and the district number. Once confirmed by the executive committee, this information is widely publicized. To avoid duplication, it is recommended that no more than five deputies give their reports at the same time. No less than one week beforehand, the executive committee provides informational material to the deputy. The material given to deputies of the Moscow city soviet for the fall of 1983 included twenty-four pages describing in considerable detail, and with many statistics, the efforts of the soviet to fulfill the various indices of its economic and social plan, as well as some shorter discussion of the activities of its administrative organs and of the standing committees.[36]

The meeting itself is supposed to be opened by a representative of the executive committee if held in the district, or by a trade union officer if at a workers' collective. Officers of the meeting—usually a president and a secretary—are elected, and an agenda is approved. The reports themselves are not regulated, but ideally deputies are to report on the activities of the soviet (based on the materials made available to them) and on their own activities as representatives of the district—their participation in debates, their work implementing mandates, what they have done to re-

nykh Sovetov pered izbirateliami, kollektivami i obshchestvennym organizatsionnyi." Descriptions in the specialist literature indicate that these procedures are intended for use generally. See Barabashev and Sheremet, *Sovetskoe stroitel'stvo*, pp. 504–510; and *Kommentarii k zakonu o statuse narodnykh deputatov v SSSR* (1983), pp. 166–173.

[36] Executive Committee of the Moscow City Soviet, "O deiatel'nosti Mosgorsoveta v 1983 godu: Informatsionnyi material dlia deputatov pered trudovymi kollektivami," Moscow, November, 1983.

spond to proposals, suggestions, and criticisms from previous meetings, their efforts in the standing committees, what is ahead for the district, and so on. If there are several deputies, each takes one or another aspect of work within the soviets, and each accounts for his own activity. Such reports are not always encountered in practice if data from the region of Sverdlovsk are any indication. There, only 35.6 percent of the reports given there in 1980–81 included information that could be considered complete by these standards.[37]

For citizens who want to communicate their demands regarding community affairs, the most important part of these meetings is the discussion of the reports. Here the constituent has the opportunity to raise questions or to make complaints about the work of the soviets, or to offer proposals about what should be done in the district. At the local level, these concerns are usually parochial and pragmatic, not unlike those received through the voter mandates. Interviews with deputies in the Lenin district revealed that housing was mentioned most often, followed by law and order, public works, children's services, and health. Similar concerns are heard elsewhere in the Soviet Union, although variations reflecting different levels of economic development and different regions are likely.[38] For example, Leizerov reports the following breakdown of items that resulted from forty-five meetings held in the more rural district of Slonimskii in Belorussia in 1977. Out of the sixty-eight demands and propositions received, seventeen sought repairs of public roads, nine were concerned with fence construction, five with irrigation systems and water supply, three with kindergartens, three with building cemeteries, two with electrification, and one each with public services, road construction,

[37] Kriazhkov, "Otchet deputata," p. 29.
[38] Ibid., p. 30. Kriazhkov's data, e.g., indicate that one-third of the proposals dealt with housing and everyday services.

bridge construction, work in the schools, the construction of an apartment building and a new store, and the improvement of work at another store.[39]

Frequency of participation in this portion of the meeting is much more difficult to determine and probably also varies from one district to another. In the soviets of the Sverdlovsk region in 1980–81, an average of 4.3 percent of those attending the meetings actually took part, not including the official representatives or the deputies themselves.[40] Following public participation, each deputy has a chance to respond and to explain what is already being done, or what he will do, to resolve the issues raised. A simple majority vote of those present is then taken on whether to approve the deputy's work, and also on any proposals or critical remarks to be included in the minutes of the meeting. Generally, though not always, the report is approved without negative comment.[41]

In the districts of Moscow, the secretary keeps the minutes (*protokol*) in standardized form. They include the place, date, and length of the meeting, the number attending, the names of officials present, the number participating in the debates, a short summary of the report(s) given, criticisms and propositions offered by those present, the signatures of the officers of the meeting, and suggestions about the organization of the meeting itself.[42] The deputies fill out similar forms. Within two days, both sets of records are sent on to the executive committee with a request for appropriate action. Apparently, such criticisms and propositions are taken seriously. In the case of the Slonimskii

[39] Leizerov, *Konstitutsionnyi printsip glasnosti*, p. 123.

[40] Kriazhkov, "Otchet deputata," p. 34.

[41] The data from Sverdlovsk suggest that in 90 percent of the cases the report is approved without critical comment (ibid., p. 35).

[42] A copy of the forms used for the minutes in the Lenin district (and elsewhere in Moscow) was made available to me. At the top of the first of two pages is the heading "Protokol sobraniia izbiratelei microraiona po otchety deputata," Prilozhenie no. 2.

district of Belorussia described above, of the sixty-eight demands received at forty-five meetings held in the fall of 1977, twelve found their way into the plan for the following year, five were deemed too expensive, and the remainder were acted on.[43]
    This process is supposed to work. But how often do deputies live up to the requirements for meetings? What kind of attendance is there? The data in Table 5-3 show that almost all deputies today report at least twice a year to their constituents. The evidence regarding attendance is much more varied, but one feature stands out: a large number of people come to one or more of these meetings

TABLE 5-3. Deputy Reports to Constituents, 1983

Level of soviet	Percent of deputies giving two or more reports to constituents	No. of meetings to hear reports	No. of constituents attending (in thousands)	Average attendance per meeting	Average attendance as percent of average constituency size[a]
Regional[b]	97.5	64,366	10,390.5	161.4	4
Okrug	92.6	2,141	160.9	75.2	8
Raion	96.9	466,017	46,986.3	100.8	32
City	97.2	518,818	39,805.9	76.7	20
City borough	96.2	219,709	19,514.9	88.8	21
Settlement	97.5	371,364	14,492.4	39.0	52
Village	98.0	2,310,008	67,484.2	29.2	65
For all levels:	97.6	3,952,423	198,835.1	50.3	—

SOURCES: *Nekotorye voprosy (statisticheskii sbornik)*, 1983, p. 32. For 1982 election data, *Itogi vyborov*, 1982.
[a] Based on figures from the June 20, 1982 election.
[b] Includes data for autonomous regions (separate data not available).

[43] Leizerov, *Konstitutsionnyi printsip glasnosti*, p. 123.

in a year, although multiple attendance by some individuals makes it difficult to determine what percentage of the total population is actually involved. Because the ratio of deputies to constituents is greater as one descends the hierarchy, average attendance declines as one moves from the higher level soviets to the lower ones. At the same time, it appears that the smaller the district is, the larger the percentage of that district in attendance (see Table 5-3, last column).[44] The greatest amount of participation as a percentage of the population clearly takes place in the rural areas. The variation in average attendance by republic is also substantial, ranging from a high of 96.5 per meeting in Armenia to about 45 per meeting in the Latvian and Russian republics.[45]

The data conceal as much as they reveal. For one thing, there is considerable variation from one district to another; in some districts almost all the constituents attend, while in other districts relatively few do.[46] The difference in quality of these meetings is even more difficult to determine. Some meetings live up to expectations, but others reportedly have people reading newspapers, snoozing, or gossiping with friends while the deputy drones on about the indices of plan fulfillment in the last quarter. Still other meetings suffer from a lack of decorum on the part of those present. One deputy confided to the author his aversion to giving reports before his district constituents be-

[44] Data from Sverdlovsk show that while only 2 percent of the population at the regional level hear reports from regional deputies, this figure climbs to about 15 percent in the cities, and 67.6 percent in the villages (Kriazhkov, "Otchet deputata," pp. 33–34). Similar findings are reported from a Siberian study conducted by V. M. Vinogradov, "Ob opyte v Vostochnoi Sibiri," in *Voprosy teorii i praktiki sovetskogo gosudarstveniia*, vol. 77, Juridical Series, issue 11, part 2 (University of Irkutsk, 1970), p. 63.

[45] *Nekotorye voprosy*, 1983, p. 32.

[46] Leizerov, *Konstitutsionnyi printsip glasnosti*, p. 127. Bezuglov has urged that a certain number of attendants be required in order for a meeting to acquire legitimacy ("Otchety deputatov pered izbirateliami," *SGiP*, no. 8 [1968], p. 103).

cause mostly senior citizens showed up and often made unrealistic demands while remaining indifferent to the procedures that such meetings required of him.

There are other problems related to the presentation of reports to constituents. One of the most frequently mentioned is the practice of giving group reports where several deputies appear at a single meeting but one reports for the others. Soviet specialists uniformly condemn this practice, and, as Bezuglov points out, it is a violation of the deputies' constitutional obligation to report before the electorate.[47] Another shortcoming concerns the amount and quality of information the deputy receives from the executive committee. Such information is understandably likely to portray the work of the soviet in flattering tones, but lacking critical pungency, the deputies' reports can easily be monumental bores, and the absence of candor erodes whatever credibility deputies may have with their constituents. Although deputies now have the right to demand further details and are encouraged to discuss shortcomings openly, they may be inhibited from doing so, not only by a lack of experience or time but also by the presence of precisely those officials to whom their criticisms would be addressed.[48] There is also disagreement about what should be included in the reports. Most scholars urge a narrower, practical focus, while some would apparently prefer that the reports be general statements of how the soviets are reflecting the current policy line of the party.[49] The one deficiency that virtually all the specialists appear to agree on is the lack of legislation governing the

[47] Bezuglov, *Deputat v Sovete*, p. 71. See also Barabashev and Sheremet, *Sovetskoe stroitel'stvo*, p. 504.

[48] Kriazhkov, "Otchet deputata," p. 30, discusses this problem and urges legislation to give the deputy greater access to information. Bezuglov has suggested (*Deputat v Sovete*, p. 7) that executive committee members not attend the reports because it takes attention away from the deputies and undermines their authority.

[49] See discussion in Leizerov, *Konstitutsionnoyi printsip glasnosti*, p. 125. Bezuglov opposes any standard format (*Deputat v Sovete*, p. 74).

conduct of the meetings at which deputies give their reports; in the absence of such regulation, the problems mentioned here are likely to continue.

Despite these deficiencies, the usefulness of the deputy reports as a way for constituents to communicate community concerns, as well as to receive information about what is happening in their districts, should not be underestimated. A great many people attend at least one of these sessions each year—nearly 200 million in 1983, averaging more than fifty per meeting. There is no evidence that attendance is legally required or coerced, and the matters discussed are of sufficient importance to attract the interest of those concerned with the quality of local life. Moreover, there is evidence that this practice has grown in the post-Stalin period. In 1949 only 25.3 percent of the deputies reported annually to their constituents; in 1957, this rose to 66.5 percent, and by 1961 it reached 80.8 percent. As of 1969, more than 95 percent of the deputies reported at least once a year.[50] As a result of the 1972 Law on the Status of Deputies, the frequency of deputy meetings with constituents has also increased substantially. In 1969 only 38 percent of the deputies gave more than one report a year, but by 1983 this figure had grown to 97.6 percent.[51] Like the voter mandates, however imperfectly they may function in practice, the meetings to hear reports serve citizens and decision-makers alike as a forum in which problems of community life can be aired.

Submitting "Proposals, Declarations, and Complaints"

The preelection meetings at which voter mandates are presented, and the postelection meetings at which deputies report to their constituents, are public forums where

[50] A. S. Pavlov, *Partiinoe rukovodstvo mestnymi Sovetami v poslevoennye gody* (Moscow: Vysshaia shkola, 1983), p. 65; "Demokratiia v deistvii," *SDI*, no. 6 (1970), p. 96.

[51] "Demokratiia v deistvii," p. 96; *Nekotorye voprosy organizatsionnoi raboty*, 1984, p. 28.

Soviet citizens can express their opinions on matters of common interest. Beside these, however, there are a variety of channels individuals can use to make direct, personal contact with the deputies in order to communicate what are officially referred to as "proposals, declarations, and complaints." These three terms have distinct meanings, which are significant, although often overlooked in practice. Proposals (*predlozheniia*) contain the suggestions of a constituent, or of several constituents jointly, about how to improve the work of local government. These are more likely to be advanced at times when the agenda for an upcoming session of the soviet is published, or in connection with a public discussion of draft legislation. Substantively, "proposals" are aimed at matters of general community interest. Declarations (*zaiavleniia*) are more specific in nature and may involve either appeals for help with a personal situation, or resolution of a community problem resulting from failure of one or another agency to perform its functions properly. When there is a question of whether the legal rights of the petitioner have been violated, the individual may file a formal complaint (*zhalob*), which may ultimately require court action.[52]

While proposals and declarations may be acted upon by the government agencies to which they are directed, complaints must be reviewed by those to whom the objects of the complaint are subordinated.[53] It is clear from official Soviet documents, as well as the writings of specialists,

[52] Examination of proposals, declarations, and complaints is stipulated by article 19 of the 1972 Law on the Status of Deputies. These definitions follow V. I. Vasil'ev's discussion in *Kommentarii k zakonu o statuse narodnykh deputatov v SSSR* (1983), pp. 156–157.

[53] The procedures on proposals, declarations, and complaints are governed by an edict of the Presidium of the Supreme Soviet, "O poriadke rassmotrenniia predlozhenii, zaiavlenii i zhalob grazhdan," originally adopted on April 12, 1968, and amended with relatively minor changes on June 25, 1980, *Vedomosti Verkhovnogo Soveta*, 1980, no. 11, item 192. See sections 3, 5, 9, 15 on complaints, and the legal responsibility of those violating the law.

that the procedures for making proposals, declarations, and complaints are intended to provide citizens with an avenue of appeal against bureaucratic indifference or infringement while at the same time providing a source of information to the government about the problems it must address. The procedures are presented as an institutional reflection of the ideological imperatives implicit in the communal model of direct democracy: workers must control those who administer.[54]

The communication of these direct, personal appeals may be accomplished orally or in writing and can be directed to members of the executive committee, administrators, party members, or the press, as well as to the deputies. Indeed, the deputies appear to be something of a court of last resort, to be turned to only if satisfaction is not obtained elsewhere, especially for those who lack personal ties to the people who make the decisions. An informal survey by the author of twenty-six law students at Moscow State University was suggestive. Faced with a problem, twenty-two students would go to the director of their workplace or to friends to get it resolved, and only one indicated that he would go to a deputy first, although more (seven) did so as a second or third choice.

The primary target of such citizen appeals would appear to be members of the executive committees and department heads. A study of how citizens communicate with government, based on a survey of 1,020 respondents in the industrial city of Taganrog in the early 1970s, found that the average number of conversations per month with workers in administrative organs was 1,450, while those

[54] See the preamble to the edict noted in footnote 53. A Central Committee resolution on this subject was published in *Pravda*, April 4, 1981: "O merakh po dal'neishemu uluchsheniiu raboty s pis'mami i predlozheniiami v svete reshenii XXVI s'ezda KPSS." A concise review of the history and theory as well as the literature up to 1973 can be found in N. N. Kazakevich, "Analiz i obobshchenie pisem i ustnykh obrashchenii v gosudarstvennykh organov," *SGiP*, no. 10 (1973), pp. 29–35.

with deputies averaged 545.[55] Friedgut's survey of 300 Soviet émigrés to Israel disclosed a similar pattern. About one-third of his respondents reported having directly contacted the authorities at least once. Over half their contacts were with administrators; deputies were second, followed by contacts with the Party, and the press. In volume, 84 of a total of 160 contacts had been with an administrator, 30 with a deputy.[56]

Since the administrators are most able to resolve the citizens' problems, such a choice is wholly understandable. However, the volume of demands made to administrators is formidable. In Moscow alone, in 1983, the executive committee received 61,716 written requests, administrative departments received 155,955, and the city borough executive committees received 135,727. In addition, 21,779 individuals came to the city soviet for personal conferences—an average of nearly 90 visits per working day—while another 118,094 went to the city borough executives.[57] As both Friedgut and Osborn note, the sheer numbers involved make shifting some of the burden to the deputies even more desirable; they can at least act as a filter, taking care of less-important items themselves and passing the remainder on to those who can deal properly with them.[58] Moreover, for those who feel unfairly dealt with, the deputy represents someone who cannot as easily be set aside; as a backup, the deputy may be prevailed upon to press the elector's case.

Opportunities for registering proposals and complaints are numerous, and more often than not they are written.

[55] Grushin and Onikova, *Massovaia informatsiia v sovetskom promyshlennom gorode*, p. 379.

[56] Friedgut, "The Soviet Citizen's Perception of Local Government," in Jacobs, *Soviet Local Politics and Government*, p. 123.

[57] *Biulleten' ispolkoma Moskovskogo Soveta*, no. 7 (April 1984), pp. 28–30.

[58] Friedgut, *Political Participation in the USSR*, pp. 208, 224–227. See also Robert J. Osborn, "Public Participation in Soviet City Government" (Ph.D. dissertation, Columbia University, 1963), p. 165.

In addition to letters to the authorities, disgruntled citizens may record their objectives in a notebook kept for that purpose at all places of work. For example, most forms of mass transportation carry a sign informing riders about how they can make dissatisfactions with the transit system known. Oral communication, however, is generally considered by psychologists and politicians alike to be more effective.

How the Deputies Respond

For deputies, oral requests from constituents that require a formal response take place during consulting hours, called a *priyom*.[59] These are supposed to be held in electoral districts at a time and place convenient for constituents. While deputies are required by law to conduct priyoms, the details of organization and procedure are not specified. In most cases, according to practice and the scholarly literature,[60] the local deputy will set aside two hours in the evening once or twice a month for this purpose. The priyom is conducted at the same place throughout the deputy's term of office, usually at the building of the executive committee, an *agitpunkt*, a "red corner," or at the offices of the *zhek*, the local committee that administers housing. The time and place of the priyom are advertised in announcements posted in the district or in the press. Deputies are enjoined to take only one case at a time, in private, and to conduct the interview in a manner designed to encourage openness on the part of the appli-

[59] The term *priyom* is also used to refer to the reception hours of executive agencies. An excellent description by a firsthand Western observer of the work of a city borough deputy chairman in charge of housing during reception hours is provided by Morton, "The Leningrad District of Moscow," pp. 215–217.

[60] The description of the priyom offered here comes principally from *Kommentarii k zakonu o statuse narodnykh deputatov v SSSR* (1983), pp. 157–160, and conversations with specialists, as well as my firsthand observations.

cant. They are also expected to keep a record of the interview, including the date, the problem, the name of the petitioner, and the disposition of the case. While such a record may inhibit candor, it also ensures responsibility on the part of both deputy and petitioner.

Although deputies have no independent judicial authority, they can resolve some of the issues brought to them on their own by contacting the appropriate administrator or enterprise head, or occasionally even by simply acting as a good listener. One former deputy described to the author how he listened to a pregnant woman complain about her relations with her mother-in-law for most of two separate sessions, before finally helping her find alternative housing. Requests that the deputy cannot handle are sent on, usually to administrators or representatives at a higher level. Conversely, the deputy may receive requests from those at a higher level to verify information about issues that occur in the deputy's district. In cases of complaints involving official abuse or neglect, however, the procedures are more specific. These must be decided within a month of their registration and, if they do not require documentation or special verification, within fifteen days.[61] Citizens who do not receive satisfaction have the right to appeal to higher authorities or to the courts; failure to respond to a complaint may result in dismissal of the official involved, and in some cases criminal charges may be brought. Taken together, the work of the deputy in the *priyom* resembles that of an ombudsman, who acts as an intermediary between the population at large and those who govern them.

On paper at least, the deputy's authority to intervene on behalf of constituents in their pursuit of governmental attention to their problems is substantial. In practice, how-

[61] Technically, the law does not stipulate a time period for deputies, but Vasilev considers the procedures for executive officials operative for deputies by analogy (in ibid., p. 160).

ever, a single deputy, especially a novice (as nearly half the deputies in any term are), when confronted by issues that transcend his or her particular small district, and able to devote only a limited amount of time to resolving an increasing volume of demands, is unlikely to be very effective, no matter how determined the deputy may be to help. To redress this problem, a practice that existed in the first years of Soviet power was revived in the 1950s: the organization of deputy groups. The idea is that because deputies from contiguous districts often share common problems, their effectiveness in resolving those problems will be enhanced if they act jointly.

In urban areas, deputy groups are formed on either a territorial basis or by place of work. Territorial deputy groups are often set up to coincide with the zheks, committees that administer the housing of 5,000 to 10,000 inhabitants. This makes sense because a large portion of the issues brought to deputies concern housing and its maintenance. Deputy groups are now comprised only of deputies and are formed on their own initiative. They vary in number between three and fifty, although twenty is considered optimal.[62] When a decision to form a group is made, officers are elected and confirmed by the soviet as a whole. Meetings are held as needed, but at least in the RSFSR, not less than every other month.[63] According to Barabashev and Sheremet, the authority of the deputy groups is in some respects analogous to that of the standing committees, especially with respect to oversight. Like

[62] Both Barabashev and Bezuglov emphasize the difference from earlier times. See Bezuglov, *Deputat v Sovete*, pp. 65–66; and Barabashev and Sheremet, *Sovetskoe stroitel'stvo*, p. 286. Regarding size, Bezuglov (p. 66) considers more than twenty too many.

[63] A decree governing the formation and activities of deputy groups and deputies' posts was adopted by the Presidium of the Supreme Soviet of the RSFSR on August 2, 1984 (see "Polozhenie o deputatskikh gruppakh i deputatskikh postakh v RSFSR," August 2, 1984). Similar legislation had been in effect in other republics for several years. Lithuania, e.g., had passed a similar decree in April 1979.

individual deputies, deputy groups have the right to make official inquiries.[64] As Friedgut argues, the deputy groups effectively transmit citizen requests to government, and vice versa.[65] An obvious temptation is for deputy groups to take over more of the functions of the individual deputy in contacting his constituents, and some specialists have even suggested that this is desirable. Most, however, reject this view, arguing that collective action should serve only to supplement, not to supplant, the individual contact of deputy and constituent.[66]

What is a priyom actually like? How does it work in practice? Systematic interviews with the deputies in the Lenin city borough indicated that at least the minimum official requirements were being met: all deputies held at least one priyom per month, most of them in the deputies' room of the apartment buildings in their city borough, and all were members of deputy groups, ranging in size from thirteen to twenty-two. The author was able to accompany one of these deputies to a priyom in an apartment complex in an older section of the city overlooking the Moscow River. On the way to the priyom the deputy explained that most of his work was with housing problems because his was an old district. Most Moscovite families, he said, now lived in their own apartments, but in his district 40 percent or more still had to put up with communal housing that more than the nuclear family would have to live in. When we arrived at the apartment building in which the deputies' room was located, we were let into the building by a *druzhinnik*, or local police aide, who was stationed in one of the several rooms set aside for civic or community functions in the building's basement. The deputies' room itself contained a bare table, five chairs, and little else. Office hours were from 6 p.m. to 8 p.m.

[64] Barabashev and Sheremet, *Sovetskoe stroitel'stvo*, p. 287.
[65] Friedgut, *Political Participation in the USSR*, p. 210.
[66] Bezuglov reviews this debate at some length in *Sovetskii deputat*, pp. 132–134.

Whether it was a result of the driving snow and cold that evening or the approaching holidays, we had only one visitor: a representative of the city borough party organization who stopped in to chat, and perhaps to see if the deputy was doing his duty. After he left and it became increasingly unlikely that anyone else was coming, the deputy showed me the logbook in which the records of previous visits are kept, as if to convince me that constituents really do come. According to the log for 1984, twenty-nine visits had taken place in the course of fifty-nine priyoms. In 1983 there had been sixty visits. What follows is a representative selection of what took place at some of the meetings in 1984.

1/21/84   A mother and daughter are living in a 25-square-meter apartment. The mother is getting remarried. The daughter had asked the district housing administrative for her own room but had received no response. The deputy promises to support her case. Result unknown.

3/5/84   An older citizen, speaking for others as well, requested that an elevator be constructed in his apartment. The deputy later brought the matter to the city borough executive committee, which decided to appropriate the necessary funds at their weekly conference.

8/6/84   A woman complains that the sanitary conditions in her apartment building are so bad that it constitutes a violation of the health code; the housing she is in is uninhabitable. She is told to get a certificate to this effect from the Sanitary Control Commission. If she receives it, the city borough executive committee must find her new housing.

9/4/84   A teacher in the *mikroraion* (microdistrict) makes a case for construction of a new children's playground in the district; she requests that this proposal be placed on the agenda of the next meeting of the deputy group. The deputy promises to do so.

11/5/84 A female veteran of World War II presently lives with her family in a five-room apartment and is seeking her own flat. She had initially approached her deputy about this in early October. The deputy sent her to the housing committee of the district executive committee, but by November 5 she still had received no answer, so she is again appealing to her deputy. The matter was later discussed at the deputy's housing commission (*zhilishche komissii*), which promised to support her application to receive an apartment in 1985.

11/6/84 A mother and daughter live in a small apartment. The daughter recently married, and the new couple are asking their mother to find other housing. The mother refuses, insisting on her right to live in the apartment. A confrontation developed, and the mother has come to the deputy to ask for a determination of her rights. The deputy holds a hearing at which a representative of the district housing administration and a representative from the daughter's enterprise are present, in addition to the principals involved and the deputy. Agreement could not be reached, and the matter was sent to the courts.

It is difficult to determine just how typical of practice elsewhere in the Soviet Union these observations are, but they are probably not atypical, at least for urban areas. They are at least suggestive of both the problems and the possibilities offered by the priyom as a mechanism for constituent contact. On the negative side, it seems clear that these consulting hours are underutilized; at half of them, no one came.[67] Whether this is because of lack of knowl-

[67] The figures from this part of the Lenin district appear to be lower than those for other areas; Friedgut, e.g., cites an Armenian study show-

edge on the part of constituents, or whether they believe there is little the deputy can do, is difficult to tell. When constituents did come, the deputy was often unable to do much more than point them in the right direction, but the deputy was helpful to citizens in some cases. The importance of the deputy's role as a kind of reference service for people unfamiliar with the workings of the state bureaucracy should not be underestimated. Pointing constituents in the right direction is a substantial portion of the work of elected representatives in the United States as well. Finally, the case of the teacher seeking a playground suggests that citizens do have the opportunity to initiate action on matters of general interest to the local community.

Aside from the problem of getting citizens to make greater use of the priyom, it is clear that not all deputies are performing their duties as well as they are supposed to. The CPSU Central Committee resolution of January 22, 1957, "On Improving the Work of the Soviets and Strengthening Their Ties with the Masses," made it clear that many deputies held no consultation hours or, if they did, were frequently absent. And an August 29, 1967 CPSU, resolution, "On Improving Work with the Examination of Letters and the Organization of the Priyom," chastised deputies who did hold priyom regularly for doing so poorly, for ignoring legitimate complaints, or for dealing with them in a "formal" way. While there is little or no published statistical data to determine whether these resolutions resulted in improved deputy performance, re-

---

ing deputies receiving an average of eight visits per year (Friedgut, *Political Participation in the USSR*, p. 230). The differences may be attributed to the method of reporting, but both cases indicate that the deputies' priyomy is frequented far less than the priyomy of the administrative organs. In the case of Moscow city, an average of over seventy people per working *day* in 1983 made use of the executive committee priyom (*Biulleten' ispolkoma Moskovskogo Soveta*, no. 7 [April 1984], p. 30). Morton describes one executive committee member receiving thirty-one visitors in the course of one four-and-a-half hour *priyom* ("The Leningrad District of Moscow," p. 207).

168   Chapter 5

cent party documents indicate that little has changed. According to one resolution, "On Measures for Further Improving Work with Letters and Propositions in the Light of the 26th Congress" (April 4, 1981),

> Serious omissions exist in the examination of the oral and written concerns of citizens. An indifferent, bureaucratic attitude toward legal and well-founded requests and declarations is tolerated, and there are instances of previous requests being ignored, causing them to be sent on to higher organizations and institutions, thereby perpetuating the runaround in satisfying their wishes.[68]

Other Forms of Constituent Contact

The opportunities Soviet citizens have to communicate their concern about local affairs examined so far have a well-developed institutional basis. Certain patterns of practice have evolved over time, and the procedures for such participation are fairly well defined. There are, however, other ways constituents can let their representatives know what they are thinking: public discussion of draft legislation, opinion surveys and informal contacts. Though less well established in usage or law, they deserve attention because of their potential for becoming more common.

But first, we should look at public organizations that are not formally part of the organs of government. Following Soviet terminology, these can be classified into two types: (1) mass public organizations, including the Komsomol, trade unions, the DOSAAF (Society for Cooperation with the Armed Forces), the Society of the Red Cross and Red Crescent, the Society of Knowledge (Znanie), all-union sport societies, and so forth; and (2) the so-called "self-activating" public organization (*organy obshchestvennoi samodeiatel'nosti*), such as the local volunteer militia (*druzhiny*),

---

[68] *Pravda*, April 4, 1981, p. 1. See also Chernenko's speech to the April 1984 Plenum of the Central Committee quoted in Chapter 3, footnote 1.

parents' committees (for schools), housing, street, and residential committees, the women's soviets, and various clubs. The former constitute local branches of national organizations and are administratively subordinated to them, while the activities of the latter are bounded by the territory in which they are located. Public organizations are also organized within the workplace.[69] The number of participants in these organizations is enormous, and they do provide, in an indirect way, another channel for articulation of citizen interests. In particular, Blair Ruble describes how trade unions provide a variety of channels for expressing demands related to the workplace, although, as he points out, their potential is infrequently realized in practice.[70] However, communication of demands for political action is a secondary purpose for these organizations; in practice they function more to carry out decisions than to initiate them, often mobilizing the population on behalf of regime-sponsored courses. Because the chief interest of the present work is with direct constituent contact involving the deputies, a more detailed discussion of these groups as instruments of public participation is not offered here.[71]

[69] For a more detailed description of the differences between types of public organizations, see Barabashev and Sheremet, *Sovetskoe stroitel'stvo*, pp. 521–559.

[70] Blair A. Ruble, *Soviet Trade Unions* (Cambridge: Cambridge University Press, 1981), esp. chap. 5. See also Hill, *Soviet Politics, Political Science, and Reform*, pp. 103–104.

[71] Friedgut devotes a chapter to the "self-help" organizations in *Political Participation in the USSR*, pp. 235–288. As he correctly observes (pp. 243, 263), they generally operate under the direction of the executive committee and especially its Organizational-Instructional department. While deputies may become involved with such organizations in particular cases and are expected to enlist the aid of such organizations in carrying out their duties, it is the executive committee and its departments that have primary responsibility for the activity of the "self-help" organizations. Legislative expression of this relationship can be found in the union-republic statutes on the residential committees adopted since 1980. See Chapter 1, footnote 24, *Sbornik normativnikh aktov*, pp. 791ff. A de-

Public Discussion of Draft Legislation

Since the Soviet Constitution of 1977 went into effect, increasing attention has been given to the direct participation of citizens in the discussion and adoption of legislation. Several articles of the Constitution stimulated this interest and are indeed the only present legal basis for this form of participation. In particular, article 5 establishes that "the most important questions of state life are submitted for nationwide discussion, and are also put up for a nationwide vote (referendum)," while article 48 states that citizens have the right to participate in "the discussion and adoption of laws and decisions of nationwide and local importance." The use of a referendum to decide a question of national policy has yet to take place, but public discussion of draft legislation has. The most widely cited example is the discussion of the draft constitution itself: 140 million citizens are supposed to have taken part and made about 400,000 propositions and suggestions, at least some of which were incorporated.[72] There have been similar discussions regarding national legislation on such subjects as education, marriage and the family, labor, and crime.[73]

tailed examination of the workings of one mass public organization (DOSAAF) can be found in William E. Odom, *The Soviet Volunteers* (Princeton: Princeton University Press, 1973).

[72] See A. I. Luk'ianov, "Konstitutsiia deistvuet, zhivet, rabotaet," *SGiP*, no. 10 (1982), p. 9; and Barabashev and Sheremet, *Sovetskoe stroitel'stvo*, p. 519. As Sharlet points out, the major decisions had already been made, and the boundaries of the discussion were made clear by those who organized it (Sharlet, *The New Soviet Constitution of 1977*, pp. 24–31). Nevertheless, even Sharlet acknowledges that "the discussion brought forth a remarkable variety of proposals on wide range of concerns" (p. 28).

[73] Peter Solomon describes how specialists participated in the making of policy on juvenile delinquency, alcoholism, and hooliganism by taking part in public discussions. See his *Soviet Criminal Rights and Criminal Policy* (New York: Columbia University Press, 1978), esp. pp. 107–126. Two articles by Western specialists show how these discussions of legislation can be used by interest groups to articulate their own points of view. Joel Schwartz and William Keech, "Group Influence and the Policy Process," *American Political Science Review* 62 (1968): 840–851 examines the educa-

While discussions of national policy are officially initiated by the Presidium of the Supreme Soviet, public discussions on local issues can be initiated by the deputies themselves and may take various forms: special meetings can be held, the media may be invited to take part, or in the case of more complicated decisions, conferences of specialists might be organized. In analyzing the results of such discussions, however, the role of the executive committee is paramount, especially its Organizational-Instructional Department.

How well do such discussions of draft decisions at the local level work in practice? In an interesting study based on a survey of 150 district and city soviet chief executives conducted by V. A. Kriazhkov in November 1982 in Sverdlovsk, the answer seems to be: not as well as they should be.[74] Asked how often discussions of draft decisions had occurred over the five years since the adoption of the Constitution, 43 percent said rarely, 50.8 percent answered that such practices took place, and only 6.8 percent indicated that this was done regularly. In probing the reasons for the apparent lack of enthusiasm, Kriazhkov was told by some that for most the idea was too new and complicated, or that clearly defined procedures were lacking. Other respondents felt that public input on their decisions was not necessary and would serve only to slow them down in their work. Criticizing this view as being incompatible with the higher need "to raise the political and legal consciousness of citizens," Kriazhkov observes that

tional policies introduced by Khrushchev in 1958, while Friedgut looked at the machine-tractor station (MTS) reforms (Theodore H. Friedgut, "Interests and Groups in Soviet Policy-Making: The MTS Reforms," *Soviet Studies* 28 [October 1976]).

[74] V. A. Kriazhkov, "Obsuzhdenie grazhdanami proektov reshenii mestnykh sovetov," *SGiP*, no. 8 (1983). The sample represents 150 executive committee presidents and vice-presidents responding out of 176 questionnaires distributed, or about 48 percent of the universe in five contiguous oblasts and the Udmurt and Bashkir Autonomous republics.

only 18.1 percent of his respondents believed that such discussions were inadvisable and that the way to increase their use is to specify the questions that should be put before the public as well as to strengthen the procedures for doing so. Other Soviet specialists, notably Leizerov and Barabashev, have also urged that lists of questions requiring public debate be included in local regulations.[75] Yet, as Kriazhkov points out, adoption of regulations is a necessary but not sufficient condition—what is needed are "changes in well-established, administrative stereotypes of thinking."[76] The 1985 Draft Program of the CPSU specifies the need to expand "the range of questions on which decisions will be made only after [public] discussion." Whether this will provide sufficient impetus for development of regulations defining how such discussions are to be conducted and on what subjects remains to be seen.[77]

At present, the discussion of draft legislation normally takes place in the press, in workers' collectives, or in public meetings of citizens at their residences. Kriazhkov's research reveals that the first two of these forums were far more likely to be used.[78] Public meetings for such purposes in residential settings are relatively rare, at least in urban areas. In the villages, however, a special type of general meeting, known as the *sel'skii skhod*, appears to of-

[75] G. V. Barabashev, "Na novom etape," *SND*, no. 6 (1981), p. 18; Leizerov, *Konstitutsionnyi printsip glasnosti*, pp. 90–92.

[76] Kriazhkov, "Obsuzhdenie grazhdanami proektov reshenii," p. 63.

[77] "The Draft Program of the CPSU," *Pravda*, October 26, 1985, part 2, sec. 4. The regulations of the city borough soviets in Moscow do contain a provision guaranteeing "the preliminary discussion of draft decisions by citizens" in six specific areas, including public safety, the environment, construction, the budget, economic planning, and the mandates (article 26, Reglament Leninskogo raionnogo Soveta Moskvy, on November 19, 1980).

[78] Kriazhkov, "Obsuzhdenie grazhdanami proektov reshenii," p. 62. Some 33.3 percent of the discussions were held in the press, 31.9 percent in workers' collectives, 30.6 percent in a combination of both, and only 4.2 percent at places of residence.

fer rural citizens broader opportunities for direct participation in local decision-making. While the origins of this
practice are to be found in the prerevolutionary period, the
continued use of the *skhody* was affirmed in the RSFSR by
special legislation in March 1927 and by a USSR decree on
September 11, 1937. Intended by Soviet authorities in that
period primarily as a forum for deciding who would be
assessed taxes and at what rate, laws adopted in 1968 in
all republics except Latvia and Tadzhikstan stipulated a
broad range of subjects to be dealt with in this manner,
including such issues as public works, the use of land,
economic planning, cultural events, the distribution of ag-
ricultural surpluses, and the preservation of law and
order.[79]

Normally, the skhody are convened by the executive
committee of the village soviet, but they may also be called
by the soviet itself or by 20 percent of the inhabitants at
their own initiative. Practice appears to dictate that 50 percent must be present to make decisions; anyone over sixteen years of age can take part. The meeting is organized
by the executive committee but is conducted by officers
elected from those present. Decisions are made by a simple majority vote. Minutes are sent to the executive committee for implementation, although this body may sus-
pend any decisions that it determines are inconsistent
with existing law.[80]

Information about how well the skhody work in practice
are sketchy. Friedgut suggests that an average attendance

---

[79] The legislative basis of the activity of the skhody in the RSFSR is
article 82 of "O poselkovom, sel'skom sovete narodnykh deputatov
RSFSR," July 19, 1968, as amended on August 3, 1979, *Vedomosti Verkhovnogo Soveta RSFSR*, 1979, no. 32, item 787. A more detailed examination
of this article is found in *Kommentarii k zakonodatel'stvu o poselkovykh i
sel'skikh Sovetakh* (Moscow: Izvestiia, 1982), pp. 430–433. Most of what follows comes from this source.

[80] Barabashev and Sheremet, *Sovetskoe stroitel'stvo*, pp. 516–517.

of between fifty and sixty people per meeting is likely.[81] Interviews with different Soviet specialists conducted by the author in the fall of 1984 indicated that the debates at village meetings were often livelier than those held among urban-dwellers; villagers, one specialist explained, were less inhibited by legal formalities because they were less familiar with them, though in their actual conduct they were more "democratic."

The Use of Public Opinion Surveys

Among Soviet specialists, there has recently been increased interest in the use of public opinion polls (*ankety*) as a means of determining citizen preferences about public policy. Although public opinion research using survey methods has been conducted since the early 1960s, much of this work has engendered controversy, especially in the field of sociology.[82] Published national polls scientifically measuring public opinion about contemporary political issues, or citizens' attitudes about government—a ubiquitous feature of American popular and scholarly publications—are far less common in the Soviet Union. The practice of elected representatives regularly commissioning polls to learn what their constituents think is even more of a novelty there. Nevertheless, according to Barabashev, "deputies can take the initiative in conducting opinion polls,"[83] and Bezuglov reports that polls are conducted annually by local soviets in Lithuania on such issues as health care, transportation, the environment, and

[81] Friedgut, *Political Participation in the USSR*, p. 154.
[82] See Jeffrey W. Hahn, "The Role of Soviet Sociologists in the Making of Social Policy," in Richard Remnek (ed.), *Social Scientists and Policy-Making in the USSR* (New York: Praeger, 1977); Archie Brown, "Political Science in the Soviet Union: A New Stage of Development?" *Soviet Studies* 36 (July 1984), pp. 326–328; and Slider, "Party-Sponsored Public Opinion Research in the Soviet Union," pp. 210–228.
[83] In *Kommentarii k zakonu*, p. 152.

leisure time.[84] Despite official encouragement, however, the use of public opinion polls has ranked low among the means used to assess public opinion. In a study carried out by the Institute of State and Law in Kalinin Oblast in the early 1970s, the employees of local government rated polls eighth out of ten possible ways to learn about public opinion, just slightly below familiarization with the materials collected by the People's Control Committees.[85] One problem inhibiting the broader use of polling is that deputies lack experience and expertise in designing survey questionnaires, so they must rely on their executive committees for assistance both in framing questions and analyzing results. Consequently, the executive committees exercise effective control over the conduct of public opinion polls, though there is as yet no legal requirement that this be so.

A second obstacle to the greater use of polls is the question of how competent the public is to render an opinion on matters of public policy. In contrast to the quantitative emphasis found in most Western research on political culture, the Soviet approach is much more qualitative: the political culture of a population is well developed or poorly developed, depending on their level of knowledge about politics (*politicheskaia gramotnost'*) and the degree to which they are active in it. Thus, the definition of "political culture" in the *Kratkii politicheskii slovar'* (*Concise Political Dictionary*) states that "one of the most important functions of political culture is educational—its purpose is the raising of the political information and competence of citizens." Further on, the reader is informed that it is only through political education that the individual "can fully manifest his citizenship qualities and on the basis of a well-devel-

---

[84] Bezuglov, *Deputat v sovete*, pp. 45–47; O. Maslova, "Kak provodito anketnye oprosy," *SDT*, no. 10 (1977), p. 78. A catalog of practical applications of survey research for local government was published in 1982 (Lebedev, *Mestnye Sovety i obshchestvennoe mnenie*).

[85] Safarov, *Obshchestvennoe mnenie i gosudarstvennoe upravlenie*, p. 100.

oped political position display political initiative and activeness in the resolution of the problems facing the government and society."[86] In the Soviet view, for public opinion to matter it must be informed. As G. Shakhnazarov wrote in 1972, "It is impossible to take part in deciding matters of state without having a clear idea of the structure of the state mechanism, the contents of the constitution and the basic branches, and without knowing the basics of governmental science."[87] The public's knowledge of political matters is not held in high esteem by those who run local government. In a study conducted in 1974–76 by the Institute of Concrete Social Research at the University of Leningrad, four categories of administrative personnel in several large cities in the RSFSR were asked whether the public knows much about the work of government. While 66 percent of the executive officers and 54 percent of the department heads thought the public had "some idea" of what was done, more than half the assistant heads and two-thirds of the staff were convinced that the public had "no idea" or "almost no idea" about what local government involved.[88]

Given these problems, the prognosis for increased use of public opinion polls to elicit citizen concerns regarding public policy is uncertain. Some scholars, like Shakhnazarov, use the issue of competence to argue for a greater, and freer, flow of information.[89] R. A. Safarov has been a leading advocate of legally requiring that public opinion be taken into account in formulating government policy. He

---

[86] "Politicheskaia kultura," in *Kratkii politicheskii slovar'* (Moscow: Politizdat, 1978), p. 318. A good review of the Soviet literature on political culture is provided by Archie Brown, "Soviet Political Culture Through Soviet Eyes," in Brown, *Political Culture and Communist Studies*, pp. 100–114.

[87] Georgi Shakhnazarov, *Sotsialisticheskaia demokratiia* (Moscow: Politizdat, 1972), p. 132.

[88] P. N. Levedev, *Sistema organov gorodskogo upravleniia* (Leningrad: Lenizdat, 1980), p. 204.

[89] Shakhnazarov, *Sotsialisticheskaia demokratiia*, pp. 135–140, 180–185.

specifically encourages the broader use of survey research tools, citing their use by Marx and Lenin and giving eight reasons why they are particularly valuable.[90] On the issue of competence, he argues forcefully that while an increase in public knowledge about governmental affairs is desirable, its absence does not diminish the value of public opinion as a barometer of what the public considers important; in this sense, whether opinion is well informed or not is irrelevant.[91]

The use of public opinion polls would be greatly enhanced by creation of a national public opinion research center, a possibility endorsed by Chernenko at the June 1983 plenum of the Central Committee. According to a recent article by Darrell Slider, such a center would be based on the experience of a Public Opinion Council established in Georgia in 1975 at the urging of Eduard Shevardnadze during his tenure as the head of the Georgian Communist Party.[92] Shevardnadze's appointment as foreign minister by Party Secretary Gorbachev clearly shows he has influence; the reference to "improving the system for study of public opinion" in the 1985 Draft Program of the CPSU may reflect his interest. As of June 1987, however, no national center for public opinion research had yet been established.

Any increase in the use of public opinion polls to determine what people think of their government, or want from it, is likely to be carefully supervised. In the first place, such usage would almost certainly be strictly controlled. Even an enthusiast like Safarov urges that legal regulations be adopted regarding who may employ polling methods and on what questions; authorized usage, he argues, should be decided by the executive organs within

[90] Safarov, *Obshchestvennoe mnenie i gosudarstvennoe upravleni*, pp. 82, 109–113.

[91] Ibid., pp. 49ff.

[92] Slider, "Party-Sponsored Public Opinion Research in the Soviet Union," esp. pp. 217–225.

defined areas of their jurisdiction.[93] Deputies would presumably have to receive permission to conduct opinion surveys. The most serious limitation to the broader use of objective survey research to discover popular political attitudes and policy preferences may be that decision-makers do not want to hear the answers. This certainly was the case with the sociological investigation in 1971. Whether a new generation of Soviet leaders will be more willing to listen to and confront difficult issues when they are raised is as yet unknown.

Informal Contact with Deputies

Citizens can also communicate their needs, problems, and proposals to deputies through direct, informal conversation. During the course of a normal day, deputies may receive contacts related to their work as an elected representative from friends, family, colleagues at work, or constituents. Whether accidental or intentional, initiated by the deputy or by constituents, what distinguishes these contacts is that they take place outside the official channels already described. Deputies are encouraged to make such contacts and are strongly urged to become familiar with their district by going door to door and conversing with constituents much in the manner of an urban committeeman or precinct captain in the United States.[94]

There is no evidence as to how conscientiously deputies do this, but there is reason to question how familiar most deputies are with the districts they represent: more often than not, they do not live in the district. Data based on a study carried out by Leizerov in Belorussia in the mid-1970s showed that in five of the city and district soviets for which he provided figures, out of 950 cases, 463 deputies (48.7 percent) lived in their district. The magnitude of the

[93] Safarov, *Obshchestvennoe mnenie i gosudarstvennoe upravleni*, pp. 112–113.

[94] See, e.g., Bezuglov, *Deputat v Sovete*, p. 44.

problem becomes more clear when it is realized that Leizerov cites this data to show how much better matters had
become in these exemplary districts! After all, a decade
earlier things had been much worse: out of 1,108 deputies
in five district soviets in Minsk, only 14 lived in the district
and another 33 lived just nearby.[95]

There are two other reasons why informal deputy-constituent links are likely to be less than optimal. For one
thing, aside from the high rate of turnover at each election, deputies who are reelected are more often than not
returned from a district other than the one they previously
represented. In a more recent study, using data from
1978–80, Leizerov indicated that the degree of reelection
from the same district had been as high as 98 percent in
one city soviet but that this was rare; in two of the soviets,
not one of the deputies who had been reelected ran in the
same district he or she had previously represented.[96] Still
another difficulty is presented by the practice of representing two or more districts at different levels of government
at the same time. Out of 1,469 deputies in sixteen district
soviets in Belorussia in 1974–76, almost one in every five
held two seats.[97] In the absence of corrective regulatory action, the problems described above will probably continue
to impede the development of close informal deputy-constituent contacts. After all, a deputy who does not live in
his or her district, and who is unlikely to be reelected from
it, will be less motivated to get to know it well, even
though electoral districts in the Soviet Union are quite small.
An equally important consequence is that citizens living in
the district are also less likely to become familiar with their
representative, a problem that we will look at later.

One final aspect of the contact that takes place between
deputy and constituent deserves attention—the problem

[95] Leizerov, *Demokraticheskie formy deiatel'nosti mestnykh Sovetov*, p. 125.

[96] Leizerov, *Konstitutsionnyi printsip glasnosti*, p. 131.

[97] Leizerov, *Demokraticheskie formy deiatel'nosti mestnykh Sovetov*, p. 113.

of bribery and corruption. That bribery and corruption exist can hardly be doubted. Especially during the anticorruption campaign in the wake of Brezhnev's passing from the scene, the degree of official misconduct at all levels became a persistent theme in the Soviet mass media, and even more so under Gorbachev's leadership.[98] How pervasive these illegal contacts are at the local level is difficult to determine. No systematic Soviet research has been published, and the scholarly literature merely hints that such practices take place, usually in the context of warning young deputies to beware of improper advances.[99]

A Western study of 1,161 former Soviet citizens who left in the last few years of Brezhnev's tenure as Party General Secretary concludes that bribery and corruption are widespread. Data from the project "Bureaucratic Encounters in the Soviet Union" conducted by the Center for Russian and East European Studies at the University of Michigan indicated that three-fourths of the respondents believed that at least half of all Soviet officials derived private material gain from their public office, and 46 percent suggested that a gift would be needed to prompt a recalcitrant official to provide proper service. In response to a question about the "main preconditions for success in life in the USSR," 42 percent mentioned "connections" (sviazy) first, 62.1 percent recommended the use of bribery or connections to get into a university, and 57.2 percent suggested the same means to get a good job after graduating. The authors of the study conclude, "Clearly, informal, and even illegal, means are those that immediately suggest themselves to Soviet people who have to interact with the state bureaucracy."[100]

Such evidence should be viewed with caution. Because the sample was not random, we must question how rep-

[98] A perusal of the *Current Digest of the Soviet Press* for 1983–1986 would yield a good sampling of such articles.
[99] See, e.g., Bezuglov, *Deputat v sovete*, p. 60.
[100] DiFranceisco and Gitelman, "Soviet Political Culture," p. 611.

resentative this opinion is even of the group it purports to reflect—77 percent of whom were Jewish and 40 percent of whom were highly educated. If it is true that Jews especially are the target of nationality quotas on access to higher education, as the article suggests, it would help explain the findings regarding higher education. Moreover, corruption is notoriously difficult to define, especially the terms *blat* (influence) and *sviazy* (connections). If a sample of, say, Americans, Italians, or Filipinos were asked how important "connections" were to gaining "success in life," would the answer be much different? What if the sample were narrowed to a disaffected group living in New York City, Rome, or Manila? Would it be surprising if 60 percent said that a bribe might help a police officer overlook a minor traffic violation, the figure reported by those interviewed by DiFranceisco and Gitelman? In the absence of other data, of course, these findings have a certain usefulness in directing our attention to phenomena that doubtless exist in Soviet political life, as they do elsewhere.

Recall

In the United States and other Western democracies, when elected representatives fail to perform their functions to the satisfaction of their constituents, the available remedy is to vote somebody else into that office at the next election. The ability to "throw the bum out" is ensured when there is a possibility of competitive multiparty elections. In the absence of alternative candidates at each election, what can Soviet voters do if they are dissatisfied with the work of their deputy? The answer Soviet authorities give is that citizens can exert direct control over their elected representative by exercising the right of recall (*otzyv*). Recall is considered an indispensable part of the *mandat imperatif* by which deputies act as "instructed delegates" whose function it is to implement the will of the people as expressed through voter mandates and at meetings held to discuss the deputies' reports. Recall is intended to be the legal guarantee that deputies who fail to do as they have been instructed can be replaced. In the words of one Soviet specialist on this question,

> The imperativeness of the deputy's mandate is understood to mean the unconditional implementation of the will of the voters in conformity with the law, and the answerability of the deputy for his actions, the strictest measure of which is the possibility of his recall by the voters. The voter mandates and the reports of the deputy, without the right of recall, would deprive the mandate of its imperative character."[101]

Like the institution of the voter mandates, the origins of the use of recall can be traced back to the Estates General in sixteenth-century France, but their approved ideological lineage is found in the description of the commune in Marx's *Civil War in France*, according to which elected councillors were "responsible and revocable at short terms." The concept was enthusiastically adopted by Lenin and indeed was the subject of the earliest piece of legislation dealing with the deputies, the decree of the Central Executive Committee of December 4, 1917, "On the Right to Recall Deputies." Drafted by Lenin with the convening of the short-lived Constituent Assembly of January 18, 1918, in mind, recall was to become a mechanism for replacing elected officials who were unsympathetic to the Bolshevik cause with those who were sympathetic.[102]

[101] A. V. Zinov'ev, "Imperativnyi kharakhter deputatskogo mandata," *Pravovodenie*, no. 1 (1984), p. 43. The late expert A. I. Lepeshkin also used this formulation ("Narodnoe predstavitel'stvo v Sovetskom gosudarstve," *SGiP*, no. 6 [1977], p. 6).

[102] Anticipating a multiparty Assembly, Lenin argued before the executive committee meeting of December 4, 1917, that popular support for other parties would change after the workers saw how their interests were being misrepresented, that they should not be stuck with representatives they no longer wanted, and that they should therefore be able to recall them (V. I. Lenin, "Draft Decree on the Right of Recall," December 2, 1917; and "Report on the Right of Recall to the Central Commit-

The right of recall was specified in article 78 of the 1918 Constitution, but left to republican level legislation in the Constitution of 1924. In these years, and especially during the process of collectivization, the right of recall was apparently widely used—or perhaps misused—as it could be employed as a tool for removing those who had any doubts about Stalin's plans for economic development. In the first half of 1931 alone, 23,000 deputies were recalled from village soviets, and 1,000 from those in urban areas.[103] Paradoxically, formal inclusion of recall as a right in article 142 of the 1936 Constitution was accompanied by its virtual disappearance from use in the twenty years that followed, a decline strongly criticized by Khrushchev and Voroshilov at the 20th Party Congress in speeches containing thinly veiled threats that a revival of its use would be directed against those "who have not justified their constituents' trust."[104]

The main reason offered in the Soviet literature for the evanescence of the use of recall after 1936 was the failure to establish procedures for doing so.[105] Leaving aside the question of whether clearly defined procedures existed prior to 1936, when recall was widely used, this deficiency was remedied by the law of October 30, 1959, on "Proce-

tee," December 4, 1917, in *Collected Works*, vol. 26, pp. 336–340. After dissolution of the Assembly, recall became a means of purging non-Bolsheviks at all levels. Popova describes this as the "main significance" of recall at this time (S. M. Popova, *Otzyv deputatov mestnykh Sovetov narodnykh deputatov* [Moscow: VIUZI, 1982], p. 16).

[103] A. I. Lepeshkin, *Kurs sovetskogo gosudarstva i prava* (Moscow: Iurid. Lit., 1961), p. 395, as cited by Friedgut, *Political Participation in the USSR*, p. 133.

[104] Khrushchev's speech, as well as portions of Voroshilov's, are translated in *Current Soviet Policies*, vol. 2 (New York: Praeger, 1957), pp. 53, 115.

[105] This point was made in the January 22, 1957, CPSU resolution on work of the deputies cited earlier and is reiterated in Popova, *Otzyv deputatov*, p. 10.

dures Governing the Recall of a Deputy of the Supreme Soviet of the USSR" and by analogous republic-level legislation adopted in 1960 for the local soviets.[106] While Soviet legislation does not specify reasons for recalling deputies, article 6 of the 1972 Law on the Status of Deputies states that those who "have not justified the voters' confidence or who have acted in a manner unworthy of their high calling" are subject to recall. This seems to mean that deputies may be recalled for failing to fulfill their legal obligations as elected officials, as well as for doing things they should not. In the first category, the specialist literature mentions failure to meet regularly with constituents, to make reports, to hold priyoms, and to work to implement voter mandates. In the second category are violations of the norms of proper conduct, such as drunkenness, "amoral behavior," public abusiveness, and poor labor discipline. According to S. M. Popova, the reasons for recall fall in the second category far more often than in the first. As she candidly notes, the social organizations responsible for initiating recall procedures are unlikely to do so for reasons related to nonperformance of duties, more often acting only when the behavior of a deputy becomes so publicly obnoxious that recall cannot be avoided.[107] Popova and Leizerov, among others, have suggested that the law on the recall of deputies would be strengthened if a list were included specifying the reasons for which action should be taken.[108]

Recall is initiated by the workers' collective that originally nominated the deputy, or by one of the mass social

[106] *Vedomosti Verkhovnogo Soveta SSSR*, 1959, no. 44, item 222; as amended 1979, no. 17, item 278. The RSFSR law "On Procedures for Recall of Local Soviet Deputies in the RSFSR" of October 27, 1960, as amended on December 12, 1979, is in *Vedomosti Verkhovnogo Soveta RSFSR*, 1979, no. 51, item 1273.

[107] Popova, *Otzyv deputata*, pp. 14–16; see also Sheremet's comments in *Kommentarii k zakonu*, p. 69.

[108] Leizerov, *Demokraticheskie formy deiatel'nosti*, p. 129.

organizations, at a meeting about which the deputy is informed. In the village soviets, proceedings can be begun by the electors themselves only at general meetings. The minutes of the initial meeting set forth the reasons for considering recall and are sent to the corresponding executive committee and its Mandate Commission to verify that proper procedures have been followed. They then submit the question to a session of the soviet that has the sole right to call for a vote by the electorate on the question of recall. Neither the executive committee, the Mandate Commission, the soviet, nor the special district commission established by them to see that the vote itself is properly conducted can raise the question of recall or decide the issue, though this apparently was once the case and, according to one informant, still takes place.[109] When the date for a recall vote is set, meetings with the electors are held where both sides may be heard and minutes are kept. A simple majority of the electors voting is needed to recall. The results are certified by the executive committee and published within five days.

The literature stresses the importance of the right of the deputy to present his or her case. In fact, the procedure is less neutral than it seems. First, raising the recall question is not a trivial matter. If the reasons offered for recall consideration prove to be frivolous, they would not survive the screening of the executive committee. By the time the question reaches the voters, therefore, there is an implicit assumption created that some grounds for recall exist. Second, there is no limit on how long the executive committee has to review the materials given it before reporting to the soviet. Because local deputies' terms are only two-and-a-half years, delay would be one way to avoid the proceedings altogether, as well as the time, trouble, and potential embarrassment that comes with them. Finally, the district

[109] Popova, *Otzyv deputatov*, p. 22. Popova was not the source regarding continued malpractice.

commission established to oversee that fairness is observed is itself comprised of four to ten representatives from precisely those organizations that originally raised the question of recall, including the local party organization. Perhaps for these reasons recall is generally considered an extreme measure, to be used only if other means fail.[110]

There are other ways to deal with a deputy who has not performed up to expectations. These include criticism of a deputy's work by constituents who hear the deputy's reports at meetings, withdrawal from office at the deputy's own request, or warnings from the executive committee or the organization who first nominated the deputy. The threat of public embarrassment may be enough to bring about the desired effect. It is possible that deputies who are not performing their duties well are encouraged to resign rather than be subjected to the embarrassment, and trouble, of the recall process, especially if no public scandal is involved. The much greater number of deputies leaving office before the end of their terms (see Table 5-4) could be interpreted in this way, although the majority seem to be related to career moves, death, or other normal circumstances. In practice, it may prove simpler just to wait until the next election and nominate someone else. In a sense, this is one way to "throw the bum out," except, of course, it is not the electorate who is making the decision to do so.

The statistics on the use of recall support the view that it is a rarely used measure, though clearly it has been used more frequently since Stalin's death, and frequently enough that it should be taken seriously by deputies. Between 1960 and 1985, approximately 10,000 deputies were recalled;[111] more than 100 of those occurred in 1961, 466 in

110 See, e.g., Sheremet's discussion in *Kommentarii k zakonu*, p. 69.

111 Zinoviev, "Imperativnyi kharakter deputatskogo mandata," reports that more than 9,000 were recalled between 1960 and 1982. Data for 1982, 1983, and 1984, available in the statistical annual *Nekotorye voprosy organizatsionnoi raboty*, suggest that the figure approaches 10,000.

TABLE 5-4. Deputies Subjected to Recall, Selected Years, 1970–84

Level of soviet	1970	1980	1982	1983	1984
Regional[a]	8	0	0	5	19
Raion	70	34	9	85	114
City	43	11	1	38	69
City borough	13	7	1	15	19
Settlement	37	15	3	26	25
Village	305	138	45	225	270
Total no. of deputies recalled	476	205	59	394	516
Total no. of deputies vacating seats	43,747	26,637	10,602	48,448	34,288
Total no. of deputies	2,065,761	2,274,861	2,285,023	2,289,859	2,290,376

SOURCES: Data for 1970 come from *SDT*, no. 6 (1971). The remaining figures come from *Nekotorye voprosy* published in 1981, 1983, 1984, and 1985, in the section entitled "Izmeneniia v sostav deputatov."

[a] Includes data for autonomous regions (separate data not available).

1963, 541 in 1968, 476 in 1970, 479 in 1974, 205 in 1980, 59 in 1982, and 394 in 1983.[112] Table 5-4 offers a more detailed picture of the use of recall by level of government over time.

These figures offer a basis for several conclusions. First, given such a large number of deputies, the use of recall is rare indeed. Even in the case of deputies vacating office

[112] The figure for 1961 is from Popova, *Otzyv deputatov*, p. 12; for 1963, see *SDT*, no. 5 (1964), p. 95; for 1968, see ibid., no. 5 (1969), p. 96; for 1970, see ibid., no. 6 (1971), p. 83. The remaining figures are found in *Nekotorye voprosy organizatsionnoi raboty* for 1976, 1981, and 1983 under the section entitled "Izmeneniia v sostav deputatov."

before their term is finished, only about one in every one hundred does so as a result of recall. Second, roughly three out of every five cases of recall occur in the rural soviets. Because rural deputies account for approximately the same portion of deputies generally, this is hardly surprising. What is something of an anomaly, however, is the decline in the use of recall, especially in the last years of the Brezhnev era, despite an increase in the number of deputies and inclusion of recall in both the 1972 Law on the Status of Deputies and the 1977 Constitution. Part of the explanation may be the more tolerant attitude toward official misconduct in Brezhnev's last years, in which case the increased number of recalled deputies in 1983 could reflect Andropov's campaign against corruption. Even Chernenko, in his speech on the soviets to the April 1984 plenary session of the Central Committee, warned officials who had become accustomed to the old ways that they had best "draw the necessary conclusions" from his criticisms of their work. Given Gorbachev's apparent commitment to continue this process, a continued rise in the number of recalls seems likely, at least for a while.

PUBLIC OPINION ABOUT THE DEPUTY'S ACTIVITIES

Soviet citizens may use any of the several mechanisms available, described above, for communicating their policy preferences or personal needs to those who represent them in local government. Some of these mechanisms are well established in law and practice, others are less so. It also seems clear that deputies expend a considerable number of man-hours trying to deal with constituency problems. In a study published in 1976, some 500 deputies in two districts in the city of Leningrad in 1969 and 1971 reported spending an average of twenty to twenty-three hours a month on deputy activities.[113] Most of the deputies interviewed by the author in the Lenin district of Moscow in 1984 spent twenty to thirty hours a month, and only one spent less than fifteen hours. Given the variety of opportunities available to citizens for contacting deputies and the evident investment of deputy time and energy in responding to them, what does the public think of the deputies' work? How often do citizens turn to their representatives, and with what expectations?

In answering these questions, the author is reminded of a chance encounter with a twenty-four-year-old student of fine arts at Moscow State University. When informed that the purpose of the author's visit to the Soviet Union was to conduct research on deputies to the local soviets, the student responded, apparently quite sincerely, by asking what a local soviet was. She had never heard of them. Also unscientific, but pointing in the same direction, were the responses of twenty-six senior law school students at Moscow State University to a questionnaire designed by the author to determine whether they had much knowledge about their deputies. While twelve students could name at least one of their representatives to the Supreme Soviet, only two could name their local deputy. Out of twenty-six, nineteen had neither met their deputy nor ever attended a meeting with the deputy; only seven knew where their city borough soviet was located. While such a sample is an inadequate basis for drawing conclusions about popular attitudes toward the deputies' work, if students in the law faculty of the most prestigious university in the Soviet Union cannot answer such questions, what can one expect of the populace at large? It could be argued that similar encounters by a Soviet professor with American students might produce similar results and that students are in general a poor indication of levels of political knowledge. Still, lacking published research on levels of

[113] Alekseev and Perfil'ev, *Printsipy i tendentsii*, p. 280.

political cognition in the Soviet Union, unscientific evidence suggests that most people do not know who their local representative is. The one published Soviet study that did ask respondents to name their local representative tends to support this conclusion: out of a total sample of 7,767 voters in Irkutsk questioned in 1961, slightly less than 10 percent could identify their district-level deputy.[114]

A more complete picture of citizens' attitudes toward the work of the deputies emerges from two studies using survey data, one by Friedgut based on interviews with 300 émigrés to Israel, which appeared in print in 1983, and the other by two Soviet social scientists using a random sample of 1,020 respondents from the industrial city of Taganrog, published in Moscow in 1980. Although subject to the same reservations about representativeness noted earlier in connection with the study of émigré opinion by DiFranceisco and Gitelman, the findings reported by Friedgut have the benefit of independent confirmation. At least in some cases, similar results were reported in Taganrog, which suggests that any anti-Soviet bias in the Friedgut study was successfully minimized.

Friedgut found that the assessment of the deputies' work by former Soviet citizens is a "mosaic of contrasts." With respect to political cognition, the evidence supports the conclusion above that most Soviets know relatively little about local government: 13 percent knew how often local elections were held, only 7.7 percent could name their local deputy, and 11.1 percent named a deputy to the Supreme Soviet, while 108 (36 percent) reported ever having met a government representative.[115] The evidence with respect to affective and evaluative orientations toward locally elected officials was more positive. While close to three of every five respondents believed that deputies

[114] V. A. Perttsik, "Puti sovershenstvovanniia deiatel'nosti deputatov mestnykh Sovetov," *SGiP*, no. 7 (1967), p. 17.

[115] Friedgut, "The Soviet Citizen's Perception of Local Government," in Jacobs, *Soviet Local Politics and Government*, p. 116.

were generally little known or unknown by the public, they did seem to think that those who were deputies were chosen for positive qualities, the most salient of which was being a leading worker.[116]

The data on how these former citizens perceived the functions of the deputies were particularly interesting. While on balance the work of the deputy is seen as more useful to the regime than to the citizen, there is recognition for this latter role as well. According to these respondents, the functions of the deputy include the following: to direct citizens to administrators (215 responses), to explain party policy (214), to inform the executive committee of citizens' needs (197), to organize the public for volunteer work (191), to engage in political activity among citizens (174), to instruct executive committees (147), to supervise the provision of services (130), and to supervise citizens' behavior (113).[117] The evaluation of the activities of the soviet itself (as distinguished from the functions of the deputy) is more favorable. While "implementation of party decisions" received the highest number of responses (249 out of 1,212), it was closely followed by the policy-making function of "decides on local development" (230 responses). When saliency is calculated, the representation of local interests to the central authorities emerges as the most important function of the soviet. Finally, the respondents in this sample expected more polite and atten-

[116] Ibid., p. 120.

[117] Ibid., p. 121. Friedgut's interpretation is that these responses indicate a perception by citizens that, when it comes to what deputies do, "service to the regime precedes service to the public," and he specifies the most frequently identified function—"to direct citizens to administrators"—as being in this category. However, in my eight years of experience as an elected official representative in suburban Philadelphia, one of the things I did most frequently in that capacity was guide otherwise unknowing citizens to the proper administrative department at the proper level of government. Whether this function, as well as others mentioned by Friedgut's respondents, constitute service to the public or to the state is debatable.

tive treatment by their elected representatives than from
the administrative apparatus. Friedgut concludes that
there is "a nucleus of cooperative and active respondents,
who, though a minority, work within established institutions for their satisfaction, and appear to have a civic sense
of competence that they may as citizens expect service and
satisfaction from official institutions."[118]

The study based on a survey of 1,020 citizens of the industrial city of Taganrog in southern Russia offers additional insight into how Soviet citizens view their deputies.
Carried out in the years 1967–74, the purpose of the study
was to determine the most effective means for informing
the population. In one section, however, the researchers
compared five channels used by citizens to contact local
organs of government: letters, personal contact with administrators, personal contact with deputies, meetings of
their workers' collective and other social organizations
(party, Union, Komsomol), and the mass media. The results indicated that nearly two of every five citizens (38
percent) had never made any effort to contact government
and that only about one out of five did so with any regu-
larity (with two-thirds of the contacts coming from only 23
percent of the population). Of the various means studied
for transmitting information to the authorities, conversation with the deputies ranked fourth out of eight in importance: 53 percent took part in meetings at their place of
work, 15 percent reported personally contacting workers
in the administration, 15 percent said they talked with the
heads of industries and other institutions, 12 percent went
to their deputies, 9 percent participated in other public
meetings, 9 percent sent letters to the editor, 9 percent
more sent letters to the organs of administration, and 5
percent wrote pieces in their factory or office newspapers.[119]

[118] Ibid., pp. 129–130.
[119] Grushin and Onikova, *Massovaia informatsia*, pp. 381–382.

Who contacts the deputies? Each of the five main "channels" of citizen contact examined by the authors was broken down by gender, age, education, and social position. Those who used the deputy as their "channel" to contact government were more likely to be women (the only one of the five categories in which this was the case) and to be older. They were less likely to have finished high school than any other group. When compared with those whose contacts were directly with administrators, individuals contacting their deputies were more likely to be workers (39 percent to 13 percent) or pensioners (21 percent to 8 percent) than members of the intelligentsia (6 percent compared with 30 percent).[120] The study also concluded that the respondents were more likely to aim their messages at administrators than at deputies by about a three-to-one ratio. The average volume of contacts per month with the former was 1,450, with the latter only 545.[121] These findings conform to the opinions of the people interviewed by Friedgut.

Focusing only on the 12 percent who reported using deputies as a channel for communicating with agencies of local government, the Taganrog research indicated that half of these had contacted their deputy only once during the deputy's term of office (at that time, the term of office was two years). Table 5-5 provides a more detailed description of deputy-constituent contact in Taganrog.

What kinds of issues are brought to the attention of deputies in Taganrog? The figures in table 5-6 show that citizen contacts with deputies are more likely to have to do with personal problems (50 percent) than problems affecting others in the community (47 percent), although this balance is not as one-sided as might be expected. More predictable is the subject matter: housing problems, public works, and retail trade are ranked first, second, and third.

[120] Ibid., p. 423.
[121] Ibid., p. 379.

TABLE 5-5. Frequency of Deputy-Constituent Contact in Taganrog, RSFSR (In Percent)

Respondent had met personally with a deputy and spoken at a constituency meeting.	2
Respondent had met personally with a deputy, and attended a constituency meeting without speaking.	5
Respondent had met personally with deputy, did not attend any constituency meetings.	5
Subtotal: those personally meeting with deputy	12
Respondent spoke at meetings, without personally meeting deputy.	2
Respondent attended meetings, without speaking or meeting deputy.	21
Respondent never attended meetings, had no contact with deputies.	65
	100%

SOURCE: Grushin and Onikova, *Massovaia informatsiia v sovetskom promyshlennom gorode*, p. 387.
NOTE: Sample = 1,020.

One interesting conclusion that emerges from Table 5-6, and indeed from the study as a whole, is that meetings in the workplace appear to be the most widely used arena for public discussion of matters of "general concern." By contrast, letters to executive and administrative officials usually deal more with individual problems (77 percent).

THE DEPUTY AS OMBUDSMAN

The evidence in this chapter gives a sketch of how the public views the work of the deputies. It is likely that only about 10 percent of Soviet citizens know who their local deputy is, and that only about 10 to 15 percent have had personal contact with their deputy. A majority of Soviet citizens, perhaps two-thirds, do not appear to be active politically—except by voting or through membership in "nongovernmental" associations, such as a trade union, the Komsomol, a workers' collective, or some other social organization. Those who are active do appear to enjoy some success in getting the government to respond to their expressed needs. As one of the mechanisms for getting action, the deputy appears to be viewed favorably, both in terms of personal characteristics and as someone who can represent constituents' interests. As for the relatively low number of those who have made contact with their deputy, it should be pointed out that Verba and Nie, in their study of political participation in the United States, found that citizen-initiated contacts with local officials ranked among the participatory acts requiring the most effort—only 20 percent reported ever having done so.[122]

There are limits to the deputy's role as representative. Deputies are not going to confront the regime over its policies in Afghanistan, nor are they going to question the leadership's wisdom in exiling Andrei Sakharov to Gorki, to name two more obvious examples of recent policy. It also seems clear that the citizen's view of local government is service-oriented and that citizens are more likely to make contact with government for personal needs, such as housing and pensions, than to make requests that would benefit the community as a whole. It must also be acknowledged that when citizens turn to local government they are more likely to turn to officials in the administration than to the deputy, in the belief that such contacts are more likely to bear fruit; the deputy is someone to whom one turns if the administrator is uncooperative.

In assessing the role of the Soviet deputy, however, it is only fair to note that protests over national policy are rarely encountered at the level of municipal government

[122] Verba and Nie, *Participation in America*, pp. 31, 52.

TABLE 5-6. Citizen Concerns and Channels of Communication, Taganrog, RSFSR (In Percent)

| Areas of Concern | Channels of Communication | | | | |
	Letters to administrators (n = 797)	Letters to editors of newspapers (n = 1,198)	Conversations with administrators (n = 4,257)	Conversations with deputies (n = 4,257)	Presentations at workplace meetings (n = 510)
Industry construction	1	14	15	5	
Transport	2	8	3	6	
Public works, everyday services	6	15	4	19	
Retail, trade, including food	3	9	6	10	2
Housing problems	33	7	13	26	
Public education	2	4	10	7	7
Culture & recreation	0	4	7	1	
Health services	3	7	12	4	0

Social security	2	4	6	4	0
Public safety	36	8	4	6	6
Problems of upbringing & family	2	5	11	0	15
Activity of organs of administration, social organizations	6	4	8	3	22
Press, radio, TV	0	6	0	0	0
Other	4	5	1	9	0
Total all areas of concern	100	100	100	100	100
TYPES OF CONCERN					
Purely personal concerns	77	46	39	50	4
General concerns	23	54	60	47	64
Concerns combining personal & public interest	0	0	0	0	32
Total all types of concern	100	100	99[a]	97[a]	100

SOURCE: Grushin and Onikova, *Massovaia informatsiia v sovetskom promyshlennom gorode*, pp. 411, 415.

[a] As given in source.

in Western democracies, although the opportunities for doing so are certainly greater. Moreover, most of the concerns of local government in these countries are also with the provision of services. Perhaps what is most unexpected and interesting in the picture of deputy-constituent contact that emerges from the data is that a substantial amount of the contact that does take place appears to be related to community needs and that, even among the émigrés interviewed by Friedgut, the deputy was perceived as having at least some policy-making role.[123] The question of what the deputy does in council is the subject of the next chapter, but on the basis of the evidence presented in this one, it would appear that as someone who represents constituents' interests the deputy functions as something of an ombudsman—at least for that minority of the population who attempt to use the deputy in that way.

[123] Friedgut, "The Soviet Citizen's Perception of Local Government," p. 122.

CHAPTER SIX

The Deputy in Council

WHEN SOVIET CITIZENS communicate their preferences
and demands to those whom they have elected, they are
actively seeking to exert influence over governmental decisions that have a bearing on their well-being, both individual and collective. In Chapter 1, we defined effective
participation as the involvement of citizens in the making
and implementation of governmental decisions affecting
their lives and emphasized the importance of constituent
contact in this process. But what, if anything, can deputies
to the local soviets do to respond to the expressed wishes
of their constituents? To what extent can the deputies take
part in the shaping of decisions that affect the communities they have been chosen to represent? In answering
these questions, we turn from the role of the deputy as a
recipient of communications from constituents to the deputy's role as a decision-maker, that is, to the deputy's
work in council. The focus will be on the activities of the
deputies related to sessions of the local soviet and to their
work in the standing committees, and on the deputies' relationship to the two other key actors in the decision-making process—the executive committee and the local party
organization.

SESSIONS OF THE LOCAL SOVIETS

.The fourteenth (and final) session of the Lenin city borough soviet for the eighteenth term (*sozyv*) was held on a
cold and snowy December 26, 1984, at the Iunost' Hotel,
not far from the Lenin Stadium in Moscow.[1] Because only

[1] To the best of my knowledge, only two other eyewitness descriptions

deputies and those with invitations are allowed to attend sessions of the soviet, there was some delay at the entrance to the hotel while people rummaged through their heavy clothing seeking proper identification, which was requested politely but firmly by an older woman standing just inside the door. The session itself took place in a large, brightly lit, modern auditorium into which I was escorted by the deputy who had arranged my invitation. We arrived just as the meeting was to begin, so most of the 250 or so deputies and other invited guests were already seated. On the stage, behind a cloth-covered table, sat members of the executive committee and a few others who had been invited to address the session—about twenty in all. A lighted podium with a microphone stood to the left of the stage.

The meeting was opened at exactly 3:00 p.m. by the president of the executive committee. The first item of business was to elect the presiding officers for the session, a male president and a female secretary, both already seated at the center of the stage. The chief presiding officer then read the draft agenda (translated below, along with the amount of time scheduled for each issue) and asked if there were any other items the deputies wanted to add:

AGENDA

*14th Session of the Lenin District Soviet of the 18th Term
December 26, 1984*

1. On the plan for economic and social development of the Lenin borough for 1985 and on the course of fulfillment of the plan for economic and social development for 1984.

---

of a local soviet session have been published since World War II: a session of the Leningrad city borough (in Moscow) in 1964 (see Morton, "The Leningrad District of Moscow: An Inside Look," p. 206) and a budgetary session of the Oktyabr' City Borough Soviet in 1970 (see Theodore H. Friedgut, "A Local Soviet at Work: The 1970 Budget and Budget Discussions of the Oktyabr' Borough Soviet of Moscow," in Jacobs, *Soviet Local Politics and Government*, chap. 9).

2. On the Lenin borough budget for 1985 and its fulfillment for 1983.
3. Information on the work of territorial groups no. 3
   and no. 6.
4. On fulfilling the decision of the 7th session of the
   18th term, "Report on the Work of Department of
   Roads and Public Works," and the critical remarks expressed by deputies in the discussion of this issue.

*Regulations and Procedures for
the Work of the Session*

to the speaker on item 1	up to 40 mins.
to the speaker on item 2	up to 20 mins.
to the speaker on item 3	up to 10 mins.
to the speaker on item 4	up to 10 mins.
to the co-reports on items 1 and 2	up to 15 mins.
to the co-reports on item 3	up to 10 mins.
to those participating in the debate	up to 10 mins.

There will be a break after one-and-one-half hours of
work.

There being no items to add, the first speaker, a business-
like woman in her late thirties, who was the head of the
planning commission and a member of the ispolkom, delivered the report (*doklad*) of the executive committee on
how well the Lenin borough had fulfilled the economic
plan for 1984 and about the basic indices and goals of the
plan for 1985.

By Western standards, the presentation of the main item
of business on the agenda seemed scripted and dry, even
ritualistic. Following what appears to be a standard format, the speaker began by praising the amount that had
been accomplished by the soviet in 1984. Seemingly end-
less statistics were offered to show that various economic
goals had been fulfilled or overfulfilled. Next came a
lengthy list of shortcomings: the industrial enterprises lo-

cated in the borough had not met their quotas in certain sectors; the assortment, quality, and availability of goods had fallen below the people's demands; labor productivity in the construction and repair organizations was still inadequate; serious problems remained in the work of the borough's food and vegetable distribution agency, and so forth. Finally, a list of the ispolkom's proposals for economic and social development in 1985 was read. The whole process took nearly all the forty minutes set aside for the speaker, who managed to invoke the name of CPSU General Secretary Konstantin Chernenko no fewer than eight times. Because most of those in the audience, including presumably all the deputies, were supposed to have received the ten-page draft decision of the executive committee beforehand, such an exercise seemed redundant, unless it was assumed that few had bothered to read it.

The reading of the ispolkom's report on the economic plan was followed by another report, this one on the budget, read by the head of the Financial Department, a woman in her mid-fifties. While similar in format, this report had the virtue of being half as long and so took only the twenty minutes set aside for it by the chairman. These two executive committee reports (*doklady*) were followed by six co-reports (*sodoklady*), each lasting five to ten minutes. Co-reports provide a chance for representatives of standing committees to evaluate the preceding reports as they affected the areas in which their standing committees exercised oversight. Co-reports were given, for example, by the chairpersons of the standing committees on budget and finance, on industry and transportation, on construction, on housing, on everyday services, and on trade. Although co-reports potentially represent an opportunity for deputies to put their concerns and differences of opinion with the ispolkom on the record, tradition seems to dictate the presentation of public consensus: any real grievances are aired and resolved beforehand. The co-reports presented at this session were at most mildly critical exhortations to do better, aimed as much at the deputies as at the ispolkom.

The presentation of the co-reports was followed by a break, during which many deputies retired to the buffet for refreshments, including plenty of coffee and tea, or talked among themselves; the number returning from the break was somewhat diminished. Those who stayed heard the liveliest speech of the day grandiloquently delivered by the borough party first secretary. A vigorous man of about sixty, the secretary was a confident public speaker whose sense of timing was adroitly mixed with touches of humour. His theme also was the economic and social plan for 1985. According to him, "the economic situation can not be considered normal, one may better say absurd . . . we demand that the ispolkom do more to improve these affairs . . . to fulfill and overfulfill the plan." Nor did he fail to provide the remedy: "greater discipline, greater organization, greater responsibility." His remarks added up to an enthusiast's pep talk, in tone similar to what a losing team hears from its coach at halftime.

Addressing the reawakened audience, the presiding officer informed them that seven people had spoken and asked if any others were scheduled to do so. Told there were none, he invited questions (*voprosy*) from deputies who had requested in writing to speak.[2] Two individuals did so. One was a woman who thought that the budget should allocate more money to health care. At this, a single member of the audience applauded enthusiastically—one of the rare instances of spontaneity during the whole session. The other speaker offered two propositions, one concerning labor discipline and one asking a minor revision in the budget figures. Both were approved unani-

---

[2] Morton reports that more than thirty written questions were read and answered briefly by the chairman of the ispolkom in the Leningrad borough case ("The Leningrad District of Moscow," p. 214). A similar procedure was followed at the previous session of the Lenin borough soviet.

mously. "Any other propositions from the deputies?" Hearing none, a vote was called on the two decisions (*resheniia*) that had been "debated": the economic plan and the budget for 1985. Not unexpectedly, the vote was also unanimous.

The third and fourth items on the agenda were dealt with by the deputies expeditiously. The fourth item was a report (*otchyot*) by the ispolkom on how it had improved its work on highway construction in the light of critical remarks made at an earlier session of the soviet and is self-explanatory. The third item, however, deserves fuller explanation. As described in the previous chapter, deputy groups consist of fifteen or twenty deputies representing contiguous districts. Because the problems faced by these districts are often overlapping, the deputies' ability to respond to the needs of their constituents may be improved if they act collectively. Spokespersons for territorial deputy groups no. 3 and no. 6 reported holding a total of about fifty such "conferences" (*zasedanii*) during their two-and-a-half-year terms, in the course of which they examined more than seventy issues related to public works, housing, food and everyday services, and education.

It became obvious from the speeches of these two deputies, however, that the purpose of the deputies' groups is to implement the decisions and policies of the soviet as much it is to communicate citizen concerns to it. Thus, the deputies spoke of organizing volunteer work brigades to repair old housing, of checking up on whether appropriate services were being provided, of organizing socialist competitions, of using the housing fund to prepare for winter, and so forth. The draft resolution, adopted unanimously and without comment by the soviet, left little room for doubt about what was expected of the deputy groups:

> To raise the responsibility of each deputy in his work, to mobilize the population of the district in fulfilling the decisions of the 26th CPSU Congress and the Plenums

of the Central Committee of CPSU, and to fulfill the adopted measures aimed at turning the district into a "model" district.[3]

From the point of view of deputy-initiated participation, the most interesting event occurred at the end of the session. Following the nomination and unanimous election of the new chief of the borough's People's Control Committee, the presiding officer recognized one of the deputies from the standing committee on education who wanted to introduce a deputy inquiry (*deputatskii zapros*). Although not on the agenda, such an inquiry has an official character and requires a response from the appropriate executive authority (see Chapter 5). In this case the deputy was a teacher at the largest school in the district, a plump, pleasant-looking, middle-aged woman, clearly determined to make her case. She noted the age of the school building, its need for repair, and that it was a danger to the children. Repairs, she said, had been promised in the 1985 plan but postponed. This was unacceptable. On behalf of the standing committee and of School 59 of the Lenin city borough school district, she demanded an explanation. The response: the executive committee will examine the inquiry and make its answer public at the next session. With this, the soviet concluded its business.

Allowing for differences attributed to regional peculiarities and the level of local government, the basic format used by the Lenin city borough was repeated at more than 300,000 sessions of the local soviets held in 1984 (see Table 6-1). For a Western observer familiar with the open contentiousness and vigorous criticism that often accompanies the conduct of business in American municipal government, the session of a soviet would seem a tame affair—indeed, a carefully choreographed presentation of tedious speeches and unanimous votes precluding sharp public

[3] "O rabote territoria'nykh deputatskikh grupp nos. 3, 6," *Reshenie Lenraisoveta goroda Moskvy*, December 26, 1984, p. 2.

TABLE 6-1. Local Soviet Sessions in 1984

Level of soviet	No. of soviets conducting sessions	No. of sessions held in 1984	Average no. of sessions per soviet	No. of sessions required by law
Regional	129	629	4.9	4
Autonomous region	8	39	4.9	4
Okrug	10	47	4.7	4
Raion	3,112	15,428	5.0	4
City	2,136	10,739	5.0	4
City borough	645	3,249	5.0	4
Settlement	3,819	22,703	5.9[a]	4–6[a]
Village	42,117	248,839	5.9[a]	4–6[a]
For all levels:	51,976	301,673	5.8	4–6

SOURCES: *Nekotorye voprosy*, 1984, p. 13; Barabashev and Sheremet, *Sovetskoe stroitel'stvo*, p. 182.

[a] The constitutions of the RSFSR, Kazakhstan, Azerbaidzhan, and Moldavia require settlement and village soviets to meet not less than six times a year, while the remaining eleven republics require not less than four sessions annually. Certain remote northern and eastern districts of the RSFSR are permitted fewer.

disagreement and inviting indifference. Yet according to Soviet law it is precisely at the sessions that deputies "resolve the most important issues within their jurisdiction" on the basis of "open, business-like discussion."[4] Contemporary Soviet legal theorists and specialists frequently quote the 1957 CPSU resolution attacking the conduct of sessions in the Stalinist period as establishing a model for how sessions should be conducted today.

[4] Article 11 of the Law on the Status of Deputies, "O statuse narodnykh deputatov v SSSR" (as amended), *Vedomosti Verkhovnogo Soveta SSSR*, 1979, no. 17, item 277.

Sessions must not be held for purposes of show or for bestowing ceremonies, or for formal approval on measures worked out beforehand, but for businesslike discussion and the resolution of real (*aktualnykh*) problems in the life of the area, region, city and district. . . . At the sessions a situation should be created which ensures the broad development of criticism and self-criticism so that deputies may thoroughly, and without haste, discuss the questions before them, express their opinions and proposals, put inquiries to the executive organs and economic managers and receive from them exhaustive answers.[5]

Yet it is clear that, almost thirty years after this was written, the divergence between theory and practice remains great. There is abundant evidence in both the scholarly literature and party resolutions to substantiate the persistence of formalism in the work of the soviets; it is not only Westerners who find them so.[6] One factor contributing to the absence of more spontaneous debate among the deputies is their large number: opening the floor to 250 participants without limits would invite chaos and paralyze the soviet in the conduct of its business. But the unwieldy number of deputies is not the main problem. The most important reason for the staged quality of most sessions is the continued dominance of the executive committee over

---

[5] Central Committee of the KPSS, "Ob uluchshenii deiatel'nosti Sovetov deputatov trudiashchikhsia i usilenii ikh sviazei s massami," January 22, 1957, *KPSS v rezoliutsiiakh* 7 (Moscow, 1971), p. 237. This formula is cited by V. I. Vasil'ev in *Kommentarii k zakonu* (1984), p. 100; Bezuglov, *Sovetskoe stroitel'stvo*, p. 330; and M. P. Shchetinina, *Deputat na sessii Soveta* (Moscow: Iurid. Lit., 1980), p. 10, among others.

[6] See e.g., Vasilev in *Kommentarii k zakonu*, p. 102, and Barabashev and Sheremet, *Sovetskoe stroitel'stvo*, pp. 222–227. These practices have also been criticized officially, e.g., "O praktike provedeniia sessii Sovetov narodnykh deputatov v Uzbekskoi SSR," *Vedomosti Verkhovnogo Soveta SSSR*, 1979, no. 37, item 607, and the speech of Konstantin Chernenko to the April 10, 1984, plenum of the Central Committee (Moscow: Politizdat, 1984), p. 8.

them, itself a legacy of the past. Few have confronted this practice more bluntly than N. G. Starovoitov. In an article published in November 1985 he wrote:

> The essential shortcomings remain window dressing, formalism, and the pursuit of quantitative rather than qualitative indicators. More than once the Central Committee has pointed out the need to achieve democracy, to suppress bureaucratic "overorganization" and formalism in relation to the conduct of sessions both in the Supreme Soviets and in many local soviets. Nonetheless, the conservative part of the local *apparat* is unwilling to part with the habits of the past, is afraid of criticism by the deputies, and frequently dominates the representative organs, the deputies. *In practice, the executive and administrative organs decide which questions will be introduced, who to invite to the sessions, and the list of speakers; they prepare the majority of reports and draft decisions, and often they prepare both the presentations and their contents.*[7]

How Deputies Can Participate in the Sessions

Despite the formal, ritualistic character of the sessions, and despite the controlling hand of the ispolkom in their preparation and conduct, there are ways the deputies can participate in the work of the sessions and influence decisions that affect their constituents. Moreover, there is evidence that opportunities for deputies to have input into this process have grown in recent years. These opportunities present themselves in three stages—before, during, and after the sessions—which we will examine in turn.

The key to controlling the work of any legislative body rests with those who define the agenda. In the case of sessions of the local soviets, decisions about when to call a session, where to hold it, what items will be discussed,

---

[7] N. G. Starovoitov, "Sessii Sovetov: teoriia, praktika, problemy," *SGiP*, no. 11 (1985), p. 7. Emphasis added.

and who will present these items are made at a meeting of the executive committee.[8] Increasingly, the items to be placed on the agenda are decided in accordance with an annual plan drawn up by the Organizational-Instructional Department of the ispolkom, which solicits suggestions from the standing committees, and from other administrative departments about what should be included. The ispolkom then discusses the recommendations of this department about what is feasible and presents a "plan of work" to the deputies for their approval at the first session of the year.[9]

Nonetheless, article 12 of the Law on the Status of Deputies guarantees deputies the right to introduce items into the agenda from the floor if they so desire. In practice this is done very rarely. According to Bezuglov, this is because the other deputies should be "psychologically prepared" for taking part in the discussion of issues and that it would be difficult to consider thoroughly a question that had not been prepared beforehand.[10] Does this mean that deputies can play little or no role in agenda-setting? Not necessarily, for as Bezuglov goes on to point out, the normal practice is for deputies to submit items be included beforehand.[11] How frequently this occurs is difficult to say, but almost all the deputies interviewed by the author indicated that this was the procedure they used, lending some credence to Bezuglov's contention. A comparison of the

---

[8] Bezuglov, *Sovetskoe stroitel'stvo*, pp. 320–321.

[9] Vasilev in *Kommentarii k zakonu*, pp. 111–112.

[10] Bezuglov, *Deputat v Sovete i izbiratel'nom okruge*, p. 15.

[11] This procedure is not uncommon in the American political practice. The agenda of the municipality in which the author was a legislator for eight years was usually determined by the chairman of the board in consultation with the managing director three days before the meeting. If any board member wanted an item included, he or she usually did so prior to this by contacting the chair, although the option of introducing an item at the meeting itself was always available when the chair invited commissioners to raise issues from past sessions or under "new business."

annual plan of the Lenin city borough with its actual agendas suggests some degree of flexibility, although changes in the schedule of items to be discussed may have been purely for administrative reasons.[12]

The number of items on an agenda is not fixed, although two or three is recommended as the norm to ensure adequate discussion.[13] The number has been steadily increasing. For example, the average number of agenda items per session in Belorussia grew from 3.0 in 1974 to 4.6 in 1980.[14] While the national average is not as high, indicating that there may be considerable regional variation for this variable, it too has grown steadily (see Table 6-2). The problem this poses, as Leizerov notes in the Belorussian case, is that the amount of time devoted to each item has decreased because the length of most sessions has not increased.[15] For this reason, and to facilitate broader participation in the discussions, Leizerov has urged that the length of sessions be increased, while Starovoitov has argued for a return to the practices of earlier years, when sessions were held more frequently.[16]

Once the items to go on the agenda have been determined, the issues themselves must be prepared, information gathered, and decisions drafted. For this, a special ad hoc committee comprised of deputies, administrators, or specialists who have a particular interest or ability pertaining to the subject under discussion may be formed; it is normally chaired by an officer of the ispolkom.[17] In recent years, two methods have been used to broaden the partic-

[12] "Plan raboty Leninskogo raionnogo Soveta na 1984 godu," approved on January 18, 1984.

[13] Bezuglov, *Sovetskoe stroitel'stvo*, p. 321.

[14] A. T. Leizerov, "Issledovanie effektivnosti sessionnoi deiatel'nosti mestnykh Sovetov," *SGiP*, no. 4 (1983), p. 57.

[15] Ibid., pp. 58–59.

[16] Leizerov, *Demokraticheskie formy*, p. 31; Starovoitov, "Sessii Sovetov," p. 7.

[17] Bezuglov, *Sovetskoe stroitel'stvo*, p. 325.

TABLE 6-2. Average Number of Issues per Session, USSR and
Belorussia, Selected Years

	Total	Areas, regions, okrugs	Districts	Cities	Boroughs in cities	Settle-ments	Villages
USSR							
1976	2.6	4.1	3.3	3.2	3.4	2.8	2.5
1980	3.0	4.3	3.8	3.6	4.0	3.2	2.9
1983	3.1	4.3	4.1	4.0	4.3	3.4	3.0
1984	3.3	4.5	4.1	4.1	4.4	3.5	3.2
Belorussia							
1976	3.3	5.6	4.1	3.7	—	3.7	3.2
1980	4.6	6.1	5.8	5.1	—	4.5	4.8

SOURCES: For USSR, *Nekotorye voprosy*, 1976, pp. 13–15; and *Nekotorye voprosy*, 1980 (1983, 1984), pp. 9–11, 13–15. For Belorussia, Leizerov, "Issledovanie effektivnosti sessionnoi deiatel'nosti mestnykh Sovetov," *SGiP*, no. 4 (1983), p. 57.

ipation not only of deputies but also of the public in general. The first of these methods is the use of questionnaires to solicit the public's input on what the problems in the district are. Leizerov describes an experiment of this sort in a rural district in Belorussia in 1978, where both deputies and their constituents were asked to evaluate the work of the district's executive committee. Some 333 propositions were forthcoming: 127 from deputies, 41 from the ispolkoms of village soviets, and 165 from the electorate.[18]

A variation of this approach is to publish the reports on agenda items or the draft decisions themselves in the local press and to invite public comment. Successful examples of this procedure are readily found in the literature on the

[18] Leizerov, *Konstitutsionnyi printsip*, pp. 83–87.

soviets.[19] As discussed in the previous chapter, deputies are also encouraged to hold meetings with their constituents to discuss certain kinds of draft legislation prior to the session at which it will be considered. It appears, however, that such efforts to solicit greater public interest occur less frequently than specialists on the soviet would want.[20] According to data from Belorussia, agendas for the sessions are often not published, and even if they are there is no information about where to send comments or criticism.[21] Without even such basic information, public participation in the preparation of sessions becomes extremely difficult. At least for the present it appears that attempts to involve deputies and their constituents in agenda-setting and decision-drafting are not ineffective when they are tried, but that the enthusiasm for such methods is greater among those writing about the soviets than it is among the members of the ispolkom who run them.

The preceding discussion underscores one of the major factors inhibiting greater involvement of the deputies in the shaping of government decisions: the availability of information. Article 11 of the Law on the Status of the Deputies obligates executive committees to provide deputies with all "materials necessary" for their participation in the sessions. Republican legislation requires that such information be available seven to 10 days before the session.[22] In practice, however, these norms are frequently violated; often deputies receive draft resolutions and copies of the

[19] Examples of such activity are discussed in Shchetinina, *Deputat na sessii Soveta*, pp. 21–25; Leizerov, *Demokraticheskie formy*, pp. 8, 12–13; Bezuglov, *Deputat v Sovete*, p. 13; and I. A. Azovkin, *Mestnye Sovety v sisteme organov vlasti* (Moscow: Iurid. Lit., 1971), p. 237.

[20] Although scholars have encouraged greater public participation along these lines, the consensus seems to be that it does not happen very often. See, e.g., Bezuglov, *Sovetskoe stroitel'stvo*, p. 327.

[21] Leizerov, *Konstitutsionnyi printsip*, pp. 80–82.

[22] See Vasilev's discussion in *Kommentarii k zakonu*, pp. 103–107.

reports only when they arrive for the session.[23] Without a chance to consider these documents beforehand, deputies learn about what they are approving only by listening to the speeches.

The opportunities for deputies to comment on or criticize the decisions are limited not only by the timeliness and quantity of information available, but also by the lack of content. In his research on the information given to deputies Michael Urban found that there was much statistical information revealing very little and that at the same time it managed to tell the deputy almost nothing about what is really being done or who was doing it. "It would be difficult to claim that ordinary deputies are supplied with information sufficient to gain much knowledge of the operations of their individual soviet or of its executive committee."[24] While it is legally possible for deputies to require information, this does not seem to take place in practice very often.[25]

As we turn from the preparation for sessions to the actual conduct of the sessions, a good place to begin is by establishing who attends. Deputies are required by law to attend each session of the soviet unless they have informed the ispolkom that they must be absent, and most deputies meet this obligation. A study of five district soviets in Belorussia in the early 1970s revealed a rate of attendance ranging between 83 percent and 93 percent, with only marginal differences when broken down by the usual social and demographic indicators.[26]

Aside from deputies, attendance is by invitation only. Unlike American practice, the meetings of elected repre-

[23] Bezuglov, *Deputat v Sovete*, p. 14; N. G. Beliaeva in Bezuglov, *Sovetskoe stroitel'stvo*, p. 328.

[24] Urban, "Information and Participation in Local Government," p. 73. Similar factors appear to limit the participation of Soviet workers in their trade unions. See Ruble, *Soviet Trade Unions*, pp. 98–99.

[25] See *Kommentarii k zakonu*, pp. 172–173, 210–214.

[26] Leizerov, *Demokraticheskie formy*, pp. 36–38.

sentatives conducting public business are not open to the citizens who elected them. Moreover, those who are invited are asked to do so only because there is some business on the agenda that directly concerns them. Thus, the overwhelming majority of these guests are the leaders of enterprises, specialists, and nonelected administrative personnel from the soviet itself.[27]

Many of those invited are scheduled to give reports, although the proportion of nondeputies speaking at the sessions has declined in recent years, at least for the city and district soviets. According to Leizerov's study of Minsk Oblast, nondeputy participants in the sessions of the district soviets in 1965 comprised 35 percent of those speaking, but this figure had declined to 12 percent by 1977. For city soviets over the same period, the portion had dropped from 28 percent to less than 2 percent.[28] While Leizerov views this development favorably because it increases the relative degree of deputy participation, he, along with Bezuglov, is also a leading proponent of opening up the session to greater attendance and even participation by the general public. A certain number of tickets to attend the sessions, they argue, should be made available to anyone from either the ispolkom or at the constituent's place of work who wants them.[29]

How can deputies participate in the session itself? As indicated by the description of the session of the Lenin city borough soviet given above, in many respects the role of the deputies is quite passive. They listen to the reports (*doklady*) of the administrative and executive organs and various topics and to the co-reports (*sodoklady*) of the appropriate standing committee representatives, which are supposed to be critical but usually are not, and then unan-

[27] Leizerov (*Konstitutsionnyi printsip*, pp. 91–93) provides data from several district soviets in Belorussia for 1975–79.

[28] Leizerov, "Issledovanie effektivnosti," p. 59.

[29] Leizerov, *Konstitutsionnyi printsip*, p. 93; A. A. Bezuglov, *Glasnost' raboty mestnykh Sovetov* (Moscow: Gosiurizdat, 1960), pp. 50–51.

imously approve these, just as they have agreed without dissent to the organizational issues on which they were asked to vote earlier. Although deputies have the right to amend the agenda any way they wish, they almost never do. That this apparent compulsion for control, this need to arrange everything beforehand, leads to boredom and indifference is not lost on Soviet specialists in local government, as the comments of Starovoitov quoted earlier make clear. Bezuglov and others have urged "sessions without reports," or conducting sessions at factories or residences (*vyezdnye sessii*), as a way to stimulate greater activity by the deputies.[30]

The deputies are not entirely without opportunities for input. Following the formal reports and co-reports, time is usually set aside for deputies to present statements (*vystupleniia*). Requests to do so may be made orally or in writing to the presiding officer; speakers are then listed in the order their requests are received. Using this procedure, deputies may introduce amendments to the draft decision being considered, which are then voted on by the soviet. The degree to which deputies participate in the "debates" in this fashion is indicated in Table 6-3. As the data show, the number of deputies per session doing this has grown in recent years.

Another way deputies can inject themselves into the discussion is to put questions (*zadavat' voprosy*) to those making reports. This can be done in oral or written form. In the villages, questions are more likely to be asked and answered orally; because the size of these soviets is smaller and the level of familiarity is greater, a good deal more open give-and-take seems to be possible in the rural areas.[31] In urban areas, questions may be answered im-

[30] Leizerov, *Konstitutsionnyi printsip*, pp. 96–97, and Bezuglov, *Sovetskoe stroitel'stvo*, pp. 336–338.

[31] The data presented in Table 6-3 show that a much higher percentage of deputies in village soviets participate than deputies in the cities and regions. See also Vasilev in *Kommentarii k zakonu*, p. 115. Several soviet

TABLE 6-3. Deputy Participation in Sessions of Local Soviets, 1976–84

Level of soviet	No. of sessions		No. of deputies participating		Percent of all deputies		Average no. of deputies participating per session	
	1976	1984[a]	1976	1984	1976	1984	1976	1984
Regional[b]	542	662	6,414	8,024	22.5	24.5	11.8	12.1
Okrug	42	47	488	496	48.5	45.5	11.6	10.6
Raion	18,018	15,428	135,843	140,148	57.8	55.2	7.5	9.1
City	12,325	10,739	92,726	99,591	34.8	34.5	7.5	9.3
City borough	3,550	3,249	32,867	34,910	27.0	25.3	9.3	10.9
Settlement	22,529	222,703	132,856	145,461	62.7	67.7	5.9	6.4
Village	255,252	248,839	1,069,501	1,161,637	79.3	85.4	4.2	4.7
For all levels:	312,249	301,673	1,470,695	1,590,267	66.5	69.4	4.7	5.3

SOURCES: *Nekotorye voprosy,* 1976; *Nekotorye voprosy,* 1984, p. 31.
NOTE: The data in this table refer to *vystupleniia* (statements, appearances), a term that does not seem to include reports of the ispolkom or department heads (*doklady* or *sodoklady*).
[a] The number of sessions required annually was reduced following adoption of 1977 Constitution.
[b] Includes data for autonomous regions.

mediately or be collected and read at the end of the session. Henry Morton describes how more than thirty questions were handled in this fashion at the session he observed in 1964. According to Morton, it was the moment of greatest interest to the deputies, but for the chairman of the executive committee "it was apparent that he relished this function least."[32] Presumably, the cause for the chair's discomfort and the deputies' interest is that having to answer questions on the record may constrain an executive officer who later tries to avoid his public commitment, or at least provide some ammunition to those who may want to criticize him if he does.

Finally, deputies can take advantage of the session to introduce proposals and comments (*zamechaniia*) that are ostensibly related to the item being discussed but that may raise matters of concern to their constituents or to some other community problem. This right was formally granted to deputies by article 15 of the 1972 Law on the Status of Deputies, which also requires a response within a specified period of time from the officials to whom they are directed. Again, such proposals may be made orally or in writing, although practice seems to dictate that they be written, at least in the urban soviets. This gives the editorial commission (*redaktsionnaia kommissiia*), formed at each session to review amendments to the draft legislation, a chance to determine whether the proposals and comments are germane to the issue being discussed. If they are, they may be introduced at once. If they are not, they are referred to the Organizational-Instructional Department of the ispolkom, which then decides who will be responsible for dealing with the deputy's problem.[33] In the absence of

scholars I interviewed in the fall of 1984, including Vasilev, Bezuglov, and Barabashev, talked about the greater informality of political life in the village soviets.

[32] Morton, "The Leningrad District of Moscow," p. 214.

[33] Bezuglov, *Sovetskoe stroitel'stvo*, pp. 341–343; Vasilev in *Kommentarii k zakonu*, pp. 124–128.

empirical data, it is difficult to say how well this procedure works in practice.[34] However, because most such proposals presumably deal with practical considerations, it seems reasonable to assume that most are processed. In the case of controversial proposals or critical comments, this procedure also provides a way for them to be resolved "offstage."

The picture of deputy participation in the work of the sessions that Soviet leaders would like to project is one in which the great majority of deputies, regardless of social background or demographic characteristics, are equally active. The statistics in Table 6-3 sustain that image, yet there is ample evidence that this is not the case and that many deputies take part in the sessions very rarely, if at all. A study conducted by the Institute of State and Law in Armenia revealed that one-third of the deputies had never spoken at a session, while another one-third had spoken only once or twice.[35] In eleven district and city soviets of Minsk Oblast in Belorussia in the fourteenth term (1973–75), 27 percent of the deputies never participated, while another 62 percent did so only once.[36]

It is also clear that a relatively small percentage of the deputies, perhaps 15 to 20 percent, tend to dominate the proceedings and to be disproportionately active. Who are they? As one familiar with empirical analyses of political participation in Western democracies might expect, data from the Armenian, Lativan, and Belorussian republics suggest that middle-aged men with higher levels of education, especially if they are employed as specialists or as leaders in government and industry, are more likely to participate than those who are not.[37] Data from the RSFSR,

[34] A hypothetical example of how it is supposed to work can be found in Bezuglov, *Deputat v Sovete*, pp. 21–22.

[35] *Upravlenie, sotsiologiia, pravo* (Moscow: Nauka, 1971), pp. 195–196.

[36] Leizerov, *Demokraticheskie formy*, p. 46.

[37] This conclusion, along with data based on the minutes of meetings and other official documents examined from 1965 to 1975 in Belorussia,

Estonia, and Latvia indicate that 70 to 80 percent are people with official positions, including enterprise managers.[38] These studies suggest that there are two identifiable groups of deputies: (1) a very active minority who have the skills and motivation to become highly active participants (sometimes referred to derisively as "staff orators") and (2) a mostly passive majority who remain silent observers out of nervousness or indifference.[39]

Still, there is evidence that the social composition of those participating in the sessions has broadened over the past two decades, more nearly reflecting the social composition of the deputies themselves. According to longitudinal data published by Leizerov, based on his continuing research into deputy activities in Minsk Oblast of Belorussia since 1965, there have been "positive changes" with respect to gender, age, occupation, and education.[40] In the Minsk district soviet the portion of female deputies taking part in the debates grew from 11.1 percent in the tenth term (1965–67) to 45.1 percent in the sixteenth term (1977–80); in village soviets for the same period, the percentage increased from 18.8 percent to 38.4 percent. With respect to age, in the district soviets of Minsk Oblast the percentage of deputies 18 to 30 years old who spoke at the session went from 19.2 percent in the fourteenth term (1973–75) to 26.5 percent in the sixteenth term (1977–80), a

---

is in Leizerov, *Demokraticheskie formy*, pp. 36–46; the summary conclusion offered here is on p. 42.

[38] A. V. Litvinova, *Povyshenie aktivnosti deputatov mestnykh Sovetov Latviiskoi SSSR* (Riga: Avtoreferat dissertatsii, Latviiskii gosudarstvennyi universitet, 1973), pp. 28–30; L. A. Grigorian, *Sovety-organy vlasti narodnogo samoupravleniia* (Moscow: Iurid. Lit., 1965), p. 118; Iu. A. Tikhomirov, *Vlast' i upravlenie v sotsialisticheskom obshchestve* (Moscow: Iurid. Lit., 1968), p. 122.

[39] The reluctance of many deputies to participate as a result of nervousness or indifference is described by Shchetinina, *Deputat na sessii Soveta*, p. 28, and Bezuglov, *Deputat v Sovete*, pp. 19–20.

[40] All data below is from Leizerov, "Issledovanie effektivnosti sessionnoi deiatel'nosti," p. 60.

development that Leizerov attributes to improved training (*ucheba*) given to the new deputies. As for occupation, in the district soviets the number of workers and peasants entering the debates rose from 8.3 percent in the twelfth term (1969–71) to 36.1 percent in the sixteenth term (1977–80), while the portion of economic administrators and specialists declined in the same period from 42.0 percent to 30.6 percent. It is difficult to determine how generalizable Leizerov's findings are for other parts of the Soviet Union. If they are, and if the number of those participating in the debates continues to grow, as the data presented in Table 6-3 indicate, then the patterns of deputy participation which prevailed in the past would appear to be changing.

One other way deputies can participate in the sessions, and one that has received considerable attention in recent years, is to use the deputy's right of inquiry (*deputatskii zapros*). The use of this right is distinguished both in form and content from the deputy's ability to put questions (*zadavat' voprosy*) during the debate. A *zapros* is directed to a specific individual, either an administrator in the government or an official in an economic enterprise within the soviet's jurisdiction. This individual is obligated to respond, and the soviet as a whole must adopt a decision as to the adequacy of their response. Moreover, also unlike a simple question (*vopros*), the right of inquiry is normally invoked when the named individuals have failed to perform their duties properly. According to one textbook, "it is resorted to as an extreme measure, that is, when deputies have been unable to achieve the elimination of serious omissions and shortcomings and the liquidation of backsliding by other means, and the necessity of bringing these matters to the attention of the soviet cannot be put off."[41]

Although R. K. Davydov and other scholars maintain that de facto use of the zapros as an instrument of deputy control over administration at the local level was in evi-

[41] Bezuglov, *Sovetskoe stroitel'stvo*, p. 344.

dence as early as the late 1940s, there is no mention of it in the laws on local government until after the CPSU Central Committee resolution on the local soviets of January 22, 1957.[42] It first becomes part of national legislation on the soviets only with the adoption of the 1972 Law on the Status of Deputies, where it received its fullest legal elaboration to date in article 15.[43]

A zapros may be introduced by a single deputy, by several deputies acting together, or by a deputies' group (see Chapter 5). Since 1983, the right to use the zapros has also been given to the standing committees, a practice strongly advocated by Davydov.[44] In all cases, only deputies from the soviet in which the zapros is introduced have the right to do this.[45] Inquiries may be expressed orally or in writing, at the session itself or prior to it. If the zapros is prepared beforehand—a practice endorsed by many legal scholars on the grounds that the quality of both the inquiry and the answer will be improved—then it must be read at the session by the presiding officer and include the identity of the official and the deputy proposing it along with the specifics of the complaint formed as a question.[46]

Zaprosy are discussed separately, usually at the end of

[42] R. K. Davydov, *Pravo deputatskogo zaprosa v sovetskom obshchenarodnom gosudarstve* (Kiev: Naukova, dumka, 1981), pp. 43–55.

[43] Despite the pleas of scholars for a more thorough legal regulation of the procedures for using the zapros, as of this writing there is no all-union or republic statute that does so. A recent attempt to draft one that could be used as a model by local soviets was published by the Sverdlovsk Legal Institute. See V. A. Kriazhkov and A. I. Potapov, *Deputatskii zapros: metodicheskie rekomendatsii* (Sverdlovsk: Iuridicheskii Institut, 1985), pp. 12–14.

[44] Davydov, *Pravo deputatskogo zaprosa*, pp. 55–57, 78. The right of standing committees to introduce zaprosy was granted in the RSFSR by article 26 of RSFSR Statute on Standing Committees, March 3, 1983, *Vedomosti Verkhovnogo Soveta RSFSR*, 1983, no. 10, item 318.

[45] This is emphasized in A. A. Bezuglov and A. T. Leizerov, *Deputatskii zapros* (Moscow: Iurid. Lit., 1980), p. 13.

[46] See, e.g., ibid., p. 31. The same authors indicate that oral inquiries occur only rarely at any level of soviet other than the village (p. 13).

the session. It may not be refused by those to whom it is addressed, unless it falls outside the soviet's jurisdiction. Unless the official has had the opportunity to prepare an answer beforehand, a time limit is established for when the official must provide one, usually by the next session. The required decision by the soviet may simply take the form of "taking the answer under advisement." Frequently, however, action on the answer is specified and someone is assigned to verify that it is carried out.[47] The statistical summary of the use of the zapros in Sverdlovsk Oblast in 1983 gives some idea of how these procedures work out in practice and what they are used for. See Table 6-4.

How often do deputies make use of their right of inquiry? As the figures in Table 6-5 indicate, the zapros is used relatively rarely. Even in 1984 it was employed on the average only two or three times in a year, depending on the level of the soviet. Soviet specialists on local government often decry the infrequency with which the right of inquiry is used, arguing that it represents an underutilized potential for strengthening the influence of the deputy over the work of the soviets and for stimulating the activity of deputy and administrator alike.[48] Yet it is clear that many deputies are either ill-prepared to use the zapros or are reluctant to engage in a confrontation with the ispolkom, whose goodwill they must cultivate to accomplish anything for their constituents. It is worth noting that most of the inquiries (more than 90 percent) are directed at individuals other than those on the ispolkom (see indicator 3, Table 6-4). Moreover, since responsibility for training new deputies rests with the ispolkom itself, a lack of enthusiasm on their part for developing this particular skill would be understandable. One result of inadequate

[47] These procedures are discussed by Vasilev in *Kommentarii k zakonu*, pp. 120–124.

[48] See, e.g., Leizerov, "Issledovanie effektivnosti sessionnoi deiatel'nosti," esp. pp. 56–57; and Bezuglov, *Sovetskoe stroitel'stvo*, p. 346.

TABLE 6-4. Use of Right of Inquiry (*Zapros*) in Sverdlovsk, 1983 (In Percents)

Indicator	City soviets	District soviets	All soviets
1. Who introduced the inquiry			
A single deputy	45	63	52
A group of deputies	24	25	24
A standing commission	19	6	14
Several commissions	1	—	1
A deputy group	11	6	9
2. Time of introduction			
Before the session	23	29	25
At the session	34	16	27
Unknown	43	55	47
3. To whom Zapros addressed			
Executive committee	6	10	7[a]
Nongovernment executives	94	90	92[a]
4. Recorded in minutes			
The inquiry	63	61	62
Answer to the inquiry	12	16	13
5. Specified in decision			
Obligations (*zadachi*)	76	92	82
Time limit	80	84	82
Who must fulfill	67	84	73
Who must verify	38	59	46
6. Subject of inquiry[b]			
Industry, construction, transport	31	63	43
Agriculture	7	n.a.	5
Trade, food, everyday services	8	8	8
Housing, public works	37	12	28
Education, culture, sports	7	10	8
Health	9	6	8
Voter mandates (*zakazy* izbiratelei*)	19	39	26

SOURCE: Kriazhkov and Potapov, *Deputatskii zapros*, p. 18.

[a] Rounded off.

[b] Some inquires may fall into more than one category.

TABLE 6-5. Use of Right Inquiry (Zapros), 1968–84

Level of soviet	No. of Inquires				No. of Inquiries per Soviet, in one year (average)				No. of deputies per inquiry (average)			
	1968	1980	1983	1984	1968	1980	1983	1984	1968	1980	1983	1984
Region, okrug	152	120	155	361	1.2	0.82	1.1	2.5	168	280	219	94
Raion	4,593	5,653	5,786	8,448	1.6	1.8	1.9	2.7	48	46	44	30
City	2,946	3,872	4,767	6,131	1.5	1.9	2.3	2.9	81	73	60	47
City borough	507	901	991	1,804	1.2	1.4	1.5	2.8	172	148	139	77
Settlement	4,589	6,093	6,908	8,810	1.3	1.6	1.8	2.3	40	35	31	24
Village	43,924	57,596	65,165	82,295	1.1	1.4	1.6	2.0	29	23	21	17
For all levels:	56,711	74,245	83,772	107,849	1.2	1.5	1.6	2.1	36	31	27	21

SOURCES: Data for 1968 from *Sovety deputatov trudiashchikhsia*, no. 5 (1969), p. 95. Data for the other years from, *Nekotorye vaprosy*, 1980, 1983, 1984.

NOTE: Averages calculated using the number of soviets and the number of deputies for these years.

training is that many, perhaps most, deputies do not know the difference between a "question" (*vopros*) and an "inquiry" (*zapros*). In one survey carried out in Pskov, V. I. Vasilev found that of 190 deputies surveyed, 45 said they had used a zapros during the current term of office: the records showed only 3 zapros had been introduced in the same period.[49]

Nevertheless, it is also clear from the data in Table 6-5 that the rate of use of the zapros grew steadily in the fifteen years between 1968 and 1983, although this growth leveled off somewhat in the last years of Brezhnev's tenure as Party General Secretary.[50] Notable in particular is the sharp increase in the use of the right of inquiry in 1984, compared with 1983. One reason for this can be found in the speech of the CPSU General Secretary, Konstantin Chernenko, to the Central Committee on April 10, 1984, in which he noted that "in recent years for all the soviets, on the average only one zapros for every thirty deputies was introduced. This figure speaks for itself, and speaks poorly."[51]

Following this speech and the CPSU resolution adopted at this plenary session, there was a dramatic increase in the use of the zapros. At first glance this would seem encouraging to those who sought such a development. On closer examination, however, much of this increase may have been due to local executive committee chairpersons seeking to improve their record by "overfulfilling their quota" for zaprosy. In an article published in *Sovety narodnykh deputatov* in May 1985, an investigative reporter found that in one rural soviet the zapros was being used at almost every session, although it had been used only once

[49] V. I. Vasil'ev, *Zakon o statuse deputatov v deistvii* (Moscow: Iurid. Lit., 1978), pp. 14–15.

[50] This is also Leizerov's conclusion, based on his analysis of national data and data from Belorussia between 1977 and 1981. See Leizerov, "Issledovanie effektivnosti sessionnoi deiatel'nosti," p. 56.

[51] *Materialy plenuma Tsk. KPSS* (Moscow: Politizdat, 1984), pp. 11–12.

in 1983. It turned out, however, that the "zapros" were really informational questions without critical content on which a vote had been taken, thus achieving the form though not the purpose of an inquiry.[52]

While data on the social composition of deputies using the zapros is scarce, there is some evidence that, as with those participating in the debates, middle-aged men with higher education and in white-collar positions tend to be more active. As is also true in the case of the debates, however, the data indicate that there have been changes since 1965 in the direction of greater participation by women, deputies under age thirty, and manual workers. In Belorussia in the sixteenth term (1977–80), some 53 percent of those using the zapros in the district soviets of Minsk Oblast were women; in the village soviets it was 41 percent (the average was 25 percent in 1969–71). Some 30 percent of those exercising the right of inquiry in the same districts in this period were under thirty years of age, roughly equal to their numerical representation in the soviets as a whole (and an increase of 12 percent from 1971 to 1973); in the villages it was 18 percent.[53]

In comparing the use of the zapros with other forms of participation in the sessions, Leizerov argues that the zapros is a good way to involve deputies who would otherwise be passive. On the basis of evidence from Lativia as well as from Belorussia, he demonstrates that the relative rate of participation of women, the young, the manually employed, and less educated is greater for those using the zapros than for those entering the debates.[54] This is so, he suggests, because less experience is needed to introduce a zapros and because its effects are more clearly visible. If

[52] A. Shiriaev, "Pochemu tak redki zaprosy, nevysok ikh avtoritet," SND, no. 5 (1985), esp. pp. 59–61.

[53] Leizerov, "Issledovanie effektivnosti sessionnoi deiatel'nosti," p. 58.

[54] Leizerov, Demokraticheskii formy, p. 51; for Latvia, see Litvinova, Poryshenie aktivnosti, p. 26.

Leizerov's findings are generalizable elsewhere in the Soviet Union, and if the use of the zapros continues to grow, the zapros represents a potentially effective mechanism for broadening the base of deputy participation in the work of the soviet.

In conformity with Lenin's reading of Marx's description of the Paris Commune, the sessional work of the deputy does not end with the closing of the session. Deputies are also responsible for overseeing implementation of the decisions they have made, a task sometimes referred to as *kontrol* or *proverka*, although these terms can be used in other contexts as well.[55] The implementation can be divided into three stages: propaganda, instruction, and verification.[56] In the first stage, the deputies are to tell the citizens what the soviet has decided. This is done in face-to-face meetings with constituents and through the mass media. Then the work of implementation must be organized, schedules drawn up, and instructions given. The main responsibility for doing this belongs to the ispolkom, but the deputy is expected to take part, or at least cooperate. Finally, the deputy is supposed to help make sure these instructions are properly carried out, reporting to the executive committee any failure to do so. While opportunities for deputies to shape the way decisions are implemented probably arise in practice, this phase of the work of the soviet is clearly dominated by the executive committee. The deputy's function seems to be more to mobilize the population to do what these organs want than to see that the interests of those they represent are not overlooked.

[55] Probably the most thorough discussion to date of *Kontrol* and the literature on it is by N. F. Selivon, *Kontrol'naia funktsiia mestnykh Sovetov narodnykh deputatov* (Kiev: Naukova dumka, 1980); see esp. chap. 2. See also B. N. Gabrichidze, "Konstitutsionnye osnovy kontrol'noi deiatel'nosti Sovetov," *SGiP*, no. 7 (1981), pp. 3–11.

[56] The approach comes from the textbook edited by Bezuglov, *Sovetskoe stroitel'stvo*, pp. 353–359.

The Standing Committees

While opportunities for most deputies to participate directly in the work of the sessions are limited, both Western and Soviet analysts have suggested that the deputy can play a far more active role in the work of the standing committees (*postoiannye komissii*).[57] In theory, these committees ensure the deputies' control over the work of executive agencies between sessions of the soviet. The scholarly literature commonly assigns the standing committees three specific functions in this regard. They are to prepare and review draft legislation, to exercise oversight (*kontrol*) with respect to administrative agencies and economic enterprises, and to help the ispolkom implement governmental decisions.[58] Although any decisions or recommendations emanating from the standing committees are purely advisory, the economic and administrative agencies to which they are directed are obligated by statute to examine them and to respond in a month's time.[59] Formally, the standing committees are created by the soviet and are supposed to be answerable only to it; they are not considered "auxiliary" (*vspomogatel'nyi*) organs of the executive committee. The latter may request, but not command, their assistance.[60]

The composition of the standing committees is also supposed to reflect their independence from the executive

[57] Friedgut, *Political Participation in the USSR*, p. 200; Jacobs, *Soviet Local Politics and Government*, p. 16; Bezuglov, *Deputat v Sovete*, p. 31.

[58] Barabashev and Sheremet, *Sovetskoe stroitel'stvo*, pp. 236–239.

[59] Legislation on the standing committees differs among the republics, but this requirement appears to hold generally. A "Statute on the Standing Committees" of the RSFSR was adopted only in 1983 (see *Vedomosti Verkhovnogo Soveta RSFSR*, 1983, no. 10, item 318, art. 23). Most other republics had already adopted statutes on the standing committees; Belorussia has had one since 1967. See *Sbornik normativnykh aktov* (see above, Chapter 1, footnote 24), p. 775.

[60] V. I. Novoselov, *Ispolkom i postoiannye komissii Soveta* (Moscow: Iurid. Lit., 1981), pp. 10–12.

committee. With the exception of rural soviets in Estonia, only deputies may be elected to membership; the election of deputies who sit on the ispolkom is forbidden.[61] In reality, the formation of the standing committees and the assignment of deputies to them are controlled by the ispolkom; its recommendations to the soviets are routinely ratified by this body at its first session. Moreover, in many republics the law allows department heads, economic managers, members of the People's Control Committee, judges, and prosecutors to sit on and even chair standing committees, which are supposed to oversee their work. In the nine city and twenty-two district soviets of Minsk Oblast in 1977–80, for example, eighty department heads were elected to standing committees, forty-four of them to committees whose function it was to oversee their departments—10 as chairpersons, 14 as vice-chairpersons, and 27 as secretaries. As many as 138 out of the 166 prosecutors and 115 out of 119 judges elected to standing committees in this period served on the committees for "socialist legality and the preservation of public order."[62] Some Soviet specialists see nothing wrong with this and would even go so far as to allow executive committee members to be elected to standing committees, although not as officers of committees that must review their work.[63] Most, however, would probably agree with Leizerov, who recommends legislation to prohibit the election of members of administrative agencies to those standing committees whose task it is to make sure they perform well.[64]

[61] Bezuglov, *Deputat v Sovete*, p. 29. Article 5 of the RSFSR "Statute on the Standing Committees."

[62] A. T. Leizerov, "Effektivnost' poriadka formirovaniia i deiatel'nosti postoiannykh komissii mestnykh Sovetov," *SGiP*, no. 3 (1982), pp. 70–71.

[63] L. A. Grigorian, *Postoiannye komissii mestnykh Sovetov* (Moscow: Iurid. Lit., 1970), pp. 29–31; S. V. Solov'eva, *Postoiannye komissii na novom etape* (Moscow: Vysshaia partiinaia shkola, Tsk. KPSS, 1963), p. 83.

[64] Leizerov, "Effektivnost' poriadka," p. 75.

One major factor making the standing committees a more likely arena for deputy participation in the work of the soviet is their smaller size. Unlike the sessions, where the average attendance above the village level is more than one hundred, the average size of a standing committee in 1985 was between five and six, ranging from about thirteen per committee at the oblast level to between four and five at the village level (see Table 6-6). While each standing committee is thus small enough to encourage even shy or nervous deputies to speak up, the system as a whole encompasses a large number of deputies: in 1985 nearly 2 million deputies were members of one or another standing committee—about 80 percent of all deputies. In addition, deputies are assisted in their work by unpaid volunteers (*aktiv*) with a particular interest or expertise in the issues before the committee. In 1984, the aktiv numbered more than 2.5 million, an average of between seven and eight per committee (Table 6-6). Although the average number of standing committees per soviet has remained steady at 6 or 7 since 1976, the number of deputies and aktiv per committee has declined somewhat. Figures for the aktiv were not published in 1985 which suggests that they have declined even further.

The areas for which the standing committees are responsible are for the most part functionally parallel to the administrative departments of the soviet. Certain standing committees are required by law, although this differs by republic. The 1983 RSFSR statute on standing committees, for example, specifies only a Credentials (*mandatnaia*) Committee, a Planning and Budget Committee, and a Committee on Socialist Legality and the Preservation of Public Order, with other commissions formed in accordance with the needs of the soviet.[65] The 1976 Kazakh statute, as amended in 1980, provides for these, but also for

[65] *Vedomosti Verkhovnogo Soveta RSFSR*, 1983, no. 10, item 318, arts. 9–12.

TABLE 6-6. Local Soviet Standing Committees, Selected Years, 1976–85

Year	No. of standing committees	Average no. of standing committees per soviet	No. of deputies on standing committees	Percent of all deputies	Average no. of deputies per standing committee	No. of aktiv (in thousands)	Aktiv per standing committee
1976	330,270	6.5	1,990,780	80.9	6.0	2,660	8.1
1980	333,547	6.5	1,833,223	80.7	5.5	2,620	7.9
1983	336,927	6.5	1,844,123	80.5	5.5	2,572	7.6
1985[a]	334,501	6.4	1,845,554	80.0	5.5	—	—
BY LEVEL OF SOVIET, 1985							
Area, region & okrug	2,262	15.4	29,918	87.4	13.2		
Raion	31,173	10.0	210,764	82.3	6.7		
City	22,997	10.8	251,041	86.3	10.9		
City borough	8,650	13.4	114,426	82.0	13.2		
Settlement	28,399	7.4	179,759	83.1	6.3		
Village	241,020	5.7	1,059,646	77.5	4.4		

SOURCES: Data for 1976, 1980, and 1983 from *Nekotorye voprosy*. Data for 1985 from *Itogi vyborov*.
[a] These data are from the first sessions following the February 24, 1985, elections.

committees on youth, on the environment, and on women.[66] The rank-ordered data provided in Table 6-7 indicate how frequently the different types of standing committees are found in Soviet local government. The fact that the average number of deputies per committee tends to rise in inverse proportion to the number of committees suggests that standing committees which appear less frequently are found only at the higher levels of government.

The large number of people involved in the work of the standing committees, and the fact that the committees parallel the functions of the administrative agencies, led some legal specialists in the early 1960s to recommend that administration be transferred to them.[67] Such proposals were consistent with Lenin's view of the soviets as "working corporations" in which citizens would voluntarily implement the decisions they made. The idea received official support in the 1961 Party Program, which proclaimed that "an increasing number of questions which now come under the jurisdiction of the departments and sections of executive bodies must be gradually referred to the standing committees of the local soviets for decision."[68] Experiments along these lines, however, were disappointing; citizen-amateurs proved to be inadequate substitutes for professionally trained administrators. Only in the rural soviets and in the soviets of small cities, where there are no branches of administration, do the standing committees appear to play a significant role in the implementation of governmental decisions.[69] While the idea has not been abandoned, the consensus now seems to be that it was

[66] *Vedomosti Verkhovnogo Soveta Kazakhskoi SSR*, 1980, no. 48, item 186, arts. 12–18.

[67] See discussion in Hill, *Soviet Politics, Political Science, and Reform*, pp. 79–81; Friedgut, *Political Participation in the USSR*, pp. 189–193; and Leizerov, *Demokraticheskie formy*, p. 109.

[68] "The 1961 Party Program," in Jan Triska (ed.), *Soviet Communism: Programs and Rules* (San Francisco: Chandler, 1962), p. 100.

[69] Barabashev and Sheremet, *Sovetskoe stroitel'stvo*, p. 252.

TABLE 6-7. Standing Committees, 1985 (Rank-Ordered by Number
of Committees)

Committee	No. of standing committees	Percent of Soviets with committee[a]	No. of deputies in committee	Average no. of deputies per committee
1. Credentials	52,040	99.9	181,518	3.5
Budget	52,032	99.9	250,584	4.8
3. Socialist Legality & Public Order	51,030	98.1	265,393	5.2
4. Agriculture	43,681	83.9	242,356	5.6
5. Culture	24,130	46.4	130,005	5.4
6. Trade, Food, & Commodities	21,801	41.9	137,525	6.3
7. Education	19,343	37.2	116,508	6.0
8. Housing, Public Works	17,030	32.7	115,934	6.8
9. Health, Social Security, Sports	16,805	32.3	111,394	6.6
10. Youth Affairs	11,375	21.9	80,482	7.1
11. Industry	6,175	11.9	54,020	8.8
12. Public Services	5,732	11.0	43,006	7.5
13. Environment	3,598	6.9	31,066	8.6
14. Construction	3,355	6.4	32,253	9.6
15. Transportation	3,009	5.7	26,570	8.8
16. Women, Maternity, Children	2,326	4.5	17,488	7.5
17. Energy	441	0.8	4,028	9.1
18. Other	598	1.2	5,430	9.1
For all committees:	334,501	100.0	1,845,554	5.5

SOURCE: *Itogi vyborov*, 1985, pp. 230–234.
[a] There were 52,041 local services as of February 24, 1985.

premature and must take into account the amount of time available to the committees, as well as the intellectual and financial resources.[70] It is significant that the 1985 CPSU Draft Program omits any reference to the transfer of administrative authority to the standing committees.

A Standing Committee at Work

The Standing Committee on Socialist Legality and the Preservation of Public Order of the Lenin city borough soviet was one of fifteen committees elected by the deputies at the first session of the eighteenth term, which began on June 20, 1982, and ended with elections to the nineteenth term on February 24, 1985. Along with the standing committees on youth affairs, planning and budget, and credentials, it is one of four required by the city borough's regulations. The close look at the work of this standing committee during the eighteenth term that is presented here is based on interviews with ten of its thirteen members, the author's attendance at its meeting of December 11, 1984, and various documentary materials on the committee's work, including agendas. While the overall quality of the work of this committee is above average, other secondary sources and interviews with specialists indicate that it is far from unique. This case study will provide some basis for evaluating the work of standing committees in general.

The composition of the standing committee reflects an effort to achieve some demographic representativeness while ensuring a balance between those with some specialized background and those who have none. In 1984, the committee included seven males and six females, ranging in age from twenty-two to sixty-three and averaging age forty-one; six of the thirteen were Party members. While three of the thirteen specialized in law at Moscow

---

[70] See, e.g., I. M. Chekharin, *Postoiannye komissii v sisteme organov mestnykh Sovetov* (Moscow: Iurid. Lit., 1972), p. 15.

State University and four held locally important party or state positions, there was also a telephone operator, a metal worker, an inspector in a bread factory, a fabric designer, and a ticket-taker for the Metro. The aktiv of the standing committee numbered eleven: five Moscow State University graduate students in law, three undergraduate law students, a teacher of law at the same institution, a notary from another borough, and a research worker from the scientific institute of the Ministry of Internal Affairs.

Following the local soviet elections of February 24, 1985, nine of the thirteen members were replaced. The composition of the standing committee, however, changed little. The balance between males and females remained the same, as did that between "specialists" and "nonspecialists." Eight of the thirteen committee members belonged to the Communist Party, instead of six. Their average age was forty, ranging between twenty and fifty-nine. It is significant that, of the four who remained from one term to the next, all could be considered "specialists": one was head of the borough Department of Internal Affairs, another taught law at Moscow State University, another was the party committee secretary at the state department store (GUM), and the fourth was referred to only as the "head of a department." The picture that emerges from this compositional analysis suggests that D. Richard Little's division of members of the USSR Supreme Soviet's standing committees into "permanents" and "transients" also holds true at the local levels of Soviet government.[71]

The patterns of participation in the work of the standing committee do not seem to be a function of whether the deputies stayed on the committee at the time of transition. Although none of the same "nonspecialists" remained from one term to the next, their levels of participation by the "nonspecialists" varied considerably. Some were con-

[71] D. Richard Little, "Soviet Parliamentary Committees After Khrushchev," pp. 41–60.

scientious in the performance of their duties, and not only attended meetings regularly but also took part in the preparation and presentation of materials; others attended only rarely. Among the "specialists," participation also varied, although all appear to have attended regularly. Of the four who were reappointed to this committee at the first session after the February 24, 1985, elections, however, only one—the secretary—exhibited a consistently high level of participation. The very active president of the Standing Committee on Socialist Legality in the previous term—a prominent law professor at Moscow State University and a veteran of several terms—was replaced as president by the dean of the law faculty of that university in order to take up an appointed position in the Moscow city soviet.

How does this standing committee work in practice? The nineteenth meeting of the Standing Committee on Socialist Legality since its term began almost two-and-a-half years earlier took place on December 11, 1984, in what appeared to be a mansion left from the prerevolutionary period and which currently served as the municipal building of the Lenin city borough soviet. Upon entering, I was escorted up a wide marble staircase with shallow steps and into a hallway lined with doorways to what must have once been bedrooms and reception halls but which now housed the offices of the city borough's ispolkom. The meeting itself was held in one of these—the office of the Organizational-Instructional Department, the purpose of which is to assist the work of the deputies.

When I arrived, there were nine deputies seated around a conference table, and four invited participants who sat in chairs that lined the walls of the room. The room itself was not large, though it had a high ceiling and contained a desk, filing cabinets, and bookcases with information for the public on the workings of the soviet. At the end of the table sat the president of the standing committee, a mantelpiece from another era at his back. The ubiquitous image of Lenin looked sternly down at the proceedings from an oyster-colored wall.

The meeting had begun at 4:30 p.m., an hour before my arrival. I was informed that this would be the case because the first items on the agenda required a discussion of specific criminal charges, and confidential testimony was being heard. According to what was written in the agenda, the standing committee was to consider a report "on the work of the district's law enforcement agencies for the prevention of bribery, embezzlement, and speculation in trade and public food establishments, in enterprises providing everyday services, and in bases (*bazakh*) distributing fruits and vegetables." I later learned that this item represented the culmination of work begun some months earlier. It seems that on the basis of a large volume of citizen complaints the borough's ispolkom had requested a joint session of three standing committees (on trade, on public food, and on legality) and asked them to investigate the truth of the charges. The particular task taken on by the Standing Committee on Socialist Legality was to determine whether contracts were being fulfilled and whether the heads of the legal-services departments of the enterprises involved had performed their duties properly. The deputies had formed "deputy posts" that conducted spot checks on the businesses in question, reporting the results of their respective standing committees. Apparently, a number of criminal charges were ultimately forthcoming, and the head of the legal-services department at the food distribution base had been relieved of his duties. At the meeting of December 11, 1984, members not only discussed these issues but also examined draft legislation intended to avoid such problems in the future, legislation that was to be considered at the next meeting of the ispolkom and presumably sent on to the soviet for ratification.

The second item on the agenda was related to the first and concerned the work of the legal services department of the vegetable and fruit association (*ob'edineniia*) of the

region. Two reports were scheduled. The first was by a
member of the aktiv, a law school graduate student, who
had been asked to check out the qualifications of the department's personnel and to see whether proper procedures were being followed. After carefully emphasizing
that his job was not to investigate whether crimes had
been committed, he indicated that "from a juridical point
of view" things had about returned to normal. After his
report, the new head of legal services, a young woman,
was invited to respond. After noting somewhat anxiously
that this was her first appearance before a standing committee, she said that she agreed with the gist of the previous report: things had been bad, but the work with
cadres was improving and a new bookkeeper had been
hired.

The floor was then opened to questions, and a lively exchange ensued. Several deputies wanted more information on the criminal proceedings. How many people were
involved? What is the prosecutor doing now? When the
reply came that this was the concern of the police and not
of the legal-services department, one deputy reminded the
speaker, "It concerns everyone." Other questions were:
What preventive propaganda measures (profilaktika) are
being taken? What is being done by the People's Control
Committee? Have violations of labor discipline been erad-
icated? Finally an older deputy gave his report. It was
quite critical. He had conducted a "raid" on October 22
and found that the contract with the collective farms had
not been met with respect to quality control and that there
were negative balances in the accounts. Despite these
shortcomings, however, the work of the new head of legal
services deserved praise. The reports were accepted with
thanks by the presiding officer.

For the third item, those invited in connection with the
previous issue left and two others came in. They represented Znanie, a public information agency specializing in
the propagandization of scientific knowledge. Approxi-

mately one year earlier, the standing committee had discussed ways to improve the public's familiarity with legal issues. In particular, it had made recommendations in this regard to Znanie. The deputy reporting on whether these recommendations had been followed reviewed the committee's earlier decision and concluded that in her opinion the tasks outlined in it had been met. She proposed that the matter "be taken from control" of the standing committee, a phrase indicating officially that no further action was needed, and that she had prepared a resolution to this effect. Two other deputies who had assisted her in verifying the outcome by conducting a "raid" on an editorial session of Znanie read brief concurring statements they had prepared. The Znanie representative was invited to respond. She agreed with most of the suggestions and then launched into a lengthy defense of their work. The issue before the committee was, or had become, noncontroversial, and after a few desultory questions and a brief sharp exchange between two of the deputies ("How would *you* have conducted this work?"), the resolution was passed without dissent.

The last two items on the agenda were dealt with relatively briefly. One concerned an assignment (*porucheniia*) the standing committee had received from the ispolkom. It concerned a fifteen-page complaint sent to the ispolkom by an instructor in a driving school. The instructor had not been trained to do this job and was now being replaced by those who were. He claimed his rights had been violated; the ispolkom asked the standing committee to determine whether this was so. The deputy reporting concluded that the complaint was not supported by the facts, adding, however, "There are definite shortcomings in the legal upbringing of the youth at this kollektiv."

For the final piece of business, the president of the committee distributed copies of a short questionnaire he had designed to study how deputies of the soviet used their right to address issues (*zadavat' voprosy*) to both the ispolkom and to the managers of enterprises in their district. He proposed asking the ispolkom to administer it at the next session of the soviet. Comment was encouraged and the discussion became quite lively; the proposal was strongly supported. Its business concluded, the standing committee adjourned at about 7:30 p.m. Afterwards the president confided to me that his real purpose in preparing the questionnaire was "political"—to get this touchy issue out into the open and onto the agenda of the ispolkom. This was an acceptable, even incontestable, way to do it.

On the basis of this description, what can be said about how well the standing committees function as a means by which deputies can take part in the work of the soviet? Using the same facts, different analysts may draw different conclusions. It is possible that my presence altered the conduct of the committee's business, although in my opinion the effect was negligible. To a large extent, the standing committee performed the functions for which it was intended. It did play a role in shaping draft legislation on a matter of concern to the community: the proper distribution of food and goods. It certainly was active in exerting oversight with respect to the management of local enterprises and the work of a major public service organization, Znanie. In both cases, spot checks (*proverki*, or raids) were used to determine whether the soviet's decisions were being carried out. Finally, the support functions that standing committees are supposed to provide were readily discernible in the efforts of the committee to improve legal propaganda and in helping the ispolkom in dealing with citizen complaints. From the point of view of deputy participation in the work of the local soviet, the levels of deputy activity and interaction were clearly much higher than they were at the session the author attended. The deputies were more openly critical, their differences of opinion more freely expressed. If the author's presence did have any effect, it probably was to introduce an ele-

ment of restraint in what might otherwise have been an
even more lively exchange.

Problems Facing the Standing Committees

The description of how one standing committee in a Moscow city borough conducts its work demonstrates what is
possible: to some extent, standing committees can provide
deputies an opportunity to participate actively in the tasks
of local government, not only in implementing decisions
but also in shaping them. But how representative is this
case study of the operations of other local soviet standing
committees? On this score, there is reason for doubt. The
Lenin city borough soviet's Standing Committee on Socialist Legality and the Preservation of Public Order met
an average of 7.6 times a year; the national average in 1984
was 4.14 times.[72] According to the deputies, the committee
gave annual reports to the soviet on their work (*otchety*),
regularly prepared reports on issues (*sodoklady*) for the sessions, and frequently rendered recommendations to the ispolkom on draft decisions and governmental operations.
This is not always the case elsewhere (Table 6-8). The fact
that the committee was chaired by a senior specialist in the
law faculty at Moscow State University surely contributed
to the committee's above-average performance.

As the data reported in Table 6-7 demonstrate, most
standing committees fall short of this model. By several
key indicators, the participation of the standing committees in the work of the soviet is quite low. In 1984, the
committees averaged less than one report (*doklad/sodoklad*)
to the sessions of their soviets a year. Although their preparation of issues for meetings of the executive committee
was nearly three times greater, the average was still less
than three a year. In the same year, only 40 percent of the
committees gave an annual report (*otchet*) on their work.
Perhaps even more striking, and clearly in contrast to the

[72] Calculated from *Nekotorye voprosy, 1984*, p. 26.

TABLE 6-8. Participation by Standing Committees in Work of Soviet, Selected Years, 1976–84

Year	No. of standing committees giving reports on issues to session (dokad/sodoklad)	Percent of standing committees giving such reports at sessions	Annual average of such reports per committee	No. of issues prepared for meetings of ispolkom (voprosy)	Average no. of issues prepared for ispolkom per committee	Percent of standing committees reporting annually on their work (otchet)
1976	377,916	73.0	1.14	893,676	2.7	47.5
1980	334,035	71.5	1.00	856,611	2.6	31.5
1983	304,870	62.2	0.91	868,422	2.6	38.9
1984	328,656	—	0.97	895,819	2.7	40.2
By Level of Soviet, 1984						
Republic/Krai	894	—	0.40	3,893	1.7	7.9
Raion	19,507	—	0.62	108,838	3.5	21.6
City	13,417	—	0.58	66,072	2.9	23.2
City borough	3,811	—	0.44	23,680	2.8	14.8
Settlement	25,996	—	0.91	77,651	2.7	39.4
Village	265,031	—	1.10	615,685	2.5	43.9

SOURCES: *Nekotorye voprosy,* 1976, 1980, 1983, 1984, pp. 23–28.
NOTE: The number of soviets and standing committees can be found in Table 6-6, except for the 1984 figures. There were 52,046 soviets in 1984 with 337,640 standing committees. Statistics for 1985 regarding standing committee participation in the work of the soviets were not available at the time of writing.

high expectations of the early 1960s the activity of standing committees in these areas has not only failed to increase but in some cases has actually declined, at least over the past decade. How can these findings be explained? Why is the apparent potential of the standing committees for active participation in the work of the soviet not more fully realized? The answers to these questions can be found in the relationship that exists between the ispolkom and the standing committee. In addition to showing what an active committee can do, the case study of the Lenin city borough Standing Committee on Social Legality also revealed that to a large extent a standing committee must rely on and interact with its executive committee if it is to succeed in accomplishing its objectives. Theoretically, the interdependence of the two bodies works to their mutual advantage. In a recent work on the subject, V. I. Novoselov described five forms this interdependence should take: "coordination" of committee activities by the ispolkom, participation of the committees in the activity of the ispolkom, assistance given by the ispolkom to the committees in carrying out their functions, the ispolkom's role in training new committee members, and material and clerical support given to the committees.[73] Novoselov's account emphasizes the independence and initiative of the standing committees. He offers examples to show what deputies have done when their recommendations went unheeded by an indifferent ispolkom. "Coordination," he insists, "does not give executive committees the right to lead the work of the standing committees."[74]

Undoubtedly, such a harmonious interaction of equals sometimes occurs, but there are at least two major reasons why this prescription is often not fulfilled in practice. The first has to do with the composition of the standing com-

[73] Novoselov, *Ispolkom i postoiannye komissii Soveta*, pp. 13ff.
[74] Ibid., p. 23.

mittees. Data from Leizerov's study of standing committees in the twenty-two district and nine city soviets of the
Minsk region in Belorussia for the sixteenth term reveal
that 68 percent of the deputies in the first case and 71 percent in the second term had no experience or expertise corresponding to the functional area of the committee on
which they served.[75] These figures declined to 36 percent
and 37 percent respectively when only the leadership of
the committees was considered. Although the level of expertise available to the committees has risen in recent
years, it varies greatly by type of committee (from 79 percent of the members of Planning and Budget Committees
to 12 percent of those on the Committees to Preserve the
Environment). Moreover, the lack of expertise is com-
pounded by the high rate of turnover of members of the
standing committees. Leizerov's data show that 85 percent
of the members of committees at the district level, 84 percent of those at the city level, and 96 percent of those at
the village level were replaced after the elections to the sixteenth term (1977–80). The corresponding figures for leaders were 65 percent, 62 percent, and 72 percent.

The data show that in most cases whatever experience
and knowledge the members of the standing committees
gain during their term of office is lost at the next election.
Nevertheless, some Soviet specialists see high levels of renewal as beneficial because they bring new people with
fresh insight into the "schools of administration," which
Lenin suggested the committees should be.[76] Others, Leizerov perhaps foremost among them, strongly recommend that those deputies reelected to the soviet be assigned to the same standing committees on which they
previously served.[77] Indeed, unless this at least is done, it

[75] The data in this section came from Leizerov, "Effektivnost' poriadka," pp. 70–73.
[76] See, e.g., Bezuglov, *Deputat v Sovete*, p. 30.
[77] Leizerov, "Effektivnost' poriadka," p. 73. See also Leizerov *Demokraticheskie formy*, pp. 95–97.

is difficult to see how the standing committees can possibly begin to assert their weight in what is now a hopelessly unequal distribution of abilities.

The second reason the relationship between the ispolkom and the standing committees is bound to be unequal has to do with time. Not only do the officers and staff of the executive committees have an advantage in experience and expertise, they also in most cases are full-time employees. Members of the standing committees, on the other hand, meet about four times a year for a few hours at each meeting and receive no time off for doing so. To deal with this problem, some scholars have suggested longer or more frequent meetings of the committees,[78] others recommend relieving the members from other forms of public service.[79] Granting released time from work, however, appears to go against Lenin's injunction that deputies perform their governmental service while continuing their jobs.

It is difficult not to conclude that for rank-and-file members of a standing committee the costs of participation relative to the benefits are high. They must master a good deal of information in a short time, not only about a subject with which they may be unfamiliar but also with political procedures that are new to them. They must do this on their own time, time already limited by other public and personal obligations. Moreover, at the end of their two-and-a-half year term, even those conscientious enough to persevere in their efforts will almost certainly be replaced. What is remarkable in the case study described earlier is not that a few of the deputies participated very rarely in the work of the standing committee, but that others became as involved as they did. It is little wonder if

[78] Leizerov, *Demokraticheskie formy*, p. 105. See also Hill's review of the literature in *Soviet Politics, Political Science, and Reform*, pp. 78–82.

[79] Starovoitov, "Sessii Sovetov," p. 12.

the balance of power between the ispolkom and the standing committees is weighted in favor of the former.

WHO GOVERNS?

The Soviet political system is typically presented in Western texts as comprised of three main structures: the organs of the Communist Party, the system of legislative councils, and the bureaucracy directed at the top by the Council of Ministers. The Presidium of the Supreme Soviet, the courts, and other actors in the political process almost invariably receive less attention.[80] In assessing the relative contributions of these bodies in functional terms, the party is generally accorded the place of first importance in the formulation of public policy; the function of the agencies of government is to implement it. It is conventional for these descriptions to treat the legislative bodies as having little or no significance. As one textbook puts it, "While the formal authority of these bodies is great, little real power is wielded by them."[81] This mode of analysis applied at the lower levels of the Soviet system leads to the conclusion that local legislatures are dominated by their executive committees and that the executive committees are told what to do by the local party organization. In such a view, the political influence of the deputy relative to the members of the ispolkom and the party is minimal at best.

How well does such a conclusion describe the political process at the local level in the Soviet Union? What is the relative contribution of these three bodies to local govern-

[80] See, e.g., the treatment of the Soviet political system found in Alex N. Dragnich and Jorgen S. Rasmussen, *Major European Governments*, 7th ed. (Chicago: Dorsey Press, 1986), pp. 551–555; Vadim Medish, *The Soviet Union*, 2nd ed. (Englewood Cliffs, N.J.: Prentice-Hall, 1984), pp. 122ff.; Leon P. Baradat, *Soviet Political Society* (Englewood Cliffs, N.J.: Prentice-Hall, 1986), part 3.

[81] Barry and Barner-Barry, *Contemporary Soviet Politics*, p. 87.

ment? After examining the relationship between the deputy and the ispolkom, and the role of the party in local politics, we will present a proposal for reconceptualizing local Soviet politics with respect to the question of who governs.

The skepticism of Western analysts regarding the role of the deputies in decision-making is not difficult to understand. On paper, the importance of the deputies in "resolving all questions of local significance" is paramount; the executive committee is elected by them and subordinated to them. The members of the ispolkom must account for their actions before the deputies.[82] But in reality the relationship between the deputies and the ispolkom is one-sided in favor of the executive agencies. The dominance of the ispolkom over the workings of local government is even acknowledged by Soviet specialists, as the passage by Starovoitov cited earlier indicates. The reasons for this dominance deserve further attention.

Much of the ispolkom's advantage derives from its status as the government between sessions of the soviet. Both the executive committee and the administrative agencies during this period have the right to make legally binding decisions. Most of them fall into the category of administrative decision-making and do not need confirmation at a subsequent session of the soviet. Even where such action is required—for example, in the case of personnel changes—there are too many deputies meeting too infrequently to allow for effective discussion. Most if not all such questions will have been arranged beforehand. Those items that do get to the soviet are decided unanimously after formal and often perfunctory "debate."

Furthermore, as a result of the system of "dual subordination" there is a whole class of decisions for which the executive and administrative agencies are responsible but

[82] Articles 145 and 146 of the RSFSR constitution, April 12, 1978, *Vedomosti Verkhovnogo Soveta RSFSR*, 1978, no. 15, item 407.

which are delegated to them by superior ministries. Over these the local deputies have little or no control. Although the question of whether the authority of the executive committee is independent of the soviet is debated by Soviet scholars, both practice and theory seem to indicate that it is.[83] Ideally, the standing committees act to ensure that ispolkom carries out the deputies' will between sessions, but as the earlier discussion on standing committees demonstrated, the standing committees lack the legal authority, the time, and the expertise to effectively control the ispolkom. Both in practice and in law it is more often the ispolkom that tells the deputies what to do.[84]

A second reason for the unequal relationship between the soviets and their executive committees has to do with their composition. As the data presented in Table 4-4 and Table 4-6 demonstrate, the composition of the soviets reflects an effort to include a fairly broad and representative cross section of the population in local government, but this is not so with their executive committees. These bodies are typically made up of middle-aged men with a higher education—in the case of presidents overwhelmingly so. Between eight and nine of every ten members of the ispolkom belong to the party. Only one in three of those on the ispolkom is replaced at each election, and for officers the rate is much lower (less than 15 percent). The high portion of middle-aged party members with higher levels of education and low rates of turnover is also characteristic of the administrative leadership, if the Lenin city borough soviet is any indication (see Table 4-7).

Moreover, *within* the executive committees there also

---

[83] See discussion in Barabashev and Sheremet, *Sovetskoe stroitel'stvo*, pp. 324–325.

[84] The right of the ispolkom to give the deputies assignments (*porucheniia*) to carry out is the subject of some dispute. A consensus seems to support it. See *Ispolnitel'nyi komitet mestnogo Soveta*, pp. 224–225. On the inequality of the balance between the ispolkom and the standing committees, see ibid., p. 199 and Leizerov, *Demokraticheskie formy*, p. 85.

appears to be an unwritten distinction between those who are officers and those who are not. For example, of the thirteen-member ispolkom of the Lenin city borough soviet, all but two were party members, all but two had higher education, all were in their forties and fifties, and of the four women, one was secretary. In the transition from the eighteenth to the nineteenth term, all six of the rank-and-file members were replaced, but among the seven officers (including five vice-presidents) there were only three new faces; the president and secretary did not change. Taken together, the evidence strongly suggests that the executive committees constitute something of an elite group—those possessing the skills and experience needed to make complex decisions. It is also likely that within this elite an even smaller group exerts disproportionate influence over the decision-making process.

Finally, the ispolkom dominates by virtue of its control over the organization of local governmental activity. Such control is especially important with regard to personnel. While the soviet as a whole retains the right to discuss and confirm appointments to administrative agencies, advisory commissions, and standing committees, in practice this is done unanimously and routinely by the deputies on the basis of the nominations put before them by the ispolkom. Interviews with Soviet deputies and specialists indicate that even this formality is occasionally violated. In addition, the ispolkom oversees the preparation of the agenda, initiates draft legislation, apparently reviews the reports by the standing committees on its proposals before the sessions, approves who will be invited to attend sessions and standing committee meetings, and controls the flow of information to the deputies, especially as it pertains to the budget. For all these reasons, the dominance of the ispolkom over the proceedings of the soviet has resulted in what Starovoitov calls a "psychological barrier" to greater deputy participation in decision-making. In the unusually candid article written in 1985, he stated:

Even now it is possible to encounter workers in the party and state apparatus who reason thus: "Why call a session of the soviet? Get the ispolkom together and let's decide." In this way they resolve a great many issues including even the important matters—not at sessions of the soviets, but by a rather narrow board [kollegiia], sometimes secretly.[85]

One proposal to redress the existing imbalance between the soviets and their executive committees is to elect a presidium that would represent the interests of the deputies between their sessions and serve their needs directly. The exact form and functions of such a body have been a matter of considerable debate among Soviet specialists.[86] Thus far, the proposal has achieved only limited acceptance: the 1980 law on the rights of oblast soviets allows the formation of such a presidium in area and regional soviets with populations over 1.5 million if permission is obtained from the appropriate Supreme Soviet. Even then, although such a presidium can make "operative decisions" on issues of current concern, the regional level ispolkom retains the right to reverse such a decision.[87] An alternative proposal is to establish a sort of separate staff, or even a standing committee, that would be independent of the ispolkom and that would service the deputies. As one deputy suggested to the author, this might help to "weaken the otherwise almost absolute dependency of the soviet on the discretion and actions of the ispolkom and its apparatus in organizing their work."[88]

If the members of the ispolkom play the starring role on

[85] Starovoitov, "Sessii Sovetov," p. 9.

[86] Two discussions of the literature on this proposal are Hill, Soviet Politics, Political Science, and Reform, pp. 82–84, and Ispolnitel'nyi komitet mestnogo Soveta, pp. 199–200.

[87] Barabashev and Sheremet, Sovetskoe stroitel'stvo, pp. 339–348.

[88] This idea is discussed and found less useful than a presidium by Bezuglov, in Ispolnitel'nyi komitet mestnogo Soveta, pp. 222–223.

the local political stage, then it is the local party organization that functions as director. As discussed at the beginning of Chapter 3, the party established its primacy in the first years of Soviet power; its right to make policy for Soviet society rests on its claim to be the sole legitimate representative of the interests of the working class. The *locus classicus* of party-state relations is the March 22, 1919, resolution of the Russian Communist Party (Bolshevik) entitled "On the Organizational Question." While clearly asserting the supremacy of the party in all matters of policy, the document is not without a certain ambiguity. On one hand, party members are enjoined to "establish complete control in the contemporary state organizations that are the soviets," but on the other hand, "the party strives to *direct* the work of the soviets, not replace them."[89] Furthermore, they are to do so "within the framework of the Soviet Constitution," a phrase that fifty-eight years later was written into the final version (though not the original) of article 6 of the 1977 Constitution acknowledging the "leading and guiding" role of the CPSU in the Soviet political system. Soviet specialists are adamant in interpreting this to mean that the organs of government, and not those of the party, make legislative decisions, that a clear boundary (*razgranichenie*) exists between the functions of the party and the state which bars the substitution (*podmena*) of the authority of the party for that of the state.[90] A new *Handbook* for deputies states this position clearly:

[89] A translation of the whole resolution can be found in Robert H. McNeal (ed.), *Resolutions and Decisions of the CPSU 1898–1964*, vol. 2 (Toronto: University of Toronto Press, 1974); the section dealing with the relationship between the party and the soviets is on pp. 88–89. Emphasis in the original.

[90] See e.g., Lukianov, *Razvitie zakonodatel'stva*, p. 302. Similar formulations can be found in E. M. Chekharin, *Sovety narodnykh deputov voploshchenie narodovlastiia* (Moscow: Iurid. Lit., 1978), pp. 34–47; *Partiia i Sovety*, pp. 197–210; A. S. Davydov, *Partiinoe rukovodstvo Sovetamu narodnykh deputatov* (Moscow: Sovetskaia Rossiia, 1983), pp. 10–12.

The article of the Constitution which states that all party organizations act "within the framework of the USSR Constitution" means that, first, party organizations may not and should not substitute for (*podmeniat'*) the organs of government; and second, they do not have the right to act contrary to the Constitution and to legislation based on it. The central party organs may, of course, recognize the necessity of introducing needed changes and amendments and issue directives to this effect to the Communist deputies of the Supreme Soviets, but until the law is changed or revoked they are obliged to abide by it.[91]

Despite the assertions that a "boundary" exists between the functions of the organs of the party and the state, there is little doubt that in practice the party controls what the soviets do. While they are careful to refer to it as "leadership," even standard Soviet treatments of this relationship accord the party a predominant influence over the formulation and implementation of policy.[92] In the words of the *Handbook*, "not one important political or organizational question is resolved by the state organs without the leading directives (*ukazanii*) of the Communist Party."[93] This is supposed to mean that local government decisions will reflect the policy directions as established by the CPSU at its Congresses, Central Committee plenary sessions, and other meetings of the party leadership. In practice, however, such directives clearly carry a sense of political, if not legal, obligation for those in the government who must carry them out. It should hardly be surprising, then, that the leadership of the local soviet makes sure its decisions conform to those of the local party organization. Although this crosses the theoretical boundary between the state

[91] *Sovety narodnykh deputatov: spravochnikh*, p. 59.
[92] See e.g., Barabashev and Sheremet, *Sovetskoe stroitel'stvo*, pp. 125–126 and also Lukianov, *Razvitie zakonodatel'stvo*, p. 306.
[93] *Sovety narodnykh deputatov: spravochnikh*, p. 64.

and the party so insistently maintained by Soviet legal scholars, there is evidence that it happens. As one recent Soviet study of city soviets concluded: "Unfortunately, sometimes the decisions of the city soviets repeat almost word-for-word the resolution of the corresponding party organs."[94]
In addition to dominating the making of policy, the party determines who will run the government. The recruitment, nomination, and training of the deputies, their executive officers, and the members of the administrative agencies are within the *nomenklatura* of the party, and no appointments to or removal from these offices takes place without at least the tacit approval of the local party organization.[95] While it is true that there is no requirement that those in government be party members, the more important the position, the more likely they are to be members. Moreover, control over candidate selection guarantees that those who are not party members share the point of view of those who are. Thus, although a majority of the local deputies (57.2 percent) elected in 1985 were not party members, 42.8 percent were. An additional 22.3 percent belonged to the Komsomol (see Table 4-3). The remaining 35 percent who had no official party affiliation were almost certainly acceptable to the party, since the nomination process would have screened out any who were not.

[94] V. S. Osnovin, *Gorodskii Sovet-organ sotsial'nogo upravlenii* (Moscow: Iurid. Lit., 1983), p. 105.

[95] The use of *nomenklatura* in reference to the soviets is noted in A. S. Davydov, *Partiinoe rukovodstvo*, pp. 37–43. See also Chapter 4, footnote 37. Until recently, relatively few details were known about how *nomenklatura* operated in practice. See, however, Michael S. Voslensky, *Nomenklatura* (New York: Doubleday, 1984), on a former prominent Soviet scholar who left the Soviet Union. Two earlier but in some respects more comprehensive descriptions are Bohdan Harasymiw, "Nomenklatura: The Soviet Communist Party's Leadership Recruitment System," *Canadian Journal of Political Science* 2 (December 1969); and Frederick C. Barghoorn, *Politics in the USSR*, 2nd ed. (Boston: Little, Brown, and Co., 1972), pp. 180–185.

Within the executive committees elected in 1985, 71 percent of the members belonged to the party, while another
8 percent were in the Komsomol. However, even this un-
derstates the party's presence because in the soviets above
the rural level, party members account for at least 85 percent of the executive committees, and Komsomol members account for another 5 percent. Among ispolkom presidents, almost all are party members, and members of the
corresponding party committee at that. Conversely, the
first secretary of the party committee usually is a member
of the ispolkom.[96] Finally, as the data for department
heads in the Lenin city borough soviet would seem to suggest (see Table 4-7), the overwhelming majority of administrators are party members of longstanding also.

Control of local government personnel ensures that the
party's policy preferences will be correctly communicated
and that those holding key positions will be members of
the Communist Party. Indeed, party members in the different agencies of local government are enjoined to form
"party groups," through which they see to it that the work
of the soviet will be coordinated with the wishes of the
corresponding party organization.[97] Party groups are
formed by those who are party members among the deputies as a whole, in the ispolkom, and in the standing
committee. Among the professional administrators, the
party's work is coordinated by primary party cells, which
are organized at the place of work—in this case, the bu-

[96] *Partiia i Sovety*, pp. 222–223. See also Bezuglov, *Sovetskoe stroitel'stvo*,
p. 81.

[97] The work of the party groups is specified in articles 68 and 69 of the
Statutes of the CPSU, *Ustav KPSS* (Moscow: Politizdat, 1984), pp. 59–60,
and they are discussed in all the standard reference works on the soviets;
see, e.g., Barabashev and Sheremet, *Sovetskoe stroitel'stvo*, pp. 138–145,
and Bezuglov, *Sovetskoe stroitel'stvo*, pp. 75–82. These works leave little
doubt about the function of the party groups. Thus, on p. 71 of *Sovety
narodnykh deputatov: spravochnik* we read: "Through these groups, the
CPSU directs the activity of the soviets from those in the village to the
Supreme Soviet of the USSR."

reaucracy—where there are at least three party members.[98] According to the rules of the CPSU, the party groups are subordinated only to their corresponding party organization and are not answerable to the party groups in the soviets at higher levels of the hierarchy.

The members of the different party groups are expected to hold meetings as the need arises. Such meetings will normally be chaired by the secretary of the corresponding party organization and will discuss the appointment of personnel, the work of individual deputies, and how well the soviet is doing in carrying out the policy directives of the party.[99] Because the party secretary normally sits on the ispolkom and a solid majority of its members belong to the party group, it can be safely assumed that there is virtually no chance that an executive committee will act contrary to the desires of the local party organization.

The relationship between the party and the state described above has led one leading Western observer of local Soviet politics, Ronald Hill, to conclude that as long as the party continues to dominate the workings of the soviets (*podmena*), "it is hard to see how a confident and effective system of local government, commanding the respect of those who work within it and of the broad mass of citizens, can develop."[100] Soviet legal scholars like Lukianov, Shakhnazarov, Barabashev, and others would reject such a contention on the grounds noted earlier that a boundary exists between "leading" and "governing"; for them, as long as the party does not actually make laws or administer them this distinction is maintained and the problem of

[98] *Ustav KPSS*, p. 60. The responsibility of party members in the standing committees is noted in *Partiia i Sovety*, p. 247.

[99] *Sovety narodnykh deputatov: spravochnik*, pp. 72–73. A description of the meetings of the party group of the Saratov oblast soviet reveals how thoroughly the party dominates the proceedings of the session (A. S. Davydov, *Partiinoe rukovodstvo*, p. 16).

[100] Ronald J. Hill, "The Development of Local Government Since Stalin's Death," in Jacobs, *Soviet Local Politics and Government*, p. 33.

podmena does not arise.[101] In reality, this is a legal fiction. Hill is quite right when he suggests that any such distinction is blurred in practice.[102] The preceding analysis shows that local soviet deputies are certainly aware of what the local party organization wants the soviet to do and perceive that they have a moral and political obligation to do it. Since the agencies of local government responsible for the preparation and execution of what the soviet does are controlled by party members, there is almost no likelihood that they will do otherwise.

The conventional view of the relative contributions to local politics by the party, the executive agencies, and the deputies presented at the beginning of this section is understandable. On the basis of the analysis presented here, it is reasonable to conclude that the party makes policy, that the ispolkom makes decisions that ensure the implementation of these policies, and that the deputies do what they are told. Such a conclusion, however, oversimplifies the realities of Soviet grassroots politics. For one thing, it ignores the fact that all members of the executive committee are themselves deputies and that leading members of the local party are often members of the executive committee. While it may be true that their importance in the formulation and implementation of policy is not derived from their status as deputies, it is incorrect to say that deputies play little or no role. This is more than a semantic distinction. To analyze local Soviet government by dividing it neatly into what the party does, what the executive and administrative agencies do, and what the deputies do is artificial and ignores the multifunctionality of local soviet agencies as well as their overlapping memberships.

A different perspective develops if one looks at local so-

[101] See Hill's excellent discussion of this in his *Soviet Politics, Political Science, and Reform*, pp. 116–123. See also Lukianov, *Razvitie zakonodatel'-stva*, pp. 301–303, and G. Kh. Shaknazarov, *Sotsialisticheskaia demokratiia* (Moscow: Politizdat, 1974), pp. 107–109.

[102] Hill, *Soviet Politics, Political Science, and Reform*, pp. 125ff.

viet politics in terms of who participates and how. In his analysis of citizen participation in Romania based on interviews with 250 deputies in four regional districts, Daniel Nelson suggests that deputies can be divided into three categories: elites, the needed, and fillers.[103] Based on the research presented in the present book, a similar typology can be offered for Soviet deputies. At the top there is an elite consisting of professionals in the party and state organs; at the highest levels they may be one and the same person. This group would include the officers of the ispolkom who have held their position for more than one term, the heads of administrative agencies, and the members of the local party committee who are actively involved in the work of the soviets as chairpersons of standing committees, as members of the ispolkom, or as deputies. Collectively numbering less than 5 percent of the deputies, these individuals—mostly well-educated men of middle age— are the decision-makers in local soviet politics.

The second group is made up of specialists, deputies who are influential by virtue of their expertise or experience and who remain as deputies for more than one term because they are useful, in some cases essential, for the efficient functioning of local government. They are not employed by either the party or the state, as are members of the elite, but hold full-time positions in enterprises or organizations formally outside of the political system. Frequently found leading standing committees, or as members of their aktiv, these individuals may become involved in local government to protect or advance the particular interests of the organization employing them. They account for perhaps another twenty to thirty percent of the deputies.

Finally, there is the rank-and-file member of the soviet

[103] Daniel Nelson, "Citizen Participation in Romania: The People's Council Deputy," in Daniel Nelson (ed.), *Local Politics in Communist Countries* (Lexington: University of Kentucky Press, 1980), pp. 90–120.

whose service as a deputy constitutes a one-term two-and-a-half-year education in the "schools of administration," as Lenin called local government. Lacking position, specialist resources, and perhaps motivation, they frequently function as an audience for the actions of more-influential deputies. While some attempt to enhance the participation of this group was evident in the "populist" policies of the Khrushchev years, the Brezhnev period marked a gradual return to the dominance of the professionals, a tendency also noted by Blair Ruble in connection with trade union officials.[104]

The attempt to understand Soviet politics through the use of elite analysis is certainly not novel.[105] However, the view that local government in the Soviet Union is dominated by a small group of party professionals who monopolize the political process while denying any real influence to those elected to represent the popular will needs to be modified. In the first place, mobility within the system is possible. For the politically ambitious, a good performance in the role of deputy may attract favorable attention from those in the party seeking new recruits or deciding who to promote; conversely, a bad performance will damage one's service record.[106] Second, even the rank and file are not wholly without opportunities to influence policy. Of the various ways examined in this chapter, the two that seem most promising are the use of the right of inquiry (*zapros*) and the deputy's participation in the work of the standing committees. Third, the deputy does have the ability to obtain attention for constituency problems and

[104] Ruble, *Soviet Trade Unions*, p. 96.

[105] Among the better efforts, see, e.g., Jerry Hough, *The Soviet Prefects* (Cambridge: Harvard University Press, 1969); Hill, *Soviet Political Elites*; Milton C. Lodge, *Soviet Elite Attitudes Since Stalin* (Columbus, Ohio: Charles E. Merrill, 1969); Bohdan Harasymiw, *Political Elite Recruitment in the Soviet Union* (New York: St. Martin's Press, 1984).

[106] This aspect of the cadre policy of the party is discussed in *Party i Sovety*, pp. 220–221.

to resolve them successfully. As noted earlier, perhaps 50 percent of the executive committee meetings are taken up with "individual" matters.[107] When asked whether they would bring constituents' problems to the attention of the soviet at its session, the deputies interviewed by the author almost always responded that they would resolve them not at the session but with the help of their executive committee, reportedly with a high rate of success.

With respect to the issue of *podmena*, the view of the local political process offered here suggests that the interaction between the party and the state is more complex than it is often presented in Western analyses. Given the overlapping memberships that exist in the leadership of the two bodies, and the problems inherent in defining what is policy and what is administration, it becomes difficult to say clearly which organ does what. It hardly makes sense to say that the party "supplants" the authority of the soviet when both bodies are led by the same people. The argument about whether the party dominates the state also underestimates the political differences between party members. Finally, for most issues resolved by local government the need for party authority simply does not arise. Only when there are jurisdictional disputes between governmental and nongovernmental agencies, or within the bureaucracy, would the party committee be likely to get directly involved.[108]

In the end, who governs? In his landmark study of municipal politics in the city of New Haven, Connecticut, Robert Dahl made this question the title as well as the subject of his book. He concluded that in the formulation of public policy "most citizens use their political resources scarcely at all," that they were citizens without politics. Real decision-making power lay in the hands of those he

[107] Lebedev, *Sistema organov gorodskogo upravleniia*, pp. 60–62.
[108] See Hough and Fainsod, *How the Soviet Union Is Governed*, pp. 508–510.

termed the "professionals." Without minimizing the differences between the two systems, it is not inappropriate to end this discussion of local Soviet government by quoting from Dahl's description of those who dominated the decision-making process in New Haven. Referring to those "professionals" both in and out of public office, Dahl writes:

> The political system of New Haven is characterized by the presence of two sharply contrasting groups of citizens. The great body of citizens use their political resources at a low level; a tiny body of professionals within the political stratum use their political resources at a high level. Most citizens acquire little skill in politics; professionals acquire a great deal. Most citizens exert little direct and immediate influence on the decisions of public officials; professionals exert much more. Most citizens have political resources they do not employ to gain influence over the decisions of public officials; consequently there is a great gap between their actual and potential influence. The professionals alone narrow the gap; they do so by using their political resources to the full and by using them with a high degree of efficiency.[109]

In the Soviet context, the "professionals" include the members of the elite as defined earlier: those deputies (less than 5 percent of the total) who work full-time in the party or state apparatus and who are the real decision-makers in local Soviet government. Most of the remaining deputies, along with most Soviet citizens, lack the time, skills, resources, or interest to become involved in making decisions. At the same time, they are not wholly without the means to influence such decisions; some of the evidence presented here suggests that efforts to do so are becoming more frequent.

[109] Robert A. Dahl, *Who Governs?* (New Haven: Yale University Press, 1961), pp. 305–306.

CHAPTER SEVEN

Is the Deputy an Effective Representative?

FROM OUR ANALYSIS, we can conclude that (1) Soviet citizens, either as deputies or through them, can and do participate effectively in their local government and (2) comparatively few Soviet citizens actually take advantage of the opportunities that do exist, although levels of participation have tended to increase over time. Before looking at the implications of these conclusions for understanding change in the Soviet political system, it is worth noting that such conclusions are at variance with much of the conventional wisdom on this subject found in Western popular and scholarly literature.

The *New York Times*, for example, in reporting Chernenko's speech on the local soviets before the Central Committee plenary session of April 10, 1984, observed that while deputies were supposed to deal with constituent concerns they in fact "do little beyond sitting through rubber-stamp sessions."[1] As for Western specialists on Soviet politics, Michael Urban is probably correct in asserting in 1982 that a majority of them would use the terms "mobilized" or "pseudo" in referring to popular participation in the Soviet Union.[2] One Westerner dismisses participation in governmental institutions in the Soviet Union as a "cha-

[1] *New York Times*, April 11, 1984, p. A12.
[2] Urban, "Information and Participation in Local Soviet Government," p. 64. While acknowledging the growth in the amount of public participation in local government, Urban maintains that it is largely devoid of real content in the sense of a "public sphere," as the term is used by Jurgen Habermas (see Urban's discussion, ibid., pp. 67–68, 83–85).

rade."[3] For others, the orientations of Soviet citizens toward their political system are characteristic of a "subject" or "subject-participant" political culture in which members of the system lack the opportunity or initiative to influence government decisions.[4] The present work does not share this view.

On the basis of the research presented here, the image of Soviet citizens as passive recipients of government policies and stoic and uncomplaining subjects lacking legitimate opportunities or the inclination to contest and shape the decisions that affect their lives is inaccurate, at least at the local level. In one respect, this conclusion is similar to one DiFranceisco and Gitelman reached based on émigré interviews. They also reject the view of Soviet citizens as inactive or ineffective in their dealings with government.[5] However, DiFranceisco and Gitelman go on to argue that "meaningful participation" takes place almost exclusively outside the formal and legitimate channels available to Soviet citizens and is primarily motivated by the desire to obtain some personal benefit; participation in "approved ways" is dismissed as "ritualistic." For this reason, they label Soviet political culture as "covert-participant."[6] Such a conclusion seems inconsistent with the evidence offered in this book,

---

[3] Donald Barry, "A Criticism of Hough's Views," in Samuel Hendel (ed.), *The Soviet Crucible* (Belmont, Calif.: Wadsworth, 1980), p. 228.

[4] Jack Gray, "Conclusions," in Archie Brown and Jack Gray (eds.), *Political Culture and Political Change* (New York: Holmes and Meier, 1977), p. 260. The term "subject-participants" is used by G. Almond and B. Powell, *Comparative Politics: A Developmental Approach* (Boston: Little, Brown, and Co., 1966), p. 273, and by Frederick C. Barghoorn, *Politics in the USSR*, 2nd ed. (Boston: Little, Brown, and Co., 1972), pp. 23–25.

[5] According to the authors, "he exhibits few of the deferential, passive attributes of the classic subject" (DiFranceisco and Gitelman, "Soviet Political Culture, pp. 618–619).

[6] Ibid., pp. 610–611, 618–619. DiFranceisco and Gitelman believe that participation is aimed almost solely at the implementation of policy; the soviet citizens' ability "to influence policy decisions, even indirectly, is practically nil."

which documents the use by many Soviet citizens of various legal means for communication of public as well as private concerns to those in local government. Not all Western analyses dismiss popular participation within existing Soviet political institutions as an exercise in futility. The conclusions offered at the beginning of this chapter do not appear inconsistent with those arrived at by Theodore Friedgut. On the basis of his investigation into the perceptions of Soviet local government held by recent émigrés to Israel, Friedgut discerns "a nucleus of cooperative and active respondents, who, though a minority, work within established institutions for their satisfaction, and appear to have a civic sense of competence, a sense that they may, as citizens, expect service and satisfaction from official institutions."[7] In a similar vein, Seweryn Bialer makes a distinction between "high politics," concerned with larger societal issues, and "low politics," which he describes as "the decisions that directly touch the citizen's daily life, the communal matters, and the conditions of the workplace." With respect to the first, Bialer finds most Soviet citizens to be apathetic. "Low politics," however, attracts far more serious attention and elicits the active participation of "a very high proportion of Soviet citizenry."[8] The evidence examined in the present work does not provide a basis for conclusions about Soviet attitudes toward "high politics," but the distinctions made by Bialer do echo the analysis of prerevolutionary Russian political culture offered earlier, which contrasted the active participation in local decisions found in many Russian villages with the absence of popular participation in deci-

---

[7] Theodore H. Friedgut, "The Soviet Citizen's Perception of Local Government," in Jacobs, Soviet Local Politics and Government, pp. 129–130.

[8] Seweryn Bialer, Stalin's Successors: Leadership Stability and Change in the Soviet Union (Cambridge: Cambridge University Press, 1980), pp. 166–167, 186–192. Although Bialer is dealing primarily with participation in party organizations, his remarks appear to be intended for other areas as well, including the soviets (see esp. p. 192).

sions of national importance. In any case, the findings reported here tend to support the views of Friedgut, Bialer, Hough, and others, which suggest in varying degrees that at least some of the political participation that takes place in the Soviet Union can be considered meaningful in the sense that it serves the interests of those who engage in it and not merely the purposes of those who govern.

POSSIBILITIES

The questions that guided the author in his research were essentially two: Are Soviet citizens able to communicate constituent concerns and preferences about policies affecting their communities to their elected representatives? What can the deputies do to ensure that the concerns of their constituents are satisfied? Answers to these questions should provide an empirical basis for our understanding of political participation in the Soviet Union. Participation was defined as the involvement of citizens in the process by which decisions affecting community life are made and implemented, and several criteria were established to determine whether such participation was effective ("meaningful"). If a close examination of the activities of locally elected Soviet deputies showed that these criteria were met in practice, then an empirical basis would be established for concluding that political participation in the Soviet Union was more than the sham that most Western literature considers it to be.

The research presented on the activity of deputies to the local soviets strongly supports the conclusion that, in this case at least, the criteria have been met. There are a number of legitimate means Soviet citizens can use to communicate their individual and community concerns to decision-makers, and some Soviet citizens do take advantage of these opportunities. Although the numbers doing so run into the millions annually, they actually account for a small portion of those who could make use of these participatory mechanisms. It also seems that, as often as not, citizens who do use the various channels available to them for contacting local government can expect some measure of attention to their concerns. Many, if not most, of these contacts are undertaken for motives of personal interest rather than for the benefit of the community as a whole. However, this is true for local government in noncommunist countries as well, and in any case advocacy of broader community interests is not wholly lacking in citizen meetings with deputies. As to the question of whether such contacts are "citizen-initiated," the interpretation offered here differs from the opinion of Friedgut, who noted a "distinct lack" of this dimension.[9] While we agree with Friedgut that much of the Soviet citizen's participatory behavior is formalistic and "devoid of content," not all of it is. When a Soviet citizen (or group of citizens) takes the time and effort—without being required to do so—to convey their concerns, and thereby tries to influence those who make decisions in local government, it is difficult to conclude that such a citizen lacks the opportunity for citizen initiative. This is true whether citizens are seeking to obtain a private benefit or a public purpose.

Where does such activity take place? Soviet elections provide only the most marginal opportunities for Soviet citizens to communicate what they want to those who govern them, and so elections cannot really be considered an effective form of political participation, even though they involve the greatest number of people. While a modest amount of citizen input can occur at nomination meetings, in conversations with canvassers (agitators), and in the marking of ballots, most of the participation is quantitative and ritualistic.

There is one notable exception to the preceding generalization: the voter mandates adopted at the preelection meetings of candidates with the electorate. Although the

[9] Friedgut, *Political Participation in the USSR*, p. 302.

procedures have become more formalized in recent years, these meetings still provide a legitimate public forum for citizens to propose policies and projects ranging from minor housing repairs and children's playgrounds to the construction of new schools and improvements in the work of public service organizations. Soviet statistics cited earlier indicate that a large number of people (fifty to one hundred) attend the meetings at which mandates are adopted. The proportion of those whose presence is required is impossible to estimate precisely. Much of what goes on at these meetings is doubtless done for the sake of form, in which participation involves little more than going through the motions; proposals made would have been discussed beforehand and received official encouragement. However, this is clearly not always the case. The evidence suggests that many who attend do so out of interest and are not reluctant to make their preferences for community action a matter of public record. At least occasionally such proposals may engender a lively debate about who gets what, when, and how in the community.

The voter mandates are not the only legitimate mechanism by which Soviet citizens can effectively have input into what their local government does. Today almost all deputies meet at least twice a year with their constituents, either at the workplace or in the district, or both. Attendance at such meetings for all levels of soviets in 1983 averaged slightly more than fifty persons (see Table 5-3). As in the case of the mandates, it is difficult to determine how many of these people were required to attend, but it appears that at least some do so voluntarily. Moreover, while the purpose of these meetings is to hear deputy reports on the work of the local soviet and the deputy's part in it, reports that can have a soporific effect on their audience, the opportunity for more open give-and-take on community or individual problems does exist in the period set aside for questions after these presentations. Many of these discussions are undoubtedly also conducted pro forma, but some deputies are more able and willing to engage in a dialogue than others. Given a self-confident deputy and an issue of sufficient local concern, such meetings can involve citizens meaningfully in community affairs. Matters of individual concern only may come up at such meetings, but they are far more likely to be brought to the deputy's attention in the office hours set aside for that purpose called the *priyom*, or through informal contact. They may also be raised through procedures for making "proposals, declarations, and complaints." All of these channels may be used to articulate concerns of interest to the larger community, but this seems to happen infrequently in practice. It also appears that deputies are a secondary target for citizen contact about private concerns. The evidence indicates that most Soviet citizens seek redress for such matters first with the administrative agencies of the local soviet; the deputy becomes at best a fallback if the administrator proves recalcitrant. Presumably, the deputy will be less easily dismissed. Other vehicles for encouraging public input into local decisions, such as public discussions of draft legislation and the use of public opinion polls, appear to be less well developed, but like the other means reviewed here they too provide an opportunity for public influence in local decisions.

In turning to the question of what deputies can do to ensure that local government is responsive to the concerns of their constituents, our research suggests that the role of many deputies in making decisions continues to be that of a spectator or, at best, a spear-carrier for those few deputies who occupy center stage—the members of the executive committee. Nowhere is this relationship clearer than in the sessions of the local soviet, which are precisely the forums where the deputies are supposed to "examine and decide the most important questions" that fall within their jurisdiction.[10] Yet even Soviet sources acknowledge that in

[10] See, e.g., *Sovety narodnykh deputatov: spravochnik*, p. 161. The phrase quoted is from article 91 of the 1977 USSR Constitution.

practice it is the ispolkom that decides what the agenda will be, who will take part in the presentations, and to a large extent what will be contained in the presentations.[11] Participation of the rest of the deputies is limited to voting unanimously for whatever resolutions are put before them.

It would be inaccurate to conclude, however, that deputies—even among the rank and file—are wholly without input into what their local governments do. In the first place, even at the sessions deputies may avail themselves of the right of formal inquiry (*deputatskii zapros*) to bring attention to an issue they feel is being ignored or improperly dealt with by those in executive or administrative positions. Even the threat of a zapros may be enough to get a recalcitrant administrator to take action. Second, many of the issues of importance in a deputy's district are apparently resolved informally in meetings where the deputy intercedes on behalf of his constituents with the appropriate department head or executive officer. It is here, or in meetings of the executive committee if necessary, that any differences of opinion will be aired. In this respect, the role of the deputy in council is akin to that of an ombudsman. Finally, the standing committees also provide deputies with an opportunity to speak their minds regarding public policy, at least in areas considered to be within the committee's jurisdiction. The case study presented in Chapter 6 suggests that some deputies take advantage of that opportunity.

Even though Soviet citizens can and do effectively participate in local government, genuine political participation, according to the criteria used in this book, seems to be very much the exception, not the rule. It is probably true that most Soviet citizens, most of the time, are only observing the forms of participation, going through the motions. However, in assessing possibilities, the impor-

[11] Starovoitov, "Sessii Sovetov," p. 7.

tant point is not how often such participation takes place but that it takes place at all. If it can be demonstrated in a few cases that Soviet citizens can and do participate meaningfully in their local government, then it is possible that they can do so anywhere in the Soviet Union and that such practices may become more widespread.

PROBLEMS

Official Soviet writing on the deputies would reject the conclusions offered here regarding political participation in the Soviet Union. In their view, genuine political participation can take place only when rule by the bourgeoisie has been overthrown and replaced by that of the working class. Because the Soviet Union has the longest experience in this regard, any suggestions that in practice most Soviet citizens do not often play a meaningful role in local Soviet politics would be unacceptable. On the contrary, Soviet spokespersons maintain that genuine political participation is ensured not only by Marxist-Leninist doctrine but also through the adoption of an increasingly comprehensive set of laws and procedures specifying the rights of citizens and their elected representatives to take part in local governance. In the official view, not only are all forms of mass political participation in the Soviet Union genuine, but the volume of such participation is so great as to include virtually the whole population.[12]

Despite Soviet claims, the research presented here—

[12] Typical of such claims is one offered in a recent publication on the Moscow city soviet, translated into English in 1984. According to the author, "The Moscow Soviet is a genuine representative body of state authority, through which almost the whole of the adult population of the capital is drawn into state administration" (V. Shapovalov, *The Moscow Soviet* [Moscow: Progress Publishers, 1984], p. 18). A similar sort of publication, dealing with the deputies, explains why only under socialism (Soviet-variety) can you have genuine participation (A. A. Bezuglov, *Soviet Deputy* [Moscow: Progress Publishers, 1973], pp. 8–22).

much of which is based on Soviet source material—indicates that relatively few Soviet citizens take advantage of the opportunities that are available for meaningful participation in local government,[13] but it is not so much that they cannot do so. This book has discussed at length the elaborate legal and theoretical basis that exists in the Soviet Union today for expanded citizen participation in government. Rather, it is that they do not take advantage of the opportunities, or at least they do not as much as they probably could. In this sense, the possibilities described in the preceding paragraphs remain largely unfulfilled.

There is evidence for this conclusion throughout the present work. Research conducted in the city of Taganrog in the RSFSR revealed that 65 percent of the respondents had never contacted their deputy or attended a constituency meeting with a deputy. Only 12 percent had met with their deputies in the space of a single term in office (see Table 5-5). Friedgut reported similar results.[14] One of the more effective means for citizens to make proposals for action to their local government discussed here is the voter

[13] Much of the Soviet claim for universality of political participation rests on voter turnout, which invariably is reported as being more than 99 percent of those eligible. As already noted, however, very little of this participation is considered "meaningful" according to the criteria established by this author. On the contrary, for the overwhelming majority of Soviet citizens their vote has at most symbolic or ritual value; many simply go through the motions to avoid drawing unwanted attention to themselves. Even the 99 percent figure is apparently exaggerated since many avoid voting by failing to use the absentee ballot (*udostoverenie na pravo golosovaniia*). Estimates of those using this means to avoid voting run between 2.5 percent and 25 percent of the electorate. See Victor Zaslavsky and Robert J. Brym, "The Structure of Power and the Functions of Soviet Local Elections," in Jacobs, *Soviet Local Politics and Government*, p. 70.

[14] Friedgut "The Soviet Citizen's Perception of Local Government," p. 117. Some 36 percent of Friedgut's respondents reported having at some time met with their representatives. This compared with the 35 percent of the Taganrog respondents who had at some time in some way done so.

mandate. Yet, although the rate of implementation is high, on the average fewer than one out of every three deputies received such a mandate in the 1982–85 term, and there was an overall decrease in the number of mandates received in comparison with the previous term (Tables 5-1 and 5-2). The meetings at which deputies report to their constituents also provide an opportunity for citizen input, but while attendance at such meetings averages around fifty people, it is clear from the Taganrog study and from data reported in a study of such meetings in Sverdlovsk Province that only about 5 percent of those attending actually take part in the proceedings, other than official representatives.[15] Nor do Soviet citizens appear to take much advantage of the opportunities for conveying concerns of a more individual nature to the deputy, either informally or through the "office hours" (*priyom*) set aside by deputies for this purpose. The data suggest that their constituents are about three times more likely to go to the ispolkom.

When it comes to the levels of actual deputy participation in the work of the soviets, the evidence also points to a gap between what is possible and what is practiced. Despite the Soviet claim that sessions are the most important forum for deputy participation in local decision-making, the data reported in Table 6-3 reveal that roughly 30 percent do not do so, while other data indicate that most of the remainder take part only once or twice during their two-and-a-half-year term.[16] As Chapter 6 points out, the deputies who do participate frequently are most likely to be those in an official position; the participatory role of the rank and file is to vote their approval, which in virtually all cases appears to be unanimous. The right of formal inquiry (*zapros*) is, as noted, a potentially useful tool by

---

[15] The data from Sverdlovsk was reported in V. A. Kriazhkov, "Otchet deputata," *Pravovedenie*, no. 3 (1983), p. 34.

[16] See, among other studies, Leizerov, *Demokraticheskie formy*, p. 46.

which deputies can participate meaningfully in the work of the sessions, but it is infrequently used. In 1984 there was an average of only about two zaprosy per soviet annually, or an average of only one zapros for every twenty-one deputies (Table 6-5).

As for the work of the standing committees, much of their potential as a vehicle for deputy participation in local government appears to be unrealized. On the average, the committees prepare less than one issue a year for sessions of the soviet, and less than three per year for the meetings of the executive committees (see Table 6-8). Only about 40 percent of the standing committees report annually on their work (otchety), although they are required to do so in some republics and the practice is strongly endorsed by scholars.[17] Perhaps more significant, by a number of important indicators the standing committees' level of activity actually declined between 1976 and 1984: fewer issue reports (doklad/sodoklad) are being prepared, and the average number of deputies per committee has declined, as has the number of nonelected participants—the aktiv (see Tables 6-6 and 6-8). In other areas the amount of standing committee activity has remained about the same. In sum, the evidence indicates that for those forms of participation which appear to offer some real opportunity for citizen input into local government in the Soviet Union, the actual levels of participation are quite low.

In much of the Soviet literature one finds references, often in passing, to the somewhat more informal character of participation in the political life of the villages and rural settlements. This impression was reinforced in a number of interviews the author had with Soviet specialists, several of whom noted that the smaller size of these units and the general personal familiarity of their members often resulted in fewer inhibitions and a freer flow of opinions. Unfortunately, good analytical work on the conduct of lo-

---

[17] Ibid., p. 103.

cal government at this level is hard to come by. However, the data presented in this work suggest that the participation in the village and rural soviets is greater, in some respects at least, than in soviets at higher levels. According to Table 4-1, for instance, the number of soviets at this level are greater (they account for about 65 percent of all deputies), but their average size is much smaller (about forty deputies per soviet). They hold more sessions annually (Table 6-1) and have a much higher percentage of deputies taking part in them (Table 6-3). Their standing committees also appear to play a more active role in the work of the soviets (Table 6-8). This last indicator reflects the absence of professional administrative staff in most villages. While not all the data indicate greater levels of participation in rural areas (there are fewer mandates per deputy and fewer zaprosy, for example), the possibility exists that such opportunities are more often used by villagers than by city folk. If so, it is tempting to speculate that contemporary practices may represent a continuation of political attitudes found in prerevolutionary Russia among the peasants—namely, that decisions concerning village life were something about which they could have a say.

Why is it that so many Soviet citizens do not take advantage of the opportunities for real political participation that do exist? After all, a legislative framework for expanded participation is now in place. Contemporary Soviet political ideology as mediated by the CPSU strongly supports it, and the evidence presented in this book shows that a sufficient amount of participation does take place in practice, to demonstrate the possibilities that exist. An important part of the answer may lie in the attitudes and orientations toward politics and government that constitute the Soviet political culture. Many Soviets do not participate more actively because they do not know how—or if they do they doubt it would do any good. There are a number of reasons for the persistence of such views, some of which have to do with how local government is organized in the Soviet Union. Others appear more subjective, a residual from earlier political experience, especially that of the Stalinist period.

In trying to understand why deputies and constituents alike do not make more frequent use of the opportunities that exist for participation in local government, it is necessary to recognize the limits of the structural framework within which their participation takes place. If we consider first the deputy's role in council, it is clear that the involvement of the vast majority of deputies consists of their attendance at sessions of the soviet and their activities on the standing committees. As far as the sessions go, there are simply too many deputies meeting too infrequently and for too short a time for more than a few of them to discuss the matters under consideration. Above the village and settlement level, the average number of deputies per soviet is well over one hundred, and they convene only about four times a year (see Table 6-1). These meetings rarely last more than three hours. Even though the range of issues falling within the jurisdiction of Soviet local government is far broader than in the West, the amount of time spent discussing the issues and reaching a decision is far less.[18] Soviet specialists argue with some justification that the large number of deputies ensures a broader diversity of opinion and a lower deputy-constituent ratio. This may be so, but if there is only the most limited opportunity for other deputies to hear those opinions, then the potential advantages of numerically superior constituency representation—as it pertains to the work of the sessions at least—would be nullified.

To some extent, the lack of more active participation by

---

[18] E.g., the municipality in which I served as councilman for eight years met in public session at least twice a month. It was not unusual for such meetings to last for several hours. Few of them took less than an hour. This does not appear to be atypical for other suburban communities of similar size (30,000). The amount of time required for the conduct of business in larger cities is, of course, even greater.

deputies in the work of the sessions appears to be a legacy of the Stalinist period. In the 1920s, each deputy represented a larger number of constituents (hence there were fewer deputies), and they met far more often.[19] The decade was also marked by a greater tolerance for the differing opinions and divided votes. By contrast, contemporary sessions of the local soviets seem less a legislative forum than a ceremony unanimously confirming decisions already made. It is interesting that a number of Soviet specialists have suggested various changes in the work of the sessions, ranging from fewer deputies to more frequent sessions lasting a longer time.[20]

In theory, the advantage of a large number of deputies is also manifest in the work of the standing committees. Given the diversity of experience and expertise among a large number of deputies, the committees should be better able to oversee the work of the administrative departments whose areas of jurisdiction they parallel. Moreover, the standing committees are small enough for each deputy to take an active part in at least one of the substantive issues dealt with by local government. However, there are two structural factors mitigating against the deputy's effectiveness in the work of the committees and, for that matter, the sessions as well. Both derive from the Marxist-

[19] The 1918 Constitution established a ratio of one deputy for every 1,000 people in the cities, and one for every 100 in the villages. City soviets were to meet once a week, village soviets twice a week. See articles 57 and 59 of the 1918 Constitution (*Sbornik normativnykh aktov*, p. 39). Presently, most soviets meet four times a year, and there is on the average about one deputy for every 400 people in the cities and one for every 45 in the villages (see Table 4-1).

[20] Some recommendations of Soviet specialists for improving the work of the sessions were examined in earlier chapters of this book. An excellent summary in English is provided by Hill, *Soviet Politics, Political Science, and Reform*, pp. 69–75. In an interview with the author on December 13, 1984, Starovoitov argued against increasing the number of sessions but suggested that they be held for a longer period of time, perhaps even several days.

Leninist conception of the elected representative as a sort of amateur custodian. One is that deputies perform their duties without released time from their full-time jobs and without compensation. The other is the conception of the soviets as "schools of administration" from which most citizens "graduate" after a single two-and-a-half-year term and which is manifest institutionally in the principle of periodic renewal. The result is that for a deputy to be at all effective in the work of the standing committees, he or she has to master a great deal of substantive and procedural knowledge in a very short period of time while fulfilling other professional, social, and familial obligations. Even those who persevere in their efforts know that about half the deputies will be replaced at the end of their term and that most of the memberships on the standing committees will have changed.

The problem of frequent deputy turnover is not likely to be resolved soon. The principle of systematic renewal for deputies was more precisely defined in the 1961 CPSU Program, which stated: "To improve the work of the soviets and bring fresh forces into them, it is desirable that at least one-third of the total number of deputies to a soviet should be elected anew each time so that new millions of working people may learn to govern the state." It was also specified that officeholders not be reelected for more than two consecutive terms, unless "the personal gifts of the official in question" make the deputy particularly "useful," in which case a three-fourths majority was needed to reelect.[21] Because almost all elections are unanimous, this latter requirement has not proven to be a serious impediment to the reelection of certain deputies for more than three terms. While the 1961 Program was aimed at correcting abuses in the past and at removing officials opposed to the policies of de-Stalinization then under way, the turnover among deputies to the local soviets has

[21] "The 1961 Program of the CPSU," in Jan F. Triska (ed.), *Soviet Communism: Programs and Rules* (San Francisco: Chandler, 1962), p. 99.

consistently exceeded the required one-third—which, as noted, undermines the effectiveness with which rank-and-file deputies can participate. While Friedgut notes that the 44.8 percent renewal rate in 1975 represented an "improvement" compared with earlier years (the rate in 1965 was 56.7 percent), this downward trend has been reversed over the ensuing decade, and in 1985 some 47.4 percent of the deputies to the local soviets had not served in the previous term.[22]

The problems created by frequent renewal and the lack of released time also affect the deputy's work with their constituents. The number of constituents per deputy is lower than in the industrialized democracies of the West, but the potential for greater deputy-constituent contact that this creates is not always met. For one thing, many deputies do not live in the districts they represent. Of those who do make the effort to get to know the district, a substantial portion are not reelected because of the principle of periodic renewal. Even among those who are reelected, it is rare for them to represent the same district for a second time.[23] As a result, many deputies are not familiar with the districts they represent, and their constituents are less likely to know who represents them. There is considerable debate among Soviet scholars about just whom the deputy represents: the workers' collective that nominated the deputy, or the territorial district to which the deputy is assigned. Some Soviet legal scholars believe that until this issue is resolved the deputy's relationship to constituents will remain ambiguous.[24]

One other organizational principle contributing to the

[22] Friedgut, *Political Participation in the USSR*, pp. 181–182. The statistics are from *Itogi vyborov*, 1985, pp. 248–249.

[23] Some Soviet specialists are quite critical of these practices. Leizerov supports his arguments with data from Belorussia showing that most deputies do not live in their district and very few are returned from the same district (Leizerov, *Konstitutsionnoi printsip glasnosti*, pp. 130–131).

[24] This ambiguity in representation was brought to the author's attention by S. A. Avak'ian in an interview on October 17, 1984.

lower levels of effective deputy participation in the work of the soviet is the Marxist-Leninist injunction against the separation of legislative and executive powers. The theoretical justification for fusing the two functions rests on the argument that those who make rules should be responsible for carrying them out. As Soviet practice has evolved, however, the executive agencies have come to dominate over the work of the legislature. Nowhere is this more significant than with respect to revenues. The main source of leverage enjoyed by Western legislative bodies is their ability to raise and spend public monies. This power ensures that administrative agencies will be responsive to the people's will as expressed through their representatives. In the Soviet system, most revenues come from above and are allocated by the executive and administrative agencies; the role of the deputies is limited to oversight and suggestions, both based on inadequate information. Soviet theorists argue that legislative control is ensured because the executive bodies are elected by and accountable to the deputies. But as we have seen, nominations are actually controlled by the CPSU and the ispolkom, and then ratified unanimously with little or no discussion by the deputies. Reports by the ispolkom to the deputies are often exercises in formalism. The dominance of the executive bodies is also, in part, a legacy of the Stalinist period, but until it is redressed Soviet citizens will have reason to doubt how much authority their deputies really have.

In understanding why many Soviet citizens make less use of the opportunities for political participation in local government than appear to be possible, only part of the explanation lies in whatever structural or organizational problems may exist. Many of these are remediable, and reforms that are either under way or being contemplated could make the system work better. Even with systemic changes, however, it is likely that levels of popular participation in local government would still remain lower than they could be. The reason is that to a significant extent the problem lies not in the system of the soviets but in how people perceive the system. In this sense, the gap between what is practiced and what seems possible is a function of political culture: it is not only what people are legally able to do that matters, but what they think they can do.

In their seminal work on comparative politics published in 1966, Gabriel Almond and Bingham Powell define political culture as "the pattern of individual attitudes and orientations toward politics among the members of a political system."[25] In elaborating what they refer to as the "subjective realm" of the individual's relationship to the political system, the authors identify three dimensions that constitute any individual's orientation toward the political system: cognitive, affective, and evaluative. Cognitive orientations refer to how much people know about the system, affective orientations to how attached they are to the system, and evaluative orientations to how well the system performs according to the individual's value preferences.[26] Taking the first of these in the context of analyzing how Soviet citizens think about their local government, it seems clear from the data presented earlier that the cognitive dimension remains less developed than it could be. Evidence from Soviet and Western publications, as well as the author's own observations, indicate that only about 10 percent of the population even know who their deputies are,[27] and few know even rudimentary information, such as where their local soviet is located, how often it meets, or how many members sit on it. When it comes to more complex procedural issues—for example, the difference

[25] Gabriel Almond and Bingham Powell, *Comparative Politics: A Developmental Approach* (Boston: Little, Brown, and Co., 1966), p. 50.

[26] A similar approach is found in Almond and Verba, *The Civic Culture*, pp. 12–13.

[27] Perttsik, "Puti sovershenstvonniia," p. 17; Friedgut, "The Soviet Citizen's Perception of Local Government," pp. 115–117; the author's interviews of thirty-eight students in the law faculty of Moscow State University, November 1984.

between a *vopros* and *zapros*, even the deputies often lack the knowledge necessary to make such a distinction.[28] But why don't Soviet citizens know more? Part of the answer is a lack of training, an issue discussed below, but lack of motivation is also a factor. It can be argued that the level of satisfaction with local government performance is so high that people do not feel a need to know more or to get involved. Such explanations are often offered to explain low voter turnouts in local elections in the United States. Yet the argument seems as disingenuous in explaining Soviet behavior as it is in excusing the voting behavior of Americans. The existence of the pervasive and notorious Soviet "second economy" alone is sufficient testimony to the discontent many Soviets feel about how well the system performs.[29] It is not because Soviet citizens are so content with how well local government is working that makes many indifferent to its workings, but rather that most still do not perceive that learning about local government, or becoming actively involved in it, will be rewarding.

If political participation in the local soviets, either as a deputy or through one, can prove useful, as argued earlier, why do so many still perceive that it is not? One answer may be the persistence of elements one would expect to find in a traditional political system with a parochial political culture.[30] The responses of law school students interviewed by the author indicate that, despite their presumable awareness of modern legal norms, they would first seek help for solving problems through family or close friends. Although the author's sample was unsystematic, this impression is supported by Friedgut's study of emi-

[28] Vasilev, *Zakon o statuse deputatov v deistvii*, pp. 14–16. The distinction between a *vopros* and a *zapros* is discussed in Chapter 5.

[29] Gregory Grossman, "The 'Second Economy' of the USSR," *Problems of Communism* 26 (September–October 1977).

[30] The term is from Almond and Verba, *The Civic Culture*, esp. pp. 17–19.

grant opinions in which only a minority sought to redress grievances through administrative means.[31] The tendency to rely on personal interaction and kinship ties rather than formal law is characteristic of traditional societies and seems to have been an important part of Muscovite political culture.[32] Yet the political culture of the prerevolutionary period was not without participatory features, especially in the village, and it is at least arguable that congruent expectations could also be renascent in contemporary Soviet political culture.

Whatever the merits of the cultural continuity argument, much of the answer lies also in the affective and evaluative orientations toward government that are a legacy of the Stalin years. In general, the legacy of the Stalinist period was to subordinate the soviets to tasks of industrialization. Whatever participatory element was present in the work of the early soviets was a luxury that could no longer be afforded and that was to be discouraged. The soviets become less and less a forum for public input into decisions and more and more an instrument for administering the five-year plans. It should hardly be surprising that the legislative activity of the deputies was reduced to ritual or dispensed with altogether, while the "real" work of local government was concentrated in the hands of those charged with the administration of state policy—the local executive committees.

The residual effects of the Stalinist period are manifest in the conduct of contemporary local Soviet government in several ways. Because their persistence seems to affect the public's evaluation of the deputy's activities, it is useful to recall some of those effects mentioned elsewhere in this book. First is the element of centralized control, also characteristic of prerevolutionary Russian political culture.

[31] "The Soviet Citizen's Perception of Local Government," pp. 126–129.

[32] See the discussion of Russian political culture in Edward L. Keenan, "Muscovite Political Folkways," *The Russian Review* 45 (1986), pp. 123–148, 156–158.

Although the discretionary authority available to the local soviets has broadened considerably in recent years, especially in areas where the local impact is greatest—such as consumer goods and services, housing, construction, land use, and environmental protection—many areas of economic administration remain almost exclusively within the jurisdiction of the central ministries. Even within the areas where local soviet authority is supposed to be greatest, decisions about how much money will be spent on what remains centrally determined. Although D. Richard Little overstates the case when he claims that "there is no record of a soviet at any level ever having rejected a government proposal," it certainly does not happen often.[33]

The element of control is also apparent horizontally in the relationship between the ispolkom and the rank-and-file deputies, and in the role played by the local party organization. If, as we have argued, the ispolkom dominates the work of the soviet, then the ispolkom itself is very much subject to the party in matters of policy and personnel; the presence of party groups in all the organs of the local soviets ensures that no actions will be taken contrary to the wishes of the local party. While Soviet legal scholars argue that this does not and should not mean the substitution of party authority for that of the state, the distinction between "leading" and "governing" is not always maintained in practice. The *subordination* of the organs of the state to those of the party undoubtedly reaches back to the decisions made shortly after the October Revolution, but the actual *substitution* of party authority appears to be a legacy of the Stalinist era, when the local soviets all but ceased to function as representative institutions.[34]

[33] D. Richard Little, "Political Participation and the Soviet System," *Problems of Communism* 29 (July–August 1980), p. 62. An apparent example to the contrary is the case of the Kuznetsk city soviet's rejection of the USSR's Agro-Industrial Ministry's plans to build a factory in their district. See "Ispolkom skazal 'net,' " *Izvestia*, January 26, 1986.

[34] The subordination of the local soviets to the Bolshevik party in 1918–

Another element of the work of the soviets that seems to reflect the past is the penchant for formalism pervading so much of what the deputies do. Whether it is a member of the ispolkom reporting at a session, or a deputy reporting to constituents, it is often *form* that is satisfied (quotas having been filled), usually devoid of critical content. Part of this is almost certainly left from a time when public officials sought the safety of anonymity—better to repeat known formulas than risk unfavorable attention by saying the wrong thing. Even in Brezhnev's time, when the risk to personal safety had diminished, it must have seemed more prudent to do what you were told than to challenge it.[35]

The passion for unanimity and public consensus so characteristic of Soviet political life from top to bottom also appears to be a remnant of the Stalin years, although, as Edward Keenan points out, the reluctance to air political differences in public has roots in traditional Russian political culture. Keenan cites an old peasant rule, "Iz izby soru ne vynesi," meaning "Do not carry your rubbish out of the hut" or, less literally, "Don't wash your dirty laundry in public."[36] Nowhere is this unanimous public face presented more elaborately than in Soviet elections. Friedgut's observation that "the Soviet system as a whole is structured against open conflict and competition" applies equally well to the behavior of deputies in the soviets and to constituents in their meetings with deputies.[37] Differences of opinion occur frequently; divided votes almost

---

19 is described in John L. H. Keep, *The Russian Revolution: A Study in Mass Mobilization* (New York: W. W. Norton, 1977); and in Israel Getzler, *Kronstadt 1917–21: The Fate of a Soviet Democracy* (Cambridge: Cambridge University Press, 1983). It is also dealt with in Chapter 3 of the present work.

[35] Such a mentality is not unknown in American democracy, especially in big cities. E.g., "To get along, go along" was the operative principle of local politics when Richard Daley was mayor of Chicago.

[36] Keenan, "Muscovite Political Folkways," p. 119.

[37] Friedgut, *Political Participation in the USSR*, p. 95.

never do. Whatever conflicts do exist are thrashed out beforehand and presented to the public as consensus opinion.

As with the other restrictive elements that remain a part of the Soviet political culture, the "objective" reasons for such public unity no longer seem as compelling as they once did. The Soviet Union in 1986 is not the "directed society" it was in 1936. It is doubtful that the system would collapse if there was more than one candidate for each office or if some deputies voted against legislation they did not agree with. Nor would the result be catastrophic if the conduct of the people's business were opened up to public scrutiny by allowing anyone interested to attend sessions of the soviet and to set aside time for them to take part. Competitive elections are not prohibited by Soviet law, and contentious public participation was not uncommon in the early soviets. On the contrary, a more authentic public dialogue, including more candid public criticism, would probably result in the people's representatives being taken more seriously than they are now, and with it the possibility of greater popular support for the institutions of government.

THE FUTURE: A SOVIET "CIVIC CULTURE"?

I am reminded of a conversation held near the end of my field research with a senior Soviet specialist who had inquired about my preliminary conclusions. I informed him that, in my opinion, the actual practice of political participation fell short of what theory called for and the law allowed. While he declined to agree with this conclusion, he did offer a larger context that was not entirely inconsistent with it. We are a country, he observed, that has endured a thousand years of history under autocratic rule. After the Revolution, the situation for much of our existence was abnormal: the civil war, Stalinism and industrialization, World War II, and the Cold War. Considering that we have had about twenty years to begin building a more democratic society, we have not done so badly.[38] Implicit in this view is the assumption that a transformation of the Soviet political culture from subject to participant is under way but that such a transformation will take time. While the analysis this book offers differs in its assessment of how much progress has been made, and while its author is probably more skeptical about how large a portion of the population will eventually become politically active, the conclusion that a basis exists for the emergence of a "civic culture" in the Soviet political system does not seem unwarranted. It can be found in the very real possibilities for political participation that are available at the local level.

This chapter emphasizes that while such possibilities exist they are not as widely used as they could be. The explanation rests on an interpretation of Soviet political culture which suggests that a certain inertia is at work in how Soviet citizens think about politics, an inertia rooted to a large degree in the experience of the Stalinist years. It appears that people's attitudes, values, and beliefs about whether they can have any input into the decisions that affect their lives at the local level have only begun to catch up with what is indeed possible. If Soviet citizens continue to experience positive results from their efforts to participate in local government, and such participation becomes routine, it is reasonable to expect that the gap between what is possible and what is practiced will narrow over time. If so, such participation would constitute an important necessary, although not sufficient, condition for the emergence of a "civic culture" in Soviet political life.[39] A

[38] A similar perspective is offered by Ronald J. Hill in his assessment of Soviet political development, "Party-State Relations and Soviet Political Development," *British Journal of Political Science* 10 (April 1980), p. 160.

[39] These conclusions regarding participation in Soviet local government and its relationship to Soviet political culture seem to support the view that political culture lags behind institutional development and political

truly "civic culture" would require a freer press and greater autonomy in the expression of interests than is presently found even on the local level, to name but two additional conditions. A "civic culture" assumes participation, but participation alone will not bring about a "civic culture."

What evidence is there to suggest that the forms of political participation discussed in this book are likely to increase? Although the level of participation in Soviet local government is relatively low, it is clear that it is growing. The past decade has seen a steady increase in the number of soviets and the number of people elected to them. In their relations with constituents, deputies now meet more often with those who elected them and are more frequently recalled by them. Although the number of voter mandates accepted has declined slightly, the mandates appear to deal with more serious issues, and the rate of implementation has risen. As to the deputies' work in the soviets, although fewer sessions were held in 1984 than in 1976, on the average more issues were discussed and more deputies took part in discussing them (Tables 6-2 and 6-3). Use of the right of deputy inquiry has become steadily more frequent (Table 6-5), and the activity of the standing committees has begun to increase again after declining in the last years prior to Brezhnev's death (Tables 6-6 and 6-8). If a longer time frame is used, the quantitative growth in the indicators of participation in the work of the local soviets becomes much more impressive. There is no area in which the changes have not been dramatic if the date of Stalin's death in 1953 is used as a benchmark.

The increases in levels of participation do not appear to be equal for all age groups. In an interesting study based

---

practice. In this sense, they would appear to confirm McCauley's argument that institutional development is a necessary, though not necessarily sufficient, precondition for attitudinal change. See Mary McCauley "Political Culture: One Step Forward, Two Steps Back," in Brown, *Political Culture and Communist Studies*, p. 19.

on data from the Soviet Interview Project, Donna Bahry found that those born after World War II, and especially after Stalin's death, were almost twice as likely to be involved in both conventional and unconventional modes of political participation. With respect to conventional behavior, Bahry found this younger generation "surprisingly positive" and went on to suggest that "despite the image of passivity that characterizes such groups, many participants felt that members like themselves could have a degree of influence over the organization's activities."[40] Although Bahry does not explicitly deal with deputies to the local soviets as a form of conventional participation, there is no apparent reason to rule out the existence of generational differences in their activities as well. If so, the process of transformation from a subject to a participant political culture may be enhanced by the transition to a newer, more active cohort.

Aside from age differences, one other factor that may contribute to increased levels of political participation and to a greater sense of political efficacy is the higher educational levels of deputies. The data provided in Table 4-5 comparing the educational levels of deputies to Belorussian level soviets in 1961 and 1982 are typical of the dramatic increase in educational level that took place over one or two generations. This is also true for officers of the executive committees of the local soviets: 55 percent of the ispolkom presidents and 67 percent of the vice-presidents had higher education in 1984—up from 33 percent and 44 percent respectively in 1976.[41] The recent emphasis on deputy training (*ucheba*) has also presumably contributed to higher levels of knowledge among deputies about how to fulfill their duties effectively. Rank-and-file deputies are expected to take part in deputy days (*dni deputata*), which

[40] Donna Bahry, "Politics, Generations, and Change in the USSR" (Soviet Interview Project, University of Illinois, Working Paper no. 20, April 1986), pp. 27ff.

[41] *Nekotorye voprosy*, 1976, 1984, pp. 40–44.

are often taught by specialists in the work of local government. Most deputies elected to the ispolkom now receive
training in special courses—including refresher courses—
designed to raise their qualifications.[42] While efforts to develop levels of political knowledge among the electorate
are not as apparent, the cognitive component of the Soviet
political culture seems likely to increase over time as a result of rising education and the civic training of those who
are elected as representatives.

Continued development of popular participation in the
work of the local soviets depends upon the policies pursued by Soviet leaders. The decision to revitalize the role
of the deputies and to reactivate the soviets after their period of dormancy in the 1930s and 1940s was an important
part of Khrushchev's attempt to build a base of popular
support for the Soviet regime and, not incidentally, for
himself. His successors chose to continue this commitment. They also enacted a legislative framework in which
it could take place and made the transfer of greater authority to the local soviets one of the hallmarks of contemporary Soviet ideology. Even Konstantin Chernenko, during his brief tenure as General Secretary, made further
improvement in the work of the soviets, especially in economic development, the theme of his remarks to the April
14, 1984, plenary session of the CPSU Central Committee.

It is still too early to say how far the new Soviet leadership under Mikhail Gorbachev will go in making good on
the promises of his predecessors relative to the soviets.
Most of the initial signs are encouraging, but not all. Con-
spicuously absent from the 1985 CPSU Draft Program, for
example, are references to transferring the administration
of local affairs more directly to the deputies through their

---

[42] In 1983, some 92 percent of the ispolkom presidents, 81 percent of
all vice-presidents, and 91 percent of the secretaries had received some
form of special training (ibid., 1984, p. 48). For a good description of how
deputies become informed, including "deputy days," see I. M. Solodovnikov, *Budni deputata* (Moscow: Iurid. Lit., 1981), pp. 36–39.

standing committees, as found in the 1961 Program. Nevertheless, the 1985 Draft does speak of a "continued increase" in the role of the Soviets in local affairs, and Gorbachev's remarks to the 27th CPSU Congress on February 28, 1985, strongly hinted that important new initiatives were under consideration.

> This is why we resolutely support the course of strengthening the independence and activeness of the local organs of power. In the Central Committee, in the Presidium of the Supreme Soviet, and in the Council of Ministers proposals are being worked out to do this. The essence of them is that each soviet be made fully and responsibly the master in everything that pertains to the satisfaction of the daily demands and needs of the people.[43]

Given continued support from the top, the importance of the local soviets in the decisions that affect the lives of most Soviet citizens will grow. Insofar as deputies are perceived as individuals who can influence those decisions on behalf of their constituents, individually or collectively, their authority is also likely to be enhanced. If the constituent contacts with elected officials that now take place at the local level continue to prove useful, it seems reasonable to expect that the attitudes of Soviet citizens toward political participation will gradually change and that the prerequisites for the emergence of a "civic culture" will be established. This is not to suggest that all or even a majority of Soviet citizens are likely to become politically active in a "meaningful" way. As indicated earlier, other than ritualistically most Soviet citizens most of the time do not participate politically. But in this respect, their behavior is not unlike that of most Americans. In this sense, the limits

[43] M. S. Gorbachev, "Doklad Tsentral'nogo Komiteta KPSS XXVII S'ezdu," in *Materialy XXVII s'ezda KPSS* (Moscow: Politizdat, 1986), p. 56.

on increased participation derive more from the same kind of disinterest in political life characteristic of many people in Western democracies (unless they are directly affected) than from the structure of local Soviet government or from Soviet ideology.

SELECTED BIBLIOGRAPHY

Introduction

THIS SELECTED BIBLIOGRAPHY contains works pertaining
to the activities of the deputies to the local soviets, in Russian and in English. Included among the English-language
works are publications cited in the present book but not
necessarily related to the deputies. In the case of works in
Russian, the criterion for inclusion was that they be published after 1977 or cited in the footnotes of this book. The
rationale for this criterion is that such works reflect
changes stemming from the adoption of the Soviet Constitution in 1977 and that other bibliographies that amply encompass citations of value prior to this time are available.
The most comprehensive of those bibliographies appears
on pages 362–379 of *Sovety narodnykh deputatov: konstitutsionnye osnovy organizatsii deiatel'nosti* (Moscow: Nauka,
1981), which covers the period from 1969 to 1980. The best
bibliographies published in the West are found in Theodore H. Friedgut's *Political Participation in the USSR*
(Princeton: Princeton University Press, 1979) and Ronald
J. Hill's *Soviet Politics, Political Science, and Reform* (New
York: M. E. Sharpe, 1980). In addition, the author of the
present work developed a comprehensive bibliography of
items from 1960 to 1984 while at the U.S. Library of Congress on short-term research grants in 1984 and 1985 from
the Kennan Institute for Advanced Russian Studies of the
Wilson Center of the Smithsonian Institution.

Those who want additional and current information on
literature in Russian dealing with the soviets are encouraged to consult two publications by the Institute of Scientific Information for the Social Sciences [Institut Nauchnoi
Informatsii po Obshchestvennym Naukam (INION)]. The

first of these is entitled *Novaia sovetskaia literatura po ob-shchestvennym naukam* (Seriia 4: Gosudarstvo i Pravo), which has provided since 1973 a monthly listing of relevant articles and chapters in books. The other is a bimonthly overview of books related to the topic: *Obshchest-vennie nauki v SSSR. Referativnyi zhurnal* (Seriia 4: Gosudarstvo i Pravo). The most important Russian-language journals in the field are *Sovety narodnykh deputatov* (*SND*), which was known by the title *Sovety deputatov trudiashchik-sia* (*SDT*) prior to 1977; *Sovetskoe gosudarstvo i pravo* (*SGiP*); and *Pravovedenie*.

Statistical data about the numbers and composition of the deputies can be found in the statistical summaries published by Izvestiia after each local election: *Itogi vyborov i sostav deputatov mestnykh Sovetov narodnykh deputatov*. These data are available from 1961 on; although until 1977 they appear under the title *Itogi vyborov i sostav deputatov mest-nykh Sovetov deputatov trudiashchiksia*. In addition, since 1973 Izvestiia has published an annual statistical profile of deputy activities, by republic and by level of government, called *Nekotorye voprosy organizatsionnoi raboty mestnykh So-vetov narodnykh deputatov* (before 1977, . . . *deputatov tru-diashchiksia*). To the best of the author's knowledge, data available from this source do not appear in Western analyses of local government in the Soviet Union other than the present one. The fifth issue of *SND* (*SDT*) also publishes some statistical data annually.

In addition to the sources of information cited thus far, there are a number of valuable reference works dealing with legislative and administrative aspects of the local soviets. A convenient collection of major legislation from 1917 to 1983 was published in 1984 by Iuridicheskaia Lite-ratura (abbreviated as Iurid. Lit. throughout) and entitled *Sbornik normativnykh aktov po sovetskomu gosudartvennomu pravu*. In addition, "commentaries" on the major laws governing the work of the soviets are available. Written by leading Soviet legal specialists and jurists, they provide a quasi-official interpretation of each law section by section. Those cited in the present work include:

Kommentarii k zakonodatel'stvu o gorodskikh, raionnykh v gorode Sovetakh narodnykh deputatov. Moscow: Izvestiia, 1983.

Kommentarii k zadonodatel'stvu o poselkovykh i sel'skikh sovetakh. 2nd ed. Moscow: Izvestiia, 1982.

Kommentarii k zakonodatel'stvu o raionnykh Sovetakh narodnykh deputatov. Moscow: Izvestiia, 1985.

Kommentarii k zakonu o statuse narodnykh deputatov v SSSR. Moscow: Iurid. Lit., 1983.

Not included in this bibliography are newspaper articles cited in the text and documentary materials relating to the work of specific soviets, in particular, materials made available to the author from the Lenin city borough soviet of Moscow. The author will consider sharing such information, as well as surveys of deputy and student opinion he conducted, with those who have a legitimate interest.

The author would like to conclude by thanking the staff of the Library of Congress for their assistance in the preparation of this bibliography, especially Dr. Robert Allen, who, though now retired, will always be present in the Library's truly remarkable Slavic and East European collection. He was a strong advocate of being aware of what you have here so that you don't needlessly duplicate your efforts over there.

MATERIALS IN RUSSIAN

Aktual'nye problemy gosudarstvovedeniia. Moscow: IGPAN, 1979.

Alekseev, Boris Konstantinovich, and Perfil'ev, M. N. *Printsipy i tendenstii razvitiia predstavitel'nogo sostava mestnykh Sovetov (sotsiologicheskoe issledovanie).* Leningrad: Lenizdat, 1976.

Atamanchuk, Grigorii Vasil'evich. *Sushochnost' sovetskogo gosudarstvennogo upravleniia*. Moscow: Iurid. Lit., 1980.

Atamanchuk, Grigorii Vasil'evich, et al., *Sovetskoe gosudarstvennoe stroitel'stvo i pravo: Kurs lektsii*. Moscow: Mysl' 1982. Second edition, 1986.

Avak'ian, Suren Adibekovich. *Gorodskoi Sovet i predpriiatiia vyshestoiashchego podchineniia*. Moscow: Iurid. Lit., 1979.

———. *Pravovoe regulirovanie deiatel'nosti Sovetov*. Moscow: Moscow State University, 1980.

———. *Sovety i rukovodstvo ekonomikoi*. Moscow: Znanie, 1985.

Azovkhin, Ivan Akimovich. *Mestnye Sovety v sisteme organov vlasti*. Moscow: Iurid. Lit., 1971.

———. "Mestnye Sovety v sisteme organov vlasti." *SND*, no. 8 (1978).

Azovkin, Ivan Akimovich, and Starovoitov, N. G. "Edinstvo sistemy Sovetov i problemy ee dal'neishnego razvitiia." *SGiP*, no. 10, (1979).

———. "Novaia Konstitutsiia i povyshenie roli Sovetov narodnykh deputatov." *SGiP*, no. 9 (1978).

———. Azovkin, Ivan Akimovich, Starovoitov, N. G. "Sovety narodnykh deputatov-politicheskaia osnova SSSR." *SGiP*, no. 11 (1982).

———. "Vazhnyi shag na puti razvitiia sovetskoi predstavitel'noi sistemy." *SGiP*, no. 10 (1980).

Azovkhin, Ivan Akimovich, and Sheremet, K. F. (eds.). *Sovety narodnykh deputatov i ekonomika*. Moscow: Nauka, 1985.

Bannykh, M. P. *Deputat i ispolkom*. Moscow: Iurid. Lit., 1979.

Barabashev, Georgii Vasil'evich. "Glavnoe zveno samoupravlenie." *SND*, no. 1 (1986).

———. "Otvetstvennost' organov upravleniia pered Sovetami." *SGiP*, no. 5 (1981).

———. "Pravovaia osnova raboty." *SND*, no. 5 (1981).

Barabashev, Georgii Vasil'evich (ed.). *Rol' mestnykh Sovetov v ekonomicheskom i sotsial'nom razvitii gorodov*. Moscow: Moscow State University, 1983.

Barabashev, Georgii Vasil'evich, and Sheremet, K. F. *KPSS i Sovety narodnykh deputatov*. Moscow: Znanie, 1978.

————. *Neposredstvennaia demokratiia v SSSR*. Moscow: Znanie, 1984.

————. Barabashev, Georgii Vasil'evich, and Sheremet, K. F. "Novaia sovetskaia konstitutsiia i nauka sovetskogo stroitel'stva." *SGiP*, no. 2 (1979).

————. *Sovetskoe stroitel'stvo*. 2nd ed. Moscow: Iurid. Lit., 1981.

Beliaeva, N. G. *Poselkovyi, sel'skii Sovet narodnykh deputatov*. Moscow: VIUZI, 1982.

Bezuglov, Anatolii Alekseevich. *Deputat v Sovete i izbiratel'nom okruge*. Moscow: Iurid. Lit., 1978.

————. *Sovetskii Deputat*. Moscow: Iurid. Lit., 1971.

Bezuglov, Anatolii Alekseevich (ed.). *Sovetskoe stroitel'stvo*. Moscow: Iurid. Lit., 1985.

Bezuglov, A. A., and Leizerov, A. T. *Deputatskii zapros*. Moscow: Iurid. Lit., 1980.

————. "Pravo deputatskogo zaprosa." *SGiP*, no. 6 (1976).

Butko, Igor' Filippovich. *Gosudarstvovedcheskie issledovaniia i praktika mestnykh Sovetov*. Kiev: Naukova dumka, 1983.

Chalyi, Petr Fedorovich. *Pravovoe polozhenie komissii pri ispolkomakh mestnykh Sovetov narodnykh deputatov*. Kiev: Naukova dumka, 1979.

Chekharin, Evgenii Mikhailovich. *Sovety narodnykh deputatov-voploshchenie narodovlastiia*. Moscow: Iurid. Lit., 1978.

Davydov, Renol'd Konstantinovich. *Pravo deputatskogo zaprosa v sovetskom obshchenarodnom gosudarstve*. Kiev: Naukova dumka, 1981.

Fritskii, O. F. *Mestnye Sovety narodnykh deputatov i upravlenie*. Kiev: Vishcha shkola, 1977.

Gabrichidze, Boris Nikolaevich. "Konstitutsionnye osnovy kontrol'noi deiatel'nosti Sovetov." *SGiP*, no. 7 (1981).

Gabrichidze, Boris Nikolaevich. *Konstitutsionnyi status organov sovetskogo gosudarstva*. Moscow: Iurid. Lit., 1982.

―――. "Mestnye Sovety i okhrana obshchestvennogo poriadka." *SGiP*, no. 2 (1983).

Gogolevskii, A. V. *Petrogradskii Sovet v gody grazhdanskoi voiny*. Leningrad: Nauka, 1982.

Grazhdanin i apparat upravleniia v SSSR. Edited by B. M. Lazarev. Moscow: Nauka, 1982.

Grigorian, Levon Armenakovich. *Postoiannye komissii mestnykh Sovetov*. Moscow: Iurid. Lit., 1970.

―――. *60 let sovetskoi gosudarstvennosti*. Moscow: Iurid. Lit., 1977.

―――. *Sovety-organy vlasti i narodnogo samoupravleniia*. Moscow: Iurid. Lit., 1965.

―――. *XXV S'ezd KPSS i aktual'nyi problemy sotsialisticheskoi demokratii v SSSR*. Moscow: Znanie, 1977.

Grigoriev, Vadim Konstantinovich, and Zhdanov, V. P. *Vybory v mestnye Sovety narodnykh deputatov i poriadok ikh provedeniia*. Moscow: Iurid. Lit., 1982.

―――. *Vybory v verkhovnye Sovety soiuznykh, avtonomnykh respublik, v mestnye Sovety narodnykh deputatov i poriadok ikh provedeniia*. Moscow: Iurid. Lit., 1980.

Grushin, B. A., and Onikova, L. A. (eds.). *Massovaia informatsiia v sovetskom promyshlennom gorode: Opyt sotsiologicheskogo issledovaniia*. Moscow: Politizdat, 1980.

Iampol'skaia, Ts. A. "Organy obshchestvennoi samodeiatel'nosti kak forma obshchestvennoi aktivnosti grazhdan." *SGiP*, no. 12 (1983).

Ispolnitel'nyi komitet mestnogo Soveta narodnykh deputatov. Edited by G. V. Barabashev. Moscow: Iurid. Lit., 1983.

Iuridicheskii spravochnik deputata mestnogo Soveta narodnykh deputatov. Edited by G. V. Barabashev and O. E. Kutafin. Moscow: Moscow State University, 1981.

Khakalo, Galina Borisovna. *Partiinoe rukovodstvo Sovetami*. Minsk: Belarus, 1981.

Kleiner, Boris Isaevich. *Razvitie funktsii mestnykh Sovetov na*

sovremennom etape. Ivanovo: Ivanovskii gosudar-
stvenyi universitet, 1985.

Koliushin, E. I. "Novoe zakonodatel'stvo o kraevykh, ob-
lastnykh sovetakh." *Pravovedenie,* no. 4 (1981).

Kompleksnye sotsial'no-pravovye issledovaniia opyt i problemy.
Moscow: Nauka, 1977.

Konev, V., and Moskalev, A. "Kak formirovat' deputatskie
kommissii?" *SND,* no. 11 (1981).

——. "Slovo deputata na sessii." *SND,* no. 10 (1981).

Korenevskaia, Elena Ignatova. *Mestnye Sovety i sotsial'noe
planirovanie.* Moscow: Iurid. Lit., 1977.

——. *Sovety narodnykh deputatov i kompleksnoe razvitie regionov.* Moscow: Sovetskaia Rossiia, 1983.

Kotok, Viktor Fomich. *Nakazy izbiratelei v sotsialisticheskom
gosudarstve.* Moscow: Nauka, 1967.

——. *Referendum v sisteme sotsialisticheskoi demokratii.*
Moscow: Nauka, 1964.

Kriazhkov, Vladimir Alekseevich. "Mestnye Sovety i in-
formirovanie grazhdan." *SGiP,* no. 10 (1981).

——. "Obsuzhdenie grazhdanami proektov reshenii
mestnykh sovetov." *SGiP,* no. 8 (1983).

——. "Otchet deputata (informatsionno-pravovye voprosy)." *Pravovedenie,* no. 3 (1983).

——. "Pravo zaprosa." *SND,* no. 2 (1983).

Kriazhkov, Vladimir Alekseevich, and Potapov, A. I. *Deputatskii zapros: metodicheskie rekomendatsii.* Sverdlovsk:
Iuridicheskii Institut, 1985.

Kulikova, Galina Borisovna. *Demokraticheskie osnovy deiatel'nosti mestnykh Sovetov v razvitom sotsialisticheskom obshchestve (1959–75).* Moscow: Nauka, 1978.

Kutafin, Oleg Emelianovich. *Konstitutsionnye osnovy obshchestvennogo stroia i politiki SSSR.* Moscow: Moscow
State University, 1985.

——. *Populiarnyi slovar-spravochnik narodnogo deputata.*
Moscow: Znanie, 1980.

Kutafin, Oleg Emelianovich, and Sheremet, K. F. *Kompe-*

tentsia mestnykh Sovetov. Moscow: Iurid. Lit., 1982; 2nd ed., 1986.

Lazarev, B. M. *Apparat upravleniia obshchenarodnogo gosudarstva.* Moscow: Iurid. Lit., 1978.

Lebedev, Pavel Nikolaevich. *Mestnye Sovety i obshchestvennoe mnenie.* Moscow: Iurid. Lit., 1982.

Lebedev, Pavel Nikolaevich (ed.). *Sistema organov gorodskogo upravlenie.* Leningrad: Leningrad University Press, 1980.

Leizerov, Arkadii Tevelevich. *Demokraticheskie formy deiatel'nosti mestnykh Sovetov.* Minsk: Belorusskii gosudarstvennyi universitet, 1977.

―――. "Effektivnost' poriadka formirovaniia i deiatel'nosti postoiannykh komissii mestnykh Sovetov." *SGiP,* no. 3 (1982).

―――. "Issledovanie dinamiki sostava deputatov mestnykh Sovetov." *SGiP,* no. 12 (1984).

―――. "Issledovanie effektivnosti sessionnoi deiatel'nosti mestnykh Sovetov." *SGiP,* no. 4 (1983).

―――. *Konstitutsionnyi printsip glasnosti raboty Sovetov narodnykh deputatov.* Minsk: Belorusskii gosudarstvennyi universitet, 1981.

Lenin, V. I. *KPSS o rabote Sovety.* Moscow: Politizdat, 1979.

Lepeshkin, A. I. "Narodnoe predstavitel'stvo v Sovetskom gosudarstve." *SGiP,* no. 6 (1977).

Lichnost' i uvazhenie k zakonom. Moscow: IGPAN, 1979.

Luk'ianov, Anatolii Ivanovich. "Konstitutsiia deistvuet, zhivet, rabotaet." *SGiP,* no. 10 (1982).

―――. *Razvitie zakonodatel'stva o sovetskikh predstavitel'nykh organakh vlasti.* Moscow: Iurid. Lit., 1978.

―――. "Sovetskaia Konstitutsiia i razvitie funktsii predstavitel'nykh organov vlasti." *SGiP,* no. 11 (1977).

Mal'tsev, V. A. "Otchetnost' kak forma kontrolia v sisteme mestnogo soveta." *Pravovedenie,* no. 2 (1978).

―――. "Statisticheskaia otchetnost' mestnykh Sovetov i ee sovershenstvovanie." *Pravovedenie,* no. 6 (1982).

Manukian, E. A. *Deputat v trudovom kollektive.* Moscow: Iurid. Lit., 1979.

Martem'ianov, V. S. "Material'no-finansovaia baza deiatel'nosti mestnykh Sovetov." *SGiP,* no. 4 (1978).

Maslennikov, V. "Uchastiye grazhdan v upravlenii." *SND,* no. 6 (1980).

Moskalev, A. V. "Sistema mestnykh Sovetov i ee sovershenstvovanie." *Pravovedenie,* no. 6 (1982).

Nagornaia, M. A. "Informatsionnoe obespechenie raboty mestnykh Sovetov." *SGiP,* no. 10 (1983).

———. *Planirovanie raboty mestnykh Sovetov.* Moscow: Iurid. Lit., 1977.

Nedogreeva, Alla Ivanovna. *Koordinatsionnaia deiatel'nost' gorodskogo Soveta narodnykh deputatov.* Kiev: Naukova dumka, 1982.

Normativnoe regulirovanie deiatel'nosti mestnykh Sovetov. Kiev: Naukova dumka, 1982.

Novoselov, Vladimir Ionovich. *Ispolkom i postoiannye komissii Soveta.* Moscow: Iurid. Lit., 1981.

———. *Na obshchestvennykh nachalakh.* Moscow: Iurid. Lit., 1978.

Organy Sovetskogo obshchenarodnogo gosudarstva. Moscow: Nauka, 1979.

Orlov, I. M. *Partinoe rukovodstvo mestnymi Sovetami.* Moscow: Vysshaia shkola, 1982.

Osnovin, V. A. *Gorodokii Sovet-organ sotsial'nogo upravlenii.* Moscow: Iurid. Lit., 1983.

Osnovy Sovetskogo gosudarstvennogo stroitel'stva i prava. Moscow: Mysl', 1979.

Partiia i Sovety. Edited by B. M. Morozov. Moscow: Politizdat, 1982.

Pavlov, Anatolii Safronovich. *Partiinoe rukovodstvo mestnymi Sovetami v poslevoennye gody.* Moscow: Vysshaia shkola, 1983.

Perttsik, Vadim Arkad'evich. "Dlia rabotnikov apparata." *SND,* no. 8 (1980).

Perttsik, Vadim A. "Puti sovershenstvovaniia deiatel'nosti deputatov mestnykh Sovetov." *SGiP*, no. 7 (1967).

———. *Realizatsiia zakonodatel'stva mestnymi Sovetami*. Moscow: Iurid. Lit., 1985.

Poliakov, I. E. "Nakazy izbiratelei-iarkoe proiavlenie sotsialisticheskoi demokratii." *SGiP*, no. 9 (1980).

Popova, S. M. *Otzyv deputatov mestnykh Sovetov narodnykh deputatov*. Moscow: Vsesoiuznyi iuridicheskii zaochnyi institut, 1982.

Predstavitel'naia sistema sotsialisticheskogo gosudarstva. Moscow: Mysl', 1981.

Priniatie reshenii mestnymi organami vlasti i upravleniia. Moscow: IGPAN, 1983.

Prokoshin, V. A. *Sovety i ekonomika*. Moscow: Sovetskaia Rossiia, 1978.

Raldugan, N. V. *Resheniia mestnykh Sovetov i ikh ispolkomov*. Moscow: Iurid. Lit., 1979.

Razvitie mestnykh organov vlasti v sotsialisticheskikh gosudarstvakh. Moscow: Nauka, 1979.

Rovovaia, S. V. "Raionnye sovety narodnykh deputatov v sisteme organov rukovodstva sel'skim khoziaistvom." in *XXVI s'ezd KPSS i voprosy razvitiia gosudarstvennogo prava, sovetskogo stroitelstva i upraveleniia*. Moscow: IGPAN, 1982.

Rukovoditeli ispolkomov: Pravovoi status i organizatsiia raboty. Moscow: Iurid. Lit., 1977.

Safarov, Rafael' Avakovich. "Obrashchenie gosudarstvennykh organov k obshchestvennomy mneniiu." *SGiP*, no. 9 (1978).

———. *Obshchestvennoe mnenie i gosudarstvennoe upravlenie*. Moscow: Iurid. Lit., 1975.

———. *Obshchestvennie mnenie v sisteme sovetskoi demokratii*. Moscow: Znanie, 1982.

Salishcheva, Nadezhda Georgievna, and Evdokimov, Iu. V. *Deputatu mestnogo Soveta*. Moscow: Znanie, 1981.

Selivanov, Anatolii Aleksandrovich. *Mestnye Sovety i molodezh'*. Moscow: Iurid. Lit., 1981.

Selivon, Nikolai Fedoseevich. *Kontrol'naia funkstiia mest-nykh Sovetov narodnykh deputatov.* Kiev: Naukova dumka, 1980.

Shchetinina, Mariia Pavlovna. *Deputat na sessii Soveta.* Moscow: Iurid. Lit., 1980.

Sheremet, Konstantin Filippovich. "Konstitutsiia SSSR i razvitie sotsialisticheskoi demokratii." *SGiP*, no. 10 (1982).

―――. *Mestnye organy vlasti sotsialisticheskogo gosudarstva.* Moscow: Nauka, 1983.

―――. *Sel'skii, poselkovyi Sovet na sovremennom etape.* Moscow: Iurid. Lit., 1969.

―――. "Sovershenstvovanie deiatel'nosti narodnykh deputatov." in *XXV S'ezd KPSS i voprosy gosudarstva i prava.* Moscow: Nauka, 1978.

Sheremet, Konstantin Filippovich, and Lazarev, B. M. *Organy gosudarstvennoi vlasti i upravleniia.* Moscow: Znanie, 1977.

Sliva, A. Ia., and Kuziakin, Iu. P. *Organizatsiia i deiatel'nost' gorodskikh Sovetov.* Moscow: VIUZI, 1982.

Smirnov, Anatolii Andreevich. "Deiatel'nost' organov gosudarstvennoi vlasti po osushchestvleniiu zakona o statuse deputatov." *SGiP*, no. 12 (1978).

―――. *Deputat mestnogo Soveta.* Moscow: Mosk. Rabochii, 1981.

―――. *Polnomochiye predstaviteli naroda.* Moscow: Iurid. Lit., 1975.

Soldatov, Sergei Aleksandrovich. *Sovety i Komsomol.* Moscow: Molodaia Gvardiia, 1980.

Solodovnikov, Ivan Mikhailovich. *Budni deputata.* Moscow: Iurid. Lit., 1981.

Solov'eva, S. V. *Sovety i nauchno-tekhnicheskii progress.* Moscow: Iurid. Lit., 1978.

Sovety narodnykh deputatov: spravochnik. Moscow: Politizdat, 1984.

Staravoitov, Nikolai Georgievich. "Demokratiia dlia vsekh." *SND*, no. 11 (1978).

Staravoitov, Nikolai Georgievich. *Izbiratelei dali nakaz*. Moscow: Znanie, 1984.

———. "Narodnyi deputat: pravovoi status i problemy ego osushchestvleniia." *SGiP*, no. 2 (1980).

———. "Organy narodovlastiia: opyt i problemy." *SND*, no. 12 (1982).

———. *Reglament Soveta i ego ispolkoma*. Moscow: Iurid. Lit., 1981.

———. "Sessii Sovetov: teoriia, praktika, problemy." *SGiP*, no. 11 (1985).

Sterpu, David Mikhailovich. *Partiinoe rukovodstvo Sovetami v usloviiakh razvitogo sotsializma, 1960–78*. Kishinev: Shtiintsa, 1981.

———. *Politicheskaia sila Sovetov v sovremennykh usloviiakh*. Kishinev: Shtiintsa, 1982.

Strekozov, V. G. *Oboronnaia rabota mestnykh Sovetov*. Moscow: Iurid. Lit., 1981.

Sukhanov, N. E. *Izbirateli dali nakaz*. Moscow: Iurid. Lit., 1981.

Tikhomirov, Iu. A. *Sotsializm i politicheskaia deiatel'nost'*. Moscow: Sovetskaia Rossiia, 1984.

———. "S uchetom obshchestvennogo mneniia." *SND*, no. 7 (1980).

Tiutiunnik, G. A. *Postoiannye komissii mestnykh Sovetov*. Moscow: Iurid. Lit., 1979.

Todyka, Iurii Nikolaevich. *Konstitutionnye osnovy organizatsii i deiatel'nosti mestnykh Sovetov narodnykh deputatov*. Kishinev: Shtiintsa, 1979.

———. *Rukovodstvo raionnykh Sovetov nizhestoiashchimi Sovetami deputatov trudiashchikhsia*. Kishinev: Shtiintsa, 1977.

Topornin, B. N. *Konstitutsionnye osnovy politicheskoi sistemy sovetskogo obshchestva*. Moscow: Mosk. Rabochii, 1978.

Vasilenkov, Petr Tarasovich. *Sovety narodnykh deputatov: organizatsiia i deiatel'nost'*. Moscow: Iurid. Lit., 1983.

Vasil'ev, Vsevolod Ivanovich. *Demokraticheskii tsentralizm v sisteme Sovetov*. Moscow: Iurid. Lit., 1973.

———. *Gorodskii sovet: zakon i praktika.* Moscow: Iurid. Lit., 1984.

———. *Zakon o statuse deputatov v deistvii.* Moscow: Iurid. Lit., 1978.

———. "Zakon zhivet, esli vypolniaetsia." *SND,* no. 11 (1981).

Viliamskii, V. S., and Emel'ianenko, A. P. *Dolzhnostnye instruktsii sluzhashchikh apparata ispolkoma.* Moscow: Iurid. Lit., 1980.

Zinov'ev, A. V. "Imperativnyi kharakter deputatskogo mandata." *Pravovedenie,* no. 1 (1984).

Zviagin, Iurii Grigorevich. *Vpervye izbrannomu v Sovet.* Moscow: Iurid. Lit., 1981.

MATERIALS IN ENGLISH

Adams, Jan S. *Citizen Inspectors in the Soviet Union: The People's Control Committee.* New York: Praeger, 1977.

Almond, Gabriel, and Verba, Sidney. *The Civic Culture.* Princeton: Princeton University Press, 1963.

———. *The Civic Culture Revisited.* Boston: Little, Brown, and Co., 1980.

Anweiler, Oskar. *The Soviets: The Russian Workers, Peasants, and Soldier Councils, 1905–21.* Translated from the German edition of 1958. New York: Pantheon Books, 1974.

Bahry, Donna. "Politics, Generations, and Change in the USSR." Soviet Interview Project, University of Illinois, Working Paper no. 20. April 1986.

Barry, Donald, and Barner-Barry, Carol. *Contemporary Soviet Politics: An Introduction.* 2nd ed. Englewood Cliffs, N.J.: Prentice-Hall, 1982.

Bezuglov, A. A. *Soviet Deputy (Legal Status).* Moscow: Progress Publishers, 1973.

Blum, Jerome. *Lord and Peasant in Russia.* Princeton: Princeton University Press, 1961.

Brown, Archie. "Political Science in the Soviet Union: A

New Stage of Development?" *Soviet Studies* 36 (July 1984).

Brown, Archie (ed.). *Political Culture and Communist Studies*. New York: M. E. Sharpe, 1984.

Brym, Robert. "The Functions of Elections in the USSR." *Soviet Studies* 30 (July 1978).

Brzezinski, Zbigniew, and Huntington, Samuel. *Political Power: USA/USSR*. New York: Viking Press, 1963.

Burks, R. V. "Political Participation Under Socialism." *Studies in Comparative Communism* 15 (Spring–Summer 1982).

Carson, George B. *Electoral Practices in the USSR*. New York: Praeger, 1955.

Churchward, L. G. "Soviet Local Government Today." *Soviet Studies* 17 (April 1966).

DiFranceisco, Wayne, and Gitelman, Zvi. "Soviet Political Culture and Covert Participation in Policy Implementation." *American Political Science Review* 78 (September 1984).

Emmons, Terence, and Vucinich, Wayne (eds.). *The Zemstvo in Russia*. New York: Cambridge University Press, 1982.

d'Encausse, Helene C. *Le Pouvoir Confisque*, published in English translation as *Confiscated Power*. New York: Harper and Row, 1982.

Friedgut, Theodore. "Citizens and Soviets: Can Ivan Ivanovich Fight City Hall?" *Comparative Politics* 10 (July 1978).

———. "Community Structure, Political Participation, and Soviet Local Government: The Case of the Kutaisi." In Henry Morton and Rudolf Tokes (eds.), *Soviet Politics and Society in the 1970s*. New York: Free Press, 1974.

———. "Interests and Groups in Soviet Policy-Making: The MTS Reforms." *Soviet Studies* 28 (October 1976).

———. *Political Participation in the USSR*. Princeton: Princeton University Press, 1979.

Frolic, B. Michael. "Decision-Making in Soviet Cities." *American Political Science Review* 66 (March 1972).

Gill, Graeme J. *Peasants and Government in the Russian Revolution.* London: Macmillan, 1979.

Gillison, Jerome. "Soviet Elections as a Measure of Dissent: The Missing One Per Cent." *American Political Science Review* 62 (September 1968).

Gitelman, Zvi. "Working the Soviet System: Citizens and Urban Bureaucracies." In Henry W. Morton and Robert C. Stuart (eds.), *The Contemporary Soviet City.* New York: M. E. Sharpe, 1984.

Hahn, Jeffrey W. "Conceptualizing Political Participation in the USSR: Two Decades of Debate." Kennan Institute for Advanced Russian Studies. Occasional Paper no. 190. 1984.

————. "Is Developed Socialism a Soviet Version of Convergence?" In Jim Seroka and Maurice Simon (eds.), *Developed Socialism in the Soviet Bloc.* Boulder, Colo.: Westview Press, 1982.

Harcave, Sidney. *First Blood: The Russian Revolution of 1905.* New York: Macmillan, 1964.

Hill, Ronald J. "The CPSU in a Soviet Election Campaign." *Soviet Studies* 28 (October 1976).

————. "Party-State Relations and Soviet Political Development." *British Journal of Political Science* 10 (April 1980): 149–166.

————. "Patterns of Deputy Selection to Local Soviets." *Soviet Studies* 25 (October 1973).

————. "Soviet Literature on Electoral Reform." *Government and Opposition* 11 (Autumn 1976).

————. *Soviet Political Elites: The Case of Tiraspol.* New York: St. Martin's Press, 1977.

————. *Soviet Politics, Political Science, and Reform.* New York: M. E. Sharpe, 1980.

Hingley, Ronald. *The Russian Mind.* New York: Charles Scribner's Sons, 1977.

Hittle, J. Michael. *The Service City: State and Townspeople in*

Russia, 1600–1800. Cambridge: Harvard University Press, 1979.

Hough, Jerry. "Political Participation in the Soviet Union." *Soviet Studies* 28 (January 1976).

Hough, Jerry, and Fainsod, Merle. *How the Soviet Union Is Governed.* Cambridge: Harvard University Press, 1979.

Jacobs, Everett M. "The Composition of Local Soviets, 1959–1969." *Government and Opposition* 7 (Autumn 1972).

―――. "Soviet Elections: What They Are and What They Are Not." *Soviet Studies* 22 (July, 1970).

Jacobs, Everett M. (ed.). *Soviet Local Politics and Government.* London: George Allen and Unwin, 1983.

Karklins, Rasma. "Soviet Elections Revisited: Voter Abstention in Noncompetitive Balloting." *American Political Science Review* 80 (June 1986).

Lane, David. *State and Politics in the USSR.* New York: New York University Press, 1985.

Lenin, V. I. *To the Population, "Democracy" and Dictatorship, and What Is Soviet Power?* Moscow: Progress Publishers, 1980.

―――. *What Is Soviet Power? Articles and Speeches.* Moscow: Progress Publishers, 1978.

Lewis, Carol, and Sternheimer, Stephen. *Soviet Urban Management.* New York: Praeger, 1979.

Little, D. Richard. "Political Participation and the Soviet System." *Problems of Communism* 29 (July–August 1980).

―――. "Soviet Parliamentary Committees after Khrushchev: Obstacles and Opportunities." *Soviet Studies* 24 (July 1972).

Medvedev, Roy. *On Socialist Democracy* (1972). Trans. by Ellen de Kadt. Random House, 1975.

Morton, Henry W. "The Leningrad District of Moscow: An Inside Look." *Soviet Studies* 20 (December 1969).

Mote, Max. *Soviet Local and Republic Elections.* Stanford, Calif.: Hoover Institution, 1965.

Nelson, Daniel. "Citizen Participation in Romania: The People's Council Deputy." In Daniel Nelson (ed.), *Local Politics in Communist Countries*. Lexington: University of Kentucky Press, 1980.

Oliver, James. "Citizen Demands in the Soviet Political System." *American Political Science Review* 63 (June 1969).

Riasanovsky, Nicholas. *A History of Russia*. 4th ed. New York: Oxford University Press, 1984.

Ruble, Blair A. *Governing Leningrad*. Berkeley: University of California Press, 1987.

————. *Soviet Trade Unions*. Cambridge: Cambridge University Press, 1981.

Savas, E. S., and Kaiser, J.A. *Moscow's City Government*. New York: Praeger, 1985.

Schulz, Donald, and Adams, Jan S. (eds.). *Political Participation in Communist Systems*. Elmsford, N.Y.: Pergamon Press, 1981.

Shapovalov, Vladimir. *The Moscow Soviet*. Moscow: Progress Publishers, 1984.

Sharlet, Robert. *The New Soviet Constitution of 1977*. Brunswick, Ohio: King's Court, 1978.

Simmons, E. J. (ed.). *Continuity and Change in Russian and Soviet Thought*. Cambridge: Harvard University Press, 1955.

Skilling, H. Gordon. "Interest Groups and Communist Politics Revisited." *World Politics* 36 (October 1983).

Slider, Darrell. "More Power to the Soviets? Reform and Local Government in the Soviet Lenin." *British Journal of Political Science* 16 (October 1986).

————. "Party-Sponsored Public Opinion Research in the Soviet Union." *Journal of Politics* 37 (February 1985): 209–229.

Solomon, Susan Gross (ed.). *Pluralism in the Soviet Union*. New York: St. Martin's Press, 1983.

Starr, S. Frederick. *Decentralization and Self-Government in*

Russia, 1830–70. Princeton: Princeton University Press, 1972.

Stewart, Philip D. *Political Power in the Soviet Union.* New York: Bobbs-Merrill, 1968.

Swearer, Howard. "Political Participation: Myths and Realities." *Problems of Communism* 9 (September–October 1960).

Taubman, William. *Governing Soviet Cities.* New York: Praeger, 1973.

Tucker, Robert. *The Soviet Political Mind.* New York: W. W. Norton, 1971.

Urban, Michael E. "Information and Participation in Local Soviet Government." *Journal of Politics* 44 (February 1982).

Weissman, Neil. *Reform in Tsarist Russia.* New Brunswick, N.J.: Rutgers University Press, 1981.

White, Stephen. *Political Culture and Soviet Politics.* New York: St. Martin's Press, 1979.

Yaney, George. *The Systematization of Russian Government.* Urbana: University of Illinois, 1973.

INDEX

Absentee ballots, 106–107
Administrative agencies, 121–122;
  composition of directors in, 123,
  124–125, 126; headed by
  women, 123; numbers and size
  of, 123
Administrative Committee, 120
Administrative subordination hi-
  erarchy, 85–89
Administrative-territorial subdivi-
  sions, 87–88
Agitators, network of, 103–104
Agitpunkt, 103, 161
Alekseev, B. K., 108
Alexander II, 50
All-peoples state, 67
All-Russian Communist Party, 62
All-Russian Congress of Soviets,
  64; First, 58; Second, 63
Almond, Gabriel, 9n, 11n, 279
Anticorruption campaigns, 180–
  181, 188
Apparat, 118–119; units of, 119–
  120
Apparatchiks, 119
April Theses, 58
Archival research, 20–21
Autocracy, 44; in "official Russia,"
  54; traditions of, 46–47
Avak'ian, S. A., 91–92

Bahry, Donna, 287
Barabashev, Georgii Vasil'evich,
  92, 95, 172, 174
Barry, Donald, 32
"Basic Authority of Area and Regional Soviets and the Soviets
  of Autonomous Regions and

Okrugs, On the," 75
"Basic Rights and Duties of the
  Village and Settlement Soviets,
  On the," 74
Belzuglov, A. A., 140–141, 174–
  175, 209; on soviet sessions,
  214–215
Bialer, Seweryn, 263
Blat, 181
Bolsheviks, 45, 58; control of, 60;
  control of villages by, 78; in mu-
  nicipal government, 58n; on so-
  viets, 62–63; takeover by, 57
Bolshevism, evolution of, 45
Boyars, 49
Brezhnev, Leonid, 71; bribery and
  corruption under, 180, 188;
  Central Committee speech of
  (May 1977), 73; developed so-
  cialism and, 8; dominance of
  professionals under, 258; for-
  malism under, 282; as General
  Secretary of party, 74; growth of
  right of inquiry under, 225;
  nomination of, 101; political life
  formulations under, 72
Bribery, 180
Brown, Archie, 10n, 11n, 41–42
Brym, Robert, 102, 107
Budget process of soviets, 128–132
*Bulletin of the Executive Committee
  of the Moscow City Soviet*, 21
"Bureaucratic Encounters in the
  Soviet Union" project, 36, 180

Campaigns, 27, 103–105
Candidacies: multiple, 95, 96–97;
  preselection of, 101–103

Catherine II, 50
Centralization, 63, 281; under Lenin and Stalin, 79; loosening of, 282
Chernenko, Konstantin, 77; on corruption, 188; revitalization of soviets under, 288; on right of inquiry, 225; speech of on local soviets, 261
Churchward, L. G., 30–31, 37–38
Cities: governing of, 31; hierarchy of, 85–87; importance of, 85
Citizen appeals, 157–161
Citizen competence, 175–176, 279–280
Citizen complaints, 158–161; deputy response to, 161–168
Citizen concerns, 193–194, 196–197; avenues open to, 30–31; communication of to decision makers, 29, 40, 267; deputies' response to, 267–268
Citizen contact, 28, 40, 168–169, 192–194, 265; with administrative organs, 36–37; deputies' response to, 161–168 (see also Deputies, citizen contact with); informal, 178–181; through proposals, declarations, and complaints, 157–160; through public discussion of draft legislation, 170–174; through public opinion surveys, 174–178; recalls, 181–188; through reports to constituents, 149–157; voter mandate and, 135–148 (see also Voter mandates)
Citizen participation, 27; broadening of, 76–79, 210–212; in campaigns, 104–105; covert, 36–37; defining characteristics of, 39–40; diversity of view on, 34–38; in draft legislation, 170–174; educational level and, 287–288; effectiveness of, 40–41; growth of,

286–290; interest groups and, 29–30; lack of historical predispositions to, 78; lack of interest in, 270–284; legal basis of, 73–74; legitimacy of, 262–264; in meetings with deputies, 150–157; need for cross-cultural definition of, 39; output-oriented, 36–37; possibilities for, 264–269; qualitative vs. quantitative, 36n; ritualistic, 262; Western skepticism about, 261–262; among younger generation, 286–287
Citizen-government channels of communication, 16, 193–194, 196–197. See also Citizen concerns, communication of to decision makers; Citizen participation
City borough deputies, 16
City boroughs, 84
City deputies, 16. See also Deputies
City soviets, 84. See also Local soviets; Soviets
City-states, 48–49
Civic competence, 16; determination of, 40–41; measuring of, 26. See also Citizen competence
Civic consciousness, development of, 34–35
Civic culture, 9; development of, 284–290; requirements for, 285–286
Civil War in France, The, 59, 182
Class conflict, "end of," 66
Clergy, 49
Code of city borough executive committees in Moscow, 118
Collectivization: of agriculture, 66n; soviets' role in, 66; village autonomy and, 78–79
Commissariat of Internal Affairs, 63
Commission to Assist the Preser-

vation of Monuments of History
and Culture, 120
Commission to Fight Drunkenness, 120
Commission on Juvenile Affairs,
120–121
Communal activity, 27
Communal model, 62; recall and,
182; and soviets, 60. *See also*
Paris Commune of 1871
Communist countries, political
participation in, 26–43
Communist Party (CPSU): control
of local government personnel
by, 253–255; decision-making
power of, 251–253; domination
of, 259; monopoly of legitimacy
of, 81; organs of, 246; policy-
making of, 252–253, 256; programs, 70–71, 76, 232, 276; relationship of with state, 255–256;
support of deputies' activities
by, 8
Communist Party Draft Program
of 1985, 172, 177, 234
Competitive balloting, 33n. *See
also* Candidacies, multiple; Elections, competitive
Congress of Soviets, 63
Connor, Walter, 32
Constituent Assembly of 1918, 64
Constituents, reports to, 149–157.
See also Citizen contact; Citizen
participation
Constitution of 1918, 183
Constitution of July 10, 1918, 63–
64
Constitution of 1936, 66–67; centralization of state by, 138; on
local soviets, 67–68; on right of
recall, 183
Constitution of 1977, 73–75; article
102 of, 139; article 6 of, 251
Corruption, 180–181; tolerance of,
188

Council of Ministers, 246
Council of Peoples' Commissars,
63
Council of Workers' Deputies, 56
Covert participation, 36–37
Credentials Committee, 230
Cultural continuity, 45–47, 281

Dahl, Robert, 259–260
Davydov, R. K., 220–221
Decision making: interest groups
and, 30; mass participation in,
30–38
Declarations, 158–161
Democracy: "genuine" vs. "not
genuine," 32–33; participation
and, 36; of peasant Russia, 52–
54
Democratic centralism, 88
Democratic liberalism, influence
of in Imperial Russia, 50–51
Democratic polity: emergence of,
38; possibility of in communist
countries, 38–39
Democratic principles: in early Soviet Russia, 79; legislative
expression of, 76
Democratization policy, 96
Department heads, appeals to,
159–160
Deputatskii zapros. *See* Zapros
Deputies, 8–17; activities of, 77,
264–265; as amateur custodians,
276; authority of to intervene
for constituents, 162–163; bribery and corruption of, 180–181;
categories of, 257–258; citizen
contact with, 149–157, 159–168,
178–181, 192–194, 265, 266–267
(*see also* Citizen contact); composition of those dominating soviet sessions, 218–220; compositional norms for, 112;
corruption of, 188; under "developed socialism," 70–76; edu-

Deputies (*cont.*)
  cational level of, 113, 114, 287–
  288; effectiveness of, 261–290;
  election terms of, 83; elections
  of, 55, 92–93; elites, 257, 260; expanded role of, 8–9, 14; importance of, 12; increasing numbers
  of, 72; lack of decision-making
  power of, 256; lack of participation by, 275–278; lack of release
  time for, 277; large number of,
  274–275; mandate of, 133–134;
  nomination of, 100–101; as ombudsman, 194–198; participation
  of in local politics, 256–258; participation of in local soviet sessions, 208–227, 271–272; percentage of female, 112; as
  political representatives, 75;
  power of in local politics, 257–
  258, 288–289; public knowledge
  of, 189–190; public opinion of,
  188–194; rapid turnover of, 276–
  277; recall of, 181–188; as representative of constituents, 134–
  135; representativeness of, 277;
  response of to citizen concerns,
  267–268; revitalization of, 288;
  role of, 82: in council, 274, in
  decision making, 199, 246–260,
  legislative, 74–75, policymaking,
  198, in standing committees,
  228–241, in voter mandates,
  142–143, 147; specialists, 257.
  See also Local deputies
Deputy groups, 204–205
Deputy *Handbook*, 251–252
Deputy reports, 149–154, 266; effectiveness of, 155–157
De-Stalinization, 8; policies, 276
Developed socialism, deputies under, 70–76
DiFranceisco, Wayne, 36, 181; on
  citizen participation, 262

Dissidents, 32
District assemblies in Imperial
  Russia, 50
District procurator, 118
District soviets, 84
Doklady, 214
Draft legislation: preparation of,
  228; public discussion of, 170–
  174
Dual subordination principle, 67,
  88–89, 122, 247–248
Duma, 49, 50; democratic ideals
  in, 79

Eastern European communist
  countries, 41–42
Economic development, 75
Efficacy, 40
Election commissions, formation
  of, 98–100
Election reconstruction, 96–97
Elections, 93–97; campaigning in,
  103–105; ceremonial nature of,
  28; competitive, 95–97, 284; effectiveness of, 28–29; lack of interest in outcome of, 95; nomination process in, 100–103;
  organization of, 97–100; participation in, 27, 106–107, 265; as
  ritual, 93–94; voting process in,
  105–107
Electoral activity, 28
Electoral districts, 97–99
Ethnic diversity, 83
Executive commissions, 114, 119,
  120–121
Executive Committee of Petrograd
  soviet, 57
Executive committees, 59; activities of, 117–118; authority of,
  121; citizen appeals to, 159–
  160; composition of, 115–117,
  248–249; control of local government by, 249–250; dominance

of, 207–208, 247–252, 278, 282;
election of, 114; in organizing
public meetings, 173; policy implementation by, 256; power of,
247–248; records of, 150; relationship of to soviets, 248–251;
relationship of to standing committees, 228–229, 243–245; responsibility of for budget process, 128–129; review of voter
mandates by, 141–142; role of in
public discussions, 171

Field research, 18–20
Five-year plans, transition to, 66n
Formal inquiry, right of. See Zapros
Formalism, 283; decline of, 71
French Estates General, 182
Friedgut, Theodore, 10n, 12, 34–
35, 107; on citizen participation,
263; on deputy renewal rate,
277; on public opinion of deputies, 190, 191–192; study of Soviet emigrés to Israel by, 24n,
280–281; "Further Increasing the
Role of the Soviets in Economic
Construction, On," 75

General Department, 119
General Strike, 56
Gentry servitors, 49
Gitelman, Zvi, 36–37, 181; on citizen participation, 262
Gorbachev, Mikhail, 95–96; appointment of Shevardnadze as
foreign minister by, 177; bribery
and corruption under, 180; commitment of to anticorruption,
188; reform efforts of, 126; revitalization of soviets under, 288;
on strengthening of local political organs, 289
Government: Bolshevik, 63–65 (see

also Bolsheviks); suggestions for
reform of, 35. See also Deputies; Local government; Local
soviets; Soviet political system;
Soviet government; Soviets
Great Purges, 66
Guberniia, 50

Harding, Neil, 61
Hill, Ronald, 35, 71, 77–78; on
Party dominance, 255–256; on
postelection meetings, 149–150
Home rule principle, 91–92
Horizontal control, 282
Horizontal subordination, 88
Hough, Jerry, 31–33

Imperial Age of Russia, 49–50
Imperial Russia political culture,
44
"Improving the Work of the Soviet Deputies, On," 138
"Improving the Work of the Soviets and Strengthening Their
Ties with the Masses, On," 68–
69, 167
"Improving Work with the Examination of Letters and the Organization of the Priyom, On,"
167
Industrialization, 55; effects of on
peasants, 79; emphasis on, 281;
soviets' role in, 66
Information: availability of, 212–
213; flow of, 36
Inquiry, right of. See Right of inquiry
Instructed delegate model, 133,
138; recall and, 181–182
Interest group pluralism, 29n
Interest groups, 29–30
Ispolkom. See Executive committees
Ivan IV, 49

Ivanovo-Voznesensk Authorized Council, 55
Ivanovo-Voznesensk textile factory strike, 138

Jacobs, Everett, 36–38, 84, 108–109, 112
Juridical bureau, 119
"Just Tsar" image, 42

Khrushchev, Nikita: criticism of soviets, 68; de-Stalinization under, 8; number of deputies under, 72; "populist" policies of, 258; "Report on the Program" of, 70; on right of recall, 183; on self-government, 70–71
Kievan Russia, 48
Kim, Jae-on, 27–29, 41
Kolkhoz system, 79
Komsomol, 30; members, 254; representation of, 112
Kontrol, 227–228, 240
Kornilov, defeat of, 59
Kotok, Viktor Fomich, 133, 139
Kraizhkov, V. A., 171–172
Kulaks, eradication of, 66–67
Kutafin, O. E., 77

Land captains, 51–52
Law on the Status of Deputies, 14, 83, 134, 149, 150; article 6 of, 184; article 7 of, 139; article 11 of, 212; article 12 of, 209; article 15 of, 217; meetings with constituents and, 157
Lebedev, P. N., 91
Legislative councils, 246
Leizerov, A. T., 113, 172, 178–179, 210–211; Minsk Oblast study of, 214; on right of inquiry, 226–227; on standing committees, 244
Lenin, V. I., 57, 59; April Theses and, 58; control of, 58–59; on deputies' performance of duties while working, 245; on professional politicians, 117; on right to recall deputies, 182; soviets and, 59–62, 232; on the state, 60; on voter mandates, 138
Lenin city borough, 19–20
Lenin city borough soviet: budget of, 130–131; membership of, 249
Lenin city borough soviet fourteenth session, 199–200, 202–205; agenda of, 200–201; regulations and procedures for, 201
Lenin district soviet composition, 111, 112
Lewis, Carol, 37
Little, D. Richard, 31–32; on centralized authority, 282; on standing committee membership, 235
Local deputies: composition of, 101–102; effectiveness of, 40; role of, 35–36. See also Deputies
Local government, 8; composition of, 253–254; expansion of, 36–38; jurisdiction of, 89–92; organization of, 80–132; soviet deputies and, 8–25. See also Local soviets; Soviet government; Village politics
Local self-government in "official Russia," 48–52
Local soviets, 30, 83; and changes in administrative-territorial subdivisions, 87–88; composition of, 107–114; efforts to revive, 35; finance of, 128–132; flow of information to, 36; hierarchy of, 84; as locus of political change, 34–36; number and size of, 86; participatory function of, 34; sessions of, 199–208: in 1984, 206t, agenda-setting in, 208–

211, attendance of, 213–214, deputy participation in, 208–227, purposes of, 206–207, shortcomings of, 207–208; units of, 119–120. *See also* Soviets

Luk'ianov, A. I., 70

Mandat imperatif. See Instructed delegate model

Mandate Commission, 120; role of in recalls, 185

Marx, Karl: on commune model, 182; on Paris Commune of 1871, 59; on soviets, 62

Marxism, conceptions of government in, 61

Marxist-Leninist doctrine: evolution of, 8; on role of elected representatives, 133

Mass media, bribery and corruption theme in, 180. *See also* Press

Mass political participation: debate over, 30–38; in West vs. Soviet Union, 33. *See also* Citizen participation; Political participation

Mass public organization, 168

Mass public organizations, 169

Masses, control of, 30

McAuley, Mary, 42–43

"Measures for Further Improving the Work of Raion and City Soviets of Working Peoples' Deputies, On," 74

"Measures for Further Improving Work with Letters and Propositions in the Light of the 26th Congress, On," 168

Medvedev, Roy, 95

Mensheviks, 56–58

Minsk Oblast: standing committees in, 229; study of, 214

Morton, Henry, 31

Moscow: as "Third Rome," 44;

city executive committee of, 115

Mote, Max, 91

Muscovite state, establishment of, 49

Nakaz izbiratelei. See Voter mandates

Narodnost. See Nationality

National policy discussions, 171

National polls, 174; obstacles to use of, 174–177

National public opinion research center, 177

Nationality, 44

Nelson, Daniel, 257

Nie, Norman, 27–29, 41

Nomenklatura system, 102

Nomination(s): Communist Party control of, 94; process of, 28, 100–103

Nongovernment associations, 195

Nonstaff departments, 126–127

Novgorod, 48–49

Novoselov, V. I., 243

Oblast soviets, 250

Oblasts, 84

October Revolution, 57

Official nationality, 44

Official Russia, 47–48; local self-government in, 48–52

Okrug soviets, 85–87

Okrugs, autonomous, 84

Oliver, James, 30

On Socialist Democracy, 95

"Organization of Work with Voter Mandates, The," 75

"Organizational Question, On the," 251

Organizational-Instructional Department, 119, 151; annual plan of, 209; responsibility of, 217; role of in public discussions, 171

Orthodox clergy, role of, 44. *See also* Clergy
Orthodoxy, 44
Output-oriented participation, 36–37
Oversight, 227, 228, 240

Paris Commune of 1871, 59–61
Participation and Political Equality, 27–29
Particularized contact, 27
Party Congresses: 8th, 65; 20th, 68–69; 22nd, 70
Party groups, 254–255
Party. *See* Communist Party
Party-state boundary, 251–253
Party-state interaction, 259
Pavlov, A. S., 71
Peasant society, 52–54
Peasants: apathy of toward government, 51; role of in decision making, 49, 78–79
People's Control Committees, 30, 229
Perfilev, M. N., 108
Peter I, 50
Peter the Great, accession of, 49–50
Petrograd Soviet, 57
Petrograd Soviet of Workers' and Soldiers' Deputies, 56–57
Planning and Budget Committee, 230
Podmena, 259
Policy, citizen influence on, 39
Political attitudes: difficulty of determining, 41–42; historical experience and, 47–48. *See also* Public opinion
Political change in Soviet Union, 35
Political efficacy, 10–11
Political participation, 8–25; in communist countries, 26–43; definition of, 27; growth of, 32;

need for reconceptualization of, 38–43; and political efficacy, 10–11. *See also* Citizen participation; Mass political participation
Political Participation in the USSR, 34
Political "professionals," 115–117, 259–260
Political reform, in Imperial Russia, 50–51
Popova, S. M., 184
Postoiannye komissii. *See* Standing committees
Powell, Bingham, 9n, 279
Presidium: to represent deputies, 250; of the Supreme Soviet, 246
Press: discussion of draft legislation in, 172; free, 286. *See also* Mass media
Priyom, 161, 162, 164, 267, 271; citizen use of, 167
"Procedure for Considering Citizens' Proposals, Applications, and Complaints, On the," 75
"Procedures Governing the Recall of a Deputy of the Supreme Soviet of the USSR," 183–184
Professional politicians, 115–117, 259–260
Proletarian Revolution and the Renegade Kautsky, 61
Proletariat, dictatorship of, 13, 62; transition from, 67
Proportional representation, 51
Proposals, 158–161
Proverka, 227
Provincial assemblies, 50
Provisional Government, 57–59
Pskov, 48–49
Public consensus, passion for, 283–284
Public councils, 127
Public forums. *See* Deputy reports; Voter mandates
Public inspectors, 127

Public instructors, 127
Public meetings, for discussion of draft legislation, 172–173
Public opinion: on deputies' activities, 188–194; surveys, 174–178
Public Opinion Council, 177
Public opinion research center, 177
Public organization, 168–169
Public policy, 38

Raion, 84
Recalls, 181–188; frequency of use of, 186–188; initiation of, 184–185; reasons for, 184
Reception Department, 119
Reconstruction policy, 96
Referendum, 135n, 170
Regional subdivisions, 83; ranking of soviets and, 84
Regional units, 84
Repartitional commune system, 53
Representative government, 8–25
Republics: autonomous, 83–84, 85; division of, 67
Research methodology, 17–25
Residual powers principle, 91–92
Responsiveness, 40
Revolution of 1905, 55
Riasanovsky, Nicholas, 49
Rigby, T. H., 33
Right of inquiry, 71, 220, 221–225, 258; increased use of, 225–226
"Right to Recall Deputies, On," 182
Romanov tsar, first, 49
Rosenberg, William, 51
Ruble, Blair, 169, 258
Rural communities, 85. See also Village politics
Russia, prerevolutionary, 47–48; local self-government in, 48–52; village politics in, 52–59

Safarov, R. A., 176–177

Sakharov, Andrei, exile of, 195
Samoupravlenie. See Self-government
Schools of administration principle, 276
Schulz, Donald, 31, 39–40
Second polity, 36–37
Self-activating public organizations, 168–169
Self-government, 82
Separation of powers principle, 278
Serfdom, beginning of, 53
Serfs, emancipation of, 50
Settlement soviets, 84
Shakhnazarov, G., 176
Sharlet, Robert, 39
Sheremet, K. F., 77, 92
Shevardnadze, Eduard, 177
Skhody, 53, 172–174
Slider, Darrell, 177
Sobory, 49
Social Revolutionaries, 58
Socialism, developed, 8, 12
Socialist Legality and the Preservation of Public Order Committee, 19, 230, 234–241
Sodoklady, 214
Sovet rabochikh deputatov. See Council of Workers' Deputies
Sovety narodnykh deputatov, 14; statistical data published in, 22
Soviet administrative organs, citizen interaction with, 36–37
Soviet Constitution: article 3 of, 8; on electoral laws, 92–93; on local government jurisdiction, 89–90
Soviet deputies. See Deputies; Local deputies
Soviet elections. See Elections
Soviet emigré sources, 22, 23–24
Soviet government: central-local division of labor in, 88–90; local-central division of labor of, 89–

Soviet government (*cont.*)
92; relationship of to autocratic
Russia, 45–47; representativeness of, 107–114. *See also* Government; Local government; Soviet political system
Soviet Local Politics and Government,
37
Soviet Political Elites, 34
Soviet political system: citizens'
perception of, 279–280; control
of by Communist Party, 251–
256, by executive committee,
247–251; deputies' role in, 256–
258; dominance of "professionals" in, 259–260; governmental
component of, 81–83; hierarchy
of, 80–92; structures of, 246. *See
also* Soviet government; Soviets
*Soviet Politics, Political Science, and
Reform*, 35
Soviet session agendas: items on,
210–211; publishing of, 211–212;
setting of, 208–210
Soviet society: common interest
of, 81–82; variegated nature of,
83
Soviets, 81; administrations and
departments of, 121–123; citizen
participation in, 126–127; composition of, 248; democratic
principles of, 73; development
of after Revolution, 59–70; division of, 67; dual subordination
system in, 89; effectiveness of,
77; elections to, 64; emergence
of, 55–59; executive committees
of, 114–118; failings of, 68–70; finance of, 128–132; institutional
expression of, 63–64; as institutions for popular participation,
62; internal organization of,
114–132; as organs of state
power, 60, 61; as part of unitary

system, 81–82; Party control
over, 64–65; ranking of, 84; regional competence of, 75; regulations pertaining to, 66n; relationship of with executive
committee, 248–251; resistance
to reform of, 126; revitalization
of, 71–72; sessions of, 67, 114
(*see also* Soviet session agenda);
staff positions in, 119–120; theoretical basis of, 76; underutiliza-
tion of powers of, 77–78; unique
position of, 12; during war and
reconstruction, 68; weakness of
in formative years, 65–66. *See
also* Local soviets
Soviets of Workers', Soldiers',
Peasants', and Farm Laborers'
Deputies, 63
St. Petersburg soviet, 56
Stalin, Joseph: death of, 286–287;
legacy of, 281–282, 285; soviets
under, 68; on voter mandates,
138
Stalinist dictatorship, 45
Stalinist political culture, 9, 10n
Standing committee deputies,
126–127
Standing committees, 228–234;
composition of, 234–235, 243–
244; deputies' participation in,
244–246, 258; ineffectiveness of,
275–276; level of activity of, 272;
levels of expertise in, 244; of local soviets from 1976 to 1985,
231; number of, 230; number of
meetings of, 241; participation
of in work of soviets, 241–243;
patterns of participation in, 235–
236; people involved in, 232;
problems of, 241–246; proceedings of, 234–241; rank-ordered
by number of committees, 233;
relationship of with executive

committee, 243, 244–245; responsibilities of, 230–232; role of in implementing government decisions, 232–234; size of, 230; specialists and nonspecialists in, 234–236; use of, 272

Staravoitov, Nikolai Georgievich, 148–149, 208, 210; on dominance of executive committee, 247, 249–250

Staroski. *See* Village elders

Starosta, 53

State: definition of, 60; withering away of, 70, 72

State and Revolution, 60–61

State of all the people, 13, 70, 73

Statistical data analysis, 21–25

"Status of the Peoples' Deputy in the USSR, On the," 74–75

Sternheimer, Stephen, 36

Supreme Soviet, 81, 83–84; Presidium of, 246

Sviazy, 181

Taxes, 129–132

Townspeople, political role of, 49

Trade unions, 30

Trotsky, Leon, 56, 59

Tsar: peasant attitude toward, 42; power of, 44, 46; relationship of with people, 44–45

Two Russias concept, 47–48

Ukrainets, P. P., 71

Unanimity, passion for, 283–284

Union-republics, 75–76, 83; capitals of, 85; subdivisions of, 84

Unitary government system, 81–83

Urban, Michael, 36, 213; on citizen participation, 261

Urban deputy groups, 163–164

Urban districts, 31

Urban settlements, 87

Vasil'ev, V. I., 225

Veche, 48

Verba, Sidney, 27–29, 41

Vertical subordination, 89

Village elders, 53, 55

Village politics, 263–264; in Imperial Russia, 52–54; informal, 272–273; organization of under soviet system, 65–66

Village soviets, 84–85

Villages, local control of, 78–79

Voluntarism, 40

Voluntary activities, abuse of, 127

Voroshilov, Klement, 69; on right of recall, 183

Voter lists, 98

Voter mandates, 105, 135–149, 182, 265–266; adoption of, 137–138; categories of, 143–144; edict of 1980 on, 139–141; effectiveness of, 147–149; frivolous, 140; funding of, 145–147; history of, 138–139; imperative character of, 137–138; implementation of, 139–143, 144–145, 148; ratio of per deputy, 137; use of, 71, 271; volume of, 136–137

Voter turnout, 106, 107

Voting, 27; avoidance of, 106–107; civic competence and, 40–41; process of, 105–107; universal participation in, 93

Vystupleniia, 215

Western elections, lack of participation in, 28–29

Westernization, commitment to, 50

White, Stephen, 47

"Within the system" participation, 27n

Workers: direct participation of, 62; representatives of, 55–56

Zadavat' voprosy, 215–217
Zamechaniia, 217
Zapros, 268, 271–272; use of, 272. *See also* Right of inquiry
Zaslavsky, Victor, 102, 107

Zemskie nachalniki, 51–52
Zemskii sobor, 49, 50
Zemstvo, 50–51; democratic ideals in, 79; flaws of, 51; termination of, 63
Zemstvo reforms, 51–52
Zheks, 161, 163
Znanie, 238–239

LIBRARY OF CONGRESS

Library of Congress Cataloging-in-Publication Data

Hahn, Jeffrey W., 1944–
Soviet grassroots: citizen participation in local Soviet government /
Jeffrey W. Hahn.

p. cm.
Bibliography: p.   Includes index.
ISBN 0–691–07767–3 (alk. paper)
1. Local government—Soviet Union—Citizen participation.
2. Political participation—Soviet Union. 3. Soviets. I. Title.
JS6055.H34 1988
320.8'0947—dc19   87–28966
                                                                      CIP